Rio or Bust

Highjacked by the Holy Spirit

Tyke Fortier

destinēe

Rio or Bust: Highjacked by the Holy Spirit
By Tyke Fortier
© Copyright 2022 by Tyke Fortier

To maintain the anonymity and protect the privacy of some individuals involved, a few names and details were changed. The occurrences in this book are from the author's memories and perspective and represent events as faithfully as possible.

Author: Tyke Fortier
Publisher: Destinee Media, www.destineemedia.com
Cover: Val McCall
Interior illustration: T.P. Wright

ISBN: 978-1-938367-72-4

TABLE OF CONTENTS

Acknowledgements..4

Map of South America...7

1. New York 8

2. New Orleans...29

3. Colombia 48

4. Ecuador 72

5. Lima, Peru...86

6. Cuzco, Peru 96

7. Machu Picchu, Peru.. 113

8. Lake Titicaca, Peru... 127

9. La Paz, Bolivia 137

10. Chile and Buenos Aires, Argentina 156

11. Rio De Janeiro, Brazil.. 201

12. London... 244

13. Florence and Paris 260

14. India and Nepal 266

15. Ibiza, Spain 286

About The Author... 313

Banana Split Misfit 315

ACKNOWLEDGEMENTS

I give loving thanks to my late husband, Peter, for removing so many stones from my path and always believing in me and my projects! His patience and support through the years have warmed my heart and held me up . . . and still do!

I want to thank Dr. Ralph McCall and his lovely wife Catherine, my dear friends, and publishers of Destinée Media! You not only triggered the idea for me to write my first book, but you have given me continued vital support and encouragement for my sequel! I can't thank you enough for initiating my motivation to tell my story. I am also forever grateful for your hands-on help! Thank you, Catherine, for your continued spot-on suggestions that helped me focus on the direction of this book's content and for laughing out loud while reading it!

Thanks to my brother and mentor, Spike Fortier. You have always been my foremost encourager, cheering me on page by page and supplying insightful advice. You have mentored me not only with my books but in *life* . . . since childhood! Your kindness, generosity, and wit have always inspired me, teaching me to laugh at myself.

Thanks to my cousin, Fran Fortier, who has also been an inspiration since childhood. Her trailblazing to Europe in the 60s ignited my ensuing wanderlust. Her interest, enthusiasm, and word-smith skills have been crucial to this book.

Thanks to Joey McLean, my ex-roommate and close friend, for, once again, diving into my project with her alluring "eagle-eyes" . . . as well as helping me fill a few pages of this book with our humorous antics together in her amazing home in New Orleans.

Thanks again to my good friend Elaine Winter for also proofreading this sequel when it was raw and somewhat illegible and for being such a devoted supporter! How you miraculously deciphered my book page by page as I wrote it is remarkable and heartwarming.

Thanks to the late Rev. Dr. Bill Maxwell and his wife, my dear friend Agnes, for their spiritual mentorship and remarkable accounts of their supernatural experiences as missionaries in Chile during the late 60s, 70s, and mid-80s.

Thanks to my talented friend and graphic designer, Val McCall, who created this book's cover with spot-on expertise. Her input on other aspects of this book has also proven crucial.

Now faith is confidence in what we hope for and assurance about what we do not see.

Hebrews 11:1 NIV

MAP OF SOUTH AMERICA

EL SALVADOR
Managua
NICARAGUA
San José
Panama
COSTA
RICA
PANAMA
Medellin
Bogotá
COLOMBIA
Cali
ECUADOR
Quito
GALAPAGOS ISLANDS
Caracas
VENEZUELA
TRINIDAD AND TOBAGO
Port-of-Spain
GUYANA
Georgetown
Paramaribo
FRENCH GUIANA
Cayenne
SURINAME
Manaus
Belém
Fortaleza
Trujillo
PERU
Machu
Picchu
Lima
Lake
Titicaca
La Paz
BOLIVIA
BRAZIL
Salvador
Brasilia
Antofagasta
PARAGUAY
Asunción
Sao Paulo
Rio de Janeiro
CHILE
Santiago
Rosario
Buenos Aires
URUGUAY
Montevideo
Concepción
ARGENTINA
South
Atlantic
Ocean
FALKLAND ISLANDS
Cape Horn

1. NEW YORK

With only half an hour until touchdown, the flight attendants routinely made their rounds with landing cards. Then, out of the blue, the seat belt signs started flashing and the pilot abruptly announced that everyone return to their seats immediately, secure their belongings, and fasten their seat belts. Up until now, the Delta cross-Atlantic flight from London to JFK had been boring. I had become accustomed to antique aircraft in developing countries that enabled me to experience the thrill that the Wright brothers must have reveled in at Kitty Hawk.

Whoa, as we hit an air pocket, kids screeched, and adults shrieked as the downdraft caused us to dive. When the flight attendants buckled up, I hunkered down, ready for some real fun! Right on, I could feel the familiar adrenaline rush I thrived on as a kid when zooming down 'thrill hill' on the Big Zephyr (roller coaster) at Pontchartrain Beach, on the lakefront in New Orleans. The sudden updraft was accompanied by a *"son et lumière"* spectacular, lightening up the heavens as the electricity flashed around us.

Nevertheless, we would soon be landing at Kennedy Airport in NYC, and my main concern was how to fill in my landing card. Profession? I'm a professional traveler – a bonafide journey junkie. I want to see it all, do it all, and meet masses of fascinating people en route. Why? Why not? Perhaps I have a low boredom threshold or a high aversion to routine. Whatever the case, I like to remain in full-forward momentum. I've been on the road non-stop for three years, and my appetite for adventure is insatiable. I instinctively know that 1975 will be an exceptional year, and I have only two weeks until the New Year is ushered in with fireworks and relentless partying that New Orleans, the 'Big Easy,' is famous for.

People often ask me if I get fed up with living out of a suitcase. The answer is NO – I thrive on the mystery of the morrow. Then I'm bullied with, "It sounds to me like you're running away from something." I smugly reply, "Spot on, I'm running away from a mediocre job that might enable me to pay the gas to get to a monotonous nine-to-five workday, pay the rent and car notes and feed myself on TV dinners, too exhausted to peel a potato. And you?" On occasion, I try to be normal, but it gets boring, so I go back to being me. I thrive on being a limited edition.

I wheel and deal to support my travel 'habit' and then convert into a clothes horse seasonally for the Prêt-À-Porter fashion shows in Florence and Paris. I return bi-annually to Kathmandu and Jaipur, India, to fuel my heart, soul, and successful jewelry enterprise. I then chill out on my idyllic island of Ibiza, afloat in the Mediterranean Sea. My favorite sales triangle - London, Paris, and Rome, has recently been reshaped into a pentagon after adding New York City and New Orleans.

It was time to touch base with my natal city, New Orleans. I wanted to reconnect with family and friends that I missed while rotating around Europe, the Far East, Africa, and everywhere in between. I hadn't been back in the US for three years. Sure, I'd seen my mom and brother, an aunt and uncle, plus a handful of friends in Europe. Still, I was looking forward to being back in the Crescent City for Christmas to see EVERYONE! I wanted to sing Carols in Jackson Square and ride through City Park, then up and down St. Charles Avenue to take in the pretentious but comforting Christmas décor, trying to spot the streetcar named Desire.

Preservation Hall would be pulsating with Dixieland's greatest rag-time stars. Toothless 'Sweet Emma' on piano and vocals, with jingling bells on both her knees. Then a solo from Cie Frazier on drums, Jim Robison on trombone, James Prevost on bass, Allan Jafe on tuba, and Narvin Kimball on banjo. YES, raw jazz at its best! I could feel the rhythm already and started to move with it!

I was craving oysters on the half-shell and spicy hot Gulf shrimp right out of the pot. Then I'd dissect some Gulf crabs, down some okra gumbo, and sip some turtle soup. Oh, to savor some crawfish *étouffée*, jambalaya, Po-boys, and beignets. Last but not least, the soul-food dish of red beans and rice chock full of ham hocks or andouille sausage. The mouth-watering Creole cuisine of New Orleans takes the sting out of the escalating crime rate, blatant bigotry, litter, and rowdy, drunken tourists. However, New Orleans is a city with a soul, and as its motto goes, "Let the good times roll."

* * *

However, I had just arrived in New York City and planned on enjoying every exhilarating minute before flying south for the winter! Within hours of my arrival, I ran into my friend Ruggero from Rome. Dressed in my full-length, multi-colored Missoni coat and coordinating fedora hat, I was gliding down the subway escalator at Times Square and 42nd Street just as Ruggero was ascending. He yodeled (Tarzan style), waved to me, and then made an Olympian leap over the center partition, lifting me off my feet in a Roman embrace as we balanced precariously on the moving steps. His Cuban girlfriend, Marta, had made it big in the Big Apple, and her fashion collection was being displayed in Bloomingdales.

Ruggero, a handsome bundle of boundless energy, informed me that his brother-in-law, a TWA agent, had some bargain-priced pre-Christmas sales on flights to anywhere. Bingo, I had my heart set on South America after soaking up some sun, fun, friends, family, and food in New Orleans – so the timing was right since I was southward bound. Done! Decided! I first prayed for discernment, then babbled off every capital in that Latin continent that I could recall.

The only catch was Ruggero insisted on cash, forbade re-routes, and stipulated that the flights be booked during the travel lull in January. The conditions were fair and coincided with my schedule, so I told him to meet me at Bendels, the iconic, high-end retailer on Fifth Avenue. Our rendezvous and 'exchange' was the following afternoon at 3 pm. Meanwhile, I spent the rest of the day combing the streets on the lookout for shops that would complement my accessories and dually check-out competition so that I could adjust my mark-up.

I had made a significant profit from my jewelry sales in the capitals of Europe. So I decided to invest my funds into something that would fill my treasure chest with a valuable return – new adventures! I'd go to Bendel's early and check out their jewelry department. Ethnic jewelry was "in," and I hadn't seen anything that compared to my silver tribal trophies in the retail area. I was evidently the first exotic vendor to hit the metropolis with the flexible silver serpent belts and antique ivory-bone bangles.

As I entered Bendels, I was blasted with a sheet of heat that severed the snow flurry from whirling into the store. There was a large jewelry section on the main floor, so I asked a perfumed, over-painted clerk if the jewelry buyer was still on the second floor. She flashed her false lashes at me and said, "NO, she's always been on the third floor." I then queried, "Is the buyer still Mrs.Goldstein?" The clerk sounded irked as she replied, "No, it's Mrs. Bernstein!" "Ah yes," I replied and sincerely hoped the clerk wouldn't get sacked for spilling the beans.

Taking the elevator straight up to the third floor, I strolled confidently down the hallway until I saw a plexiglass sign on a glossy wooden door with the name embossed in gold - Mrs. Bernstein. Not only did I pick up on accents, but I acquired attitudes when I traveled. I discovered while in New York I became unusually brazen. NYC was a hard, competitive big city, and there was no time for pleasantries.

I didn't want to waste this lady's time. The door opened, and a pert but rude young lady asked, "Are you lost?" I volleyed back, "I'd like to see Mrs. Bernstein." The secretary stared at me and said, "Impossible." I thought for a second, "Well, I've come from India via Paris, especially to see Mrs. Bernstein." Miss Know-it-All didn't believe my story. However, a voice echoed from the rear of the office complex, "Leah, let her in."

A sophisticated woman of about forty-five with red hair, nails to match, and spiked heels studied me from head to toe and asked,

"What do you have? You look like a circus, but after all, you *are* wearing Missoni, even if it's last year's model." I confidently replied, "I've got the hottest item in ethnic jewelry this side of Afghanistan (which sounded more remote than India), and it's selling at Harrods in London."

I was fortunate to hit Harrods, Harvey Nicholls, and Selfridges all on the same day and made sizable sales at each landmark. Mrs. Bernstein said, "Okay, follow me to my office, and I'll find out if you're wasting my time or not." I pulled out three snake belts from my white cloth bag and laid them softly on her mahogany desk. Her eyes widened. She admitted, "I can only buy for Bendel's on the third Friday of each month, however, if you come to my apartment, I'll invite my friends over for some bubbles after work, and we can negotiate." Hallelujah, I not only got my toe into the buyer's office at Bendel's but I was also invited into her apartment on Madison Avenue. The Dale Carnegie course I splurged on in high school was paying off.

Mrs. Bernstein scribbled her address on the back of an embossed business card with a gold Cartier pen and told me to be there Thursday at 6 pm. She then said curtly, "You can go now." It was so different in the South, where people diplomatically said what they didn't mean and meant what they didn't say. I quite liked the New Yorkers' directness – you knew where you stood and where not to stand. No time was wasted.

I nodded and strutted down the office corridor, executing a perfect pirouette, ending with a ballet leap out of the office door. The secretary, engrossed in a crossword puzzle, didn't even bother to look up. I skipped down the hallway and into the elevator, where

I then yelped, followed with, "YES MA'AM, that's how you do it!" The three weary shoppers trapped with me took a step back and then moved nearer to the door to exit with haste. I maneuvered my way back onto the main floor through petulant perfume sprayers, combative cosmetic samplers, and display racks of accessories, exiting the main entrance and onto Fifth Avenue.

I still had half an hour to kill until my rendezvous with Ruggero. My excitement enabled me to jog around the block twice to work off some nervous energy and inhale some fresh air. New York department stores are so overheated and stuffy in the winter; you must wear a sleeveless t-shirt and check in your coat.

"*Ciao Bella,*" I heard Ruggero shouting from the corner of 57th St. and 5th Ave. He was an upbeat guy with a permanent grin and laughed with ease. I had $200 in an envelope to hand him for the flights. A real bargain – seven countries in all! Flight tickets went on sale before Christmas, along with everything else in New York. Oh well, no questions asked.

We made a seamless exchange – like runners on a relay team who passed the baton without losing speed. Ruggero sprinted back to his taxi, leaped in with his perplexed passenger, and sped off without explanation. I galloped straight up 5th Ave to the Metropolitan Museum of Art and remained there until the last call at 5:15 pm. I had bought a same-day discounted ticket for the Broadway musical "Porgy and Bess" that started at 8 pm, so I had time to look for other outlets to sell my jewelry and grab a bite to eat at a deli before show-time.

Hmmm, a grilled corned beef Reuben sandwich on rye with sauerkraut, Swiss cheese, and Russian dressing. Not Kosher, but mouth-watering and filling. I discovered it was assumed I was Jewish while in New York since strangers called me 'sister' with a knowing look. I'd nod and flash them my full-lipped Semitic smile.

I had two more days in NYC before heading to New Orleans. I wanted to go to the MOMA (Museum of Modern Art) and the Frank Lloyd Wright-designed Guggenheim Museum. Oh yes, also the ice skating rink at Rockefeller Plaza and more musicals! I wanted to check out Soho – the warehouse area that had become hip since a swarm of artists, photographers, writers, designers, and 'wannabes' had moved to the eclectic area to rent a roomy loft and wait to be discovered. There was so much high-strung energy in that cradle of creativity; I got a buzz that would last for weeks.

Between museums and musicals, I marched up and down Madison, Fifth, and Lexington Avenues, as well as all the cross streets, searching for retailers that were right for my ethnic treasures. I put together an aggressive sales pitch after a few failures. I would burst into a shop and shout, "I have something you can't live without." "Oh yeah?" was the usual reply, "Don't waste my time!" My silver belts and antique ivory bangles were eye-catchers, and every shop owner caressed a belt and questioned me, "Is this *really* silver?" I only had ten belts with me and had shipped the rest in a sturdy Samsonite to my mother in New Orleans.

I knew to be punctual and arrived at Bernstein's apartment on time. It was nearly the penthouse, give or take a few floors. As I entered the lofty living quarters, I remained blasé while panning the panoramic view of the Big Apple twinkling below. The décor sang out clearly, 'I'm rich and loving it.' The posh sofas were decorated with an array of middle-aged Jewish ladies, each attempting to outdo the other - in everything.

Of course, I was the odd-ball goy (gentile) but looked Jewish enough to blend since my hair was thick, brown, and curly. My nose was appropriately long, and my XL lips were painted magenta to match my nails, coordinated with my silk blouse and the nearby vase full of lavender roses. I wore my high-waisted French flared jeans, which exaggerated my disproportionately long legs. I glanced at the coffee table filled with the remnants of *lox* (smoked salmon belly), cream cheese on matza flatbread, and sun-dried tomato hummus dip. A bottle of Moet and Chandon was nearly empty, and the chatter was loud.

Perfect conditions for unrestrained splurging! I repeated my spiel about the Thar Desert gypsies, who hand-crafted the silver belts and wore them to perform their mesmerizing cobra dance. I cleaned up at Mrs. Bernstein's cozy coffee afternoon, selling a silver belt to each of the overly-enthusiastic ladies who thought they had bargained me senseless. I decided it was a miracle, considering their shapes and sizes. Post-champagne euphoria had taken hold of their sound judgment. Perhaps they would display their belt on a pedestal as an art form or give it to a slim relative. I imagined one of my sublime snake belts fastened around the well-fed waist of the Bette Midler look-alike would double as a tourniquet, giving her rosy cheeks a purple hue.

After I pocketed the money, Mrs. Bernstein told me, "You can see yourself out now." I was not offended; I exited a winner. However, the ladies were now proud owners of a hand-crafted treasure from the Kalbelia nomad tribe of the Thar Desert of Jaipur, India, and thus richer for it!

Newton's Law became a vivid reality as I plummeted down forty-seven floors, plastered to the elevator wall with bent knees to cushion the impact. I was feeling deeply deprived that I was not Jewish. After all, Jesus was Jewish, and since I became His follower, I became acutely aware of why God had chosen such exceptional people to reveal Himself to the world. The Jewish excelled at everything except the NFL (National Football League). They outshined goys in physics, medicine, banking, retailing, composing, conducting, directing, writing, acting, art, and arithmetic - even comedy. It wasn't their fault, but it had caused them a lot of grief throughout the centuries. Overachievers are under-appreciated, as well as highly envied.

I skipped down Madison Ave gleefully singing, "It's Summertime, and the livin' is . . . ," as snowflakes ironically settled on the parked cars and pavement. All the previous night's musical/opera songs from "Porgy & Bess" kept whirling around my mind, heart, and soul. They eventually forced their way through my lips in waves of vibrato, honoring composer George Gershwin (Gershowitz), who was blessed by his Ukrainian-Jewish ancestry. I rest my case.

* * *

Making my way back to my hotel near Broadway, I'd freshen up and call my friend Clem, who I'd met in Ibiza six months earlier. He insisted that I call him when I got to New York. Clem was the spitting image of the young, swashbuckling Tyrone Power. However, his good looks had not converted him into a macho-man. He was gentle and polite, a part-time pharmacist and a full-time vegetarian – plus a stickler for good nutrition. He seemed to have innate ethics, led by a moral compass and was a certified mystery man in the early 70s.

Clem was way ahead of his time in juicing, especially green stuff, and gulping daily shots of wheatgrass. He was also the only male I knew that kindly warned about contraceptive pills adverse effects – the undisputed gateway to flower-power and promiscuity of the hippie, 'make love, not war' movement. Clem also knew how to converse with females. He was interested in music, off-Broadway plays, out-of-the-way gourmet eateries, fashion, and travel. We always had a lot to laugh about and never ran short of stories. Most importantly, we seemed to have a mutual perspective on life.

Raised in Queens, his father was willing to back him with his own pharmacy in his local neighborhood, but Clem was headed for Manhattan. He found a fourth-floor walk-up studio on 59th Street near 1st Avenue, viewing the Queensboro Bridge, explaining that he chose part-time work to enjoy life full-time. I admired Clem; at twenty-seven, he understood his needs, and his priorities were in place.

He was writing screenplays on the side and promoting the famous Ibiza liquor, *Hierbas*, which he discovered while visiting my island of Ibiza in the Med. It was a potent liquor filled with medicinal herbs – first brewed by Monks in the Middle Ages on Spain's Balearic Islands. No less than eighteen botanical elements contribute to the creation of Hierbas.

Clem had the cosmopolitan instinct to contact the owner of the Ibizan production of Hierbas, Señor Mari Mayans. Having obtained the distribution rights for the USA, he reached out to the largest alcoholic beverage companies to represent the herb-filled liquor.

My hotel, the Wellington, was old and lacked luster, but on 55th St and 7th Ave – it was smack-dab in the center of the theater district and a stone's throw to almost everything worth seeing. NYC was a walking city – the city blocks were short, and my legs were long. I dared to call Clem at work in an uptown pharmacy, and he enthusiastically said he'd whiz by my hotel at 8 pm after his shift ended. I peeked out of the revolving door when a gold vintage Cadillac De Ville convertible pulled up with Clem at the wheel. I bolted out and jumped into the passenger's seat, and we had a friendly hug over the posh armrest console that separated us.

Clem was cool but far from a hippie - however, he was a rebel. His lengthy, black hair was held back neatly in a low ponytail, and he was dressed head to toe in white, wrapped in a navy blue *peacoat*. The last time I'd seen a "Navy" peacoat was when I was ten years old. But Clem was so cool - he could pull off driving a Cadillac with white leather interior, decked out in white jeans, a white sweatshirt, and tennis shoes in the height of winter. After all, European designers searched for street fashion in the US (especially NYC) to transform the casual 'look' into designer chic.

We laughed and reminisced during the six-mile drive down to Chinatown. My waist-long curls were flying in the breeze, topped by a Woolworth's knit ski cap, and I was bundled up in a Norma Kamali coat. Norma moved the needle of design by giving birth to the sleeping bag coat. Her shop was located on East 53rd Street. The window display stopped me in my tracks as I was jogging by. She had transformed gym wear into clubwear and shaped comfy casual into unimaginable style. Kamali was dancing on the lip of a fashion volcano that would explode worldwide. She was someone to follow.

As we crunched through the snow to get to a Vietnamese restaurant on the edge of Chinatown, Clem explained the nutritional advantages of opting for The Saigon restaurant. He assured me that MSG (monosodium glutamate) was forbidden, and their products were organically cultivated. He convinced me my eyes would be brighter and my skin softer after this meal.

Growing up post-war, in the land of plenty, I thrived on greasy burgers and French fries dipped in mayonnaise from the local Louisiana-style drive-in joints. My mom prepared balanced meals at home, and all the Mars bars, Hershey Kisses, and artificially flavored nibbles I consumed didn't seem to take a toll on my vital organs. I pretended to be impressed with the healthy experience we were about to embark upon. I was twenty-seven, skinny, felt good and couldn't get wrapped up in the merits of eating organically. I ran behind a DDT truck from ages three to six in New Orleans' mosquito-infested lakefront district and survived, but I was appreciative of Clem's concern and quaint desire to avoid poison.

I pleaded with him to order quickly since my hypoglycemic symptoms had kicked in, and I was on the verge of eating the tablecloth. He explained the merits of the Vietnamese fresh spring rolls you designed at the table.

During Clem's spring roll narrative, I inhaled the rice prawn crackers and simultaneously wiped out the peanut sauce. I could feel the calorie rush calming my nerves. Phew.....I was ready to ingest those succulent spring rolls and slurp some chicken Pho, while Clem opted for the vegetarian counterpart. I wondered how an Italian boy, born and raised in Queens, could be delivered from sausage, spaghetti Bolognese, pepperoni pizza, and chicken Alfredo pasta. I heard that Catholic Priests were into exorcism; perhaps he had been delivered from the desire to eat meat . . . . ?

Clem insisted that we end the meal in *Piccola Italia* (Little Italy). It was only about a five-minute slush and slide until we were inside Café Palermo. While we were thawing out, basking in the aromatic atmosphere of espresso, I studied the framed photos covering the bullet-chipped walls. They were all action shots of Italian boxing stars such as the undefeated "Iron Chin" Rocky Marciano, "Raging Bull" Jake La Mota, "The Giant," Primo Carnera, plus a string of other memorable knock-out artists - many from NYC, boasting rags to riches stories.

Another delectable suggestion was anise biscotti (a tooth-chipping double-baked long bread infused with anise liquor.) The idea was to dip it into a piping hot cappuccino before dripping it over the tablecloth into your mouth. Clem convinced me to try a Cannoli Siciliana topped with pistachios. I thought about camping out in Café Palermo forever . . . . wearing a fashionable bullet-proof vest, of course.

* * *

Clem and I reminisced about our times together in Ibiza, including the 'in' bar *La Tierra*. The owner, Arleen, was an ex-librarian from Brooklyn who was an indisputable encyclopedia with a cryptic Jewish wit that enhanced her *Brooklyn* accent. Her cameo-white complexion offset her jet black, teased hair, complementing her Cleopatra-style eye make-up. She always wore a kaftan, and it was rumored she had a Moroccan lover hidden somewhere.

The bar drew the ex-pat American enclave that was usually tucked away in the San Juan hills – especially the draft dodgers with the girls in tow. Even though the Vietnam War was ebbing, the good life in Ibiza was exploding. Pacha Disco had opened in 1973 in a *finca* (farmhouse) about a mile from *La Tierra* (The Earth), just across the bay. This charming club ushered in a spanking new era of night-life in Ibiza.

A culture shift had taken place. Once crowded with locals in their folkloric costumes, the quaint streets of Ibiza were being transformed with a mix of multi-national hippies, artists, authors, colorful conmen, and characters of every stripe and persuasion. You could be whoever you wanted to be – fantasy personalities and titles were up for grabs. Last names were obsolete for obvious reasons, so descriptions were tacked onto first names. For example, Leather Lou, Freddie Flute, Handsome Harry, Beautiful Barry, Soho Suzie, Pink Peter, Lady Liz, and Macrobiotic Mary were some of the depictive names that identified people.

Against this backdrop, I met Clem. He was an exception to the rule. He had a good job in NYC, and he didn't dally with drugs . . . only green chlorophyll powder and juiced veggies. We sipped Hierbas at La Tierra most evenings with my two Amazon companions. The three of us girls were five foot nine, slim, with long hair and outrageous outfits. Paula, an American of Lebanese extract, had huge dark eyes and glossy black hair. Her choice of pure white apparel enhanced her toasted tan. Clem fell for her; who wouldn't? Ute, a gorgeous German model married to an Afro-American military man from Mississippi stationed in Germany, was the third Musketeer.

Clem opted for a small hotel near the ancient, esthetic, walled *Dalt Vila* (high city). The fortified pyramid-shaped 16th-century

Renaissance city was held together by 400 years of whitewashing and was topped with a grand cathedral. Nobility, along with the bishops, were perched at the top for a bird's eye view and the hierarchy descended, winding down to the simple folk at the bottom.

Dozens of cobblestone lanes were filled with magenta bougainvillea and nearly nude gypsy children, along with mongrel dogs and free-range chickens. Most of the aristocrats had moved out of the magnificent walled city into dull, comfortable dwellings that boasted running water and electricity.

Our days were spent on *Las Salinas* Beach, not far from the salt flats that attracted the Roman settlers in 123 BC. We'd then hightail it back to the Ibiza port for an afternoon *horchata* (tiger nut) power drink in view of the ferry landing. From there, we could casually scrutinize the fresh arrivals as they descended the boat from Barcelona. There was just enough time to shower and dress for La Tierra. Afterward, we'd ramble down to *Mono des Nudo* Bar (Naked Ape), then dine in style at the upstairs eatery, *Los Pasajeros* (The Passengers) or *Juanito's Pollos* (Johnny's Chickens).

It was hard to spend more than a buck on a meal, including wine and bottled water. Juanito looked like Goliath but was as gentle as a lamb, and his roasted chickens were the best in town. After an hour of warm-up disco at Lola's cave, adjacent to the ancient wall, we'd end up in Pacha by midnight, ready to rock out until they flickered the lights at 3 am.

For the grand opening of the elite club, I went as a 'basket case.' Cutting the bottom out of my Ibiza hand-woven basket, I stepped into it and swung the long rope straps around my neck. I then popped a bouquet of gladiolas into the basket and VOILÀ. I resembled a 'chicken in the basket' with spiked heels and stork-like legs. I won the masquerade contest but lost some suitors, who rated my outfit less than romantic.

Our Amazon clique's fame grew, and we were often invited to an infamous art forger's home for lunch in *Los Molinos* (The windmills). Elymr de Hory could copy any renowned artist, and he did. Although he was Hungarian, his English was superb and his American friend, Mark, clued him in on all the latest slang. Elymr had spent time in a French prison and was hiding in Ibiza, but by now, he had signed his name to his awesome artwork that resembled the old masters.

Elymr's endearing conversations always lingered on the periphery of truth and were taken with a grain of salt. He was cunningly catty and such an intriguing gossip, you felt honored to be added to his entourage . . . . even if you were to become his next verbal victim.

Clifford Irving, who lived on the road to San José with his Swiss wife, Edith, had written a best-seller about Elmyr, appropriately titled *Fake*. After a few lean years, Irving embarked on an audacious and meticulously executed autobiography, supposedly composed of interviews with the billionaire recluse Howard Hughes.

However, Hughes unexpectedly emerged briefly from his fifteen-year seclusion to testify against Clifford's almost-perfect literary crime. Meanwhile, Clifford's wife had deposited the huge advance payment from McGraw-Hill, written to H. Hughes, into a Swiss account using the name Helga Hughes. Irving's sentence was reduced to 17 months in a NYC jail, while Edith was sentenced in Switzerland.

Although Ibiza had an element of spirituality and a growing community of seekers, art and literary hoaxes were considered "soft crimes," and the hoaxers were perceived as brilliant stars. I tried to analyze what drew me to Ibiza. I think it was the unconditional acceptance I felt. There were no social standards or stigmas. The more eccentric, entrancing, or exotic you appeared, rather than how rich and famous you were, determined your celebrity status.

It was like stepping back into another era. The lack of work ethic among the foreigners removed any incentive to 'get my act together.' However, if you were in tune with the advancing boom, you knew everything was possible. As far as I was concerned, it was a great place to soak up the sun, dance, and have fun without feeling guilt or remorse. It was my special unspoiled spot to unplug and recharge. I was a working girl and deserved a good holiday. I needed a few more years of nomad lifestyle; then, I'd rethink the upcoming opportunities.

* * *

New York is a city that never sleeps, and this week Clem had the graveyard shift at the drug store where he starred as the engaging, handsome pharmacist. As we headed uptown in his golden Cadillac convertible, he confessed the weight of responsibility he felt in filling prescriptions. I admired Clem's conscience and decided he must have gleaned something from his pre-teen catechism classes as a kid growing up in Queens. Or perhaps he had an inherent sense of duty. Whatever the case, I'd have to wait until my return from South America, heading back to Europe, to experience the star-studded clubs of New York City.

Clem was a regular at all the 'in' clubs and a favorite due to his sterling behavior and untarnished good looks. In a few months, by the time I returned, Salsa would be the rage, and I was raised on Tabasco!

Along with traveling, dancing was my preferred passion and pastime. Meanwhile, I was heading to New Orleans, where I could strut my stuff and sing my heart out 'cause that swingin' city had rhythm like no other. Of course, some might argue, except for Rio. I'd soon find out since my strategy was to be in Brazil for Carnival. RIO or BUST became my hedonist motto and mantra-type battle cry!

Clem dropped me back at my hotel before midnight and gave me some valuable 'life or death' advice along the way. "Remember Tyke, go lightly on sugar – it feeds negative stuff. Also, try and avoid meat and dairy products – you know they're full of antibiotics and other junk." I nodded and looked grateful. Clem never mentioned I should be careful traveling around South America alone, so that was a pleasant relief. I figured if I could survive New Orleans, Bogota would be a breeze.

My flight was at noon, so I decided to play it safe and leave my mid-town hotel at 9 am. I'd eat breakfast at Kennedy Airport and thumb through all the fashion magazines. The polished bellhop carried my suitcases to the curb and blew his deafening police whistle until a cab screeched to a halt. I hopped in and hoped the cabby wouldn't revolt at my request to go only six blocks.

The bus terminal had the same chaotic atmosphere as the Bombay train station. My way of surviving was to sing at the top of my lungs, releasing happy hormones and dually parting the crowd . . .

like the Red Sea. I liked to travel chic, so I wore my Missoni multi-colored coat and matching fedora hat. My leather luggage, made in Rome, weighed a ton but added pizzazz to my overall 'look.'

Also, I didn't want to disappoint the autograph seekers who might mistakenly think I was Carly Simon – the famous singer and songwriter married to James Taylor. Not wanting anyone to think Carly was a snob, I kindly signed with a flair and wished them well. By now, I had accepted that my tall, lean stature, prominent mouth with full lips, and long curly brown hair were not unique. They were clearly shared with a well-known singer, so I'd go with the flow and smile.

It was only an hour to the airport on the express bus, so I spent my time wisely filing my nails and shaping my brows so I could hit the ground running in New Orleans and not waste any time. By now, I'd made friends with my kinky, curly hair and even encouraged it to fluff with a wide-toothed Afro comb.

I was wearing my soft suede, hand-printed Cavalli outfit, and felt like a million dollars. After signing nearly a dozen autographs and returning a few "I know who you are" winks from fans who didn't dare to disturb me, I chilled out in the food court, tempted to woof down a beef burger, but heeding Clem's advice, I chose an egg sandwich and natural yogurt, ugh.

My non-stop Delta flight to New Orleans was punctual and comfortable. After the plane took off and the seat-belt signs allowed, I casually moved to an empty seat on the emergency exit row to stretch my long legs. It was only a three-and-a-half-hour flight, but that would give me time to shake off my NYC aggressive attitude and re-acquire my New Orleans 'laid-back' manner. I noticed my seatmate's knees protruding into the seat in front, and he was twice my height in a seated position. He was either an NBA basketball star or a run-away freak from a traveling circus.

I made a point not to start conversations on airplanes until the descent. That way, it would be a short but sweet interaction. I cleared my throat and said, "Basketball?" He nodded and said, "Singer?" I nodded. That was it, short but sweet.

When the plane finally rolled to a stop, I hopped up to get my heavy hand luggage from the overhead compartment. The jolly giant seated next to me had to bend over in a standing position not to crack his head open on the plane's ceiling. I tried not to stare and started to sing instead. "Oh, when the saints, oh when the saints go marching in, oh yes, I want to be in that number … …."

I prayed that the doors would open to get a move on the crowded, cramped situation. We finally exited and had a quarter-mile walk to the luggage pick-up. My new friend offered to carry my hefty hand luggage. I didn't want to be offensive and refuse, so I said, "How very kind of you, sir." I wanted to show him respect and prove that I was not prejudiced.

2. NEW ORLEANS

I could see my mother and brother in the distance waving and started skipping to keep up with the long stride of my airplane buddy who was toting my bag. It was like, "Guess Who's Coming to Dinner?" I hadn't been back to New Orleans in three years and was always full of surprises. When I stopped to hug mom and bro, I asked Hercules if he needed a ride into the city, but he smiled and said, "Thanks, ma'am, but my limo will be waiting for me."

WHAM, as we stepped out of the air-conditioned airport, it felt like someone had thrown a wet blanket over me. Hello New Orleans! I could feel my hair shrinking up a few inches and my mascara starting to melt, but I was home – or was I? I must admit that I felt more culture shock returning to New Orleans than when I arrived in Europe. I believe God Almighty has a purpose for each of us in His appointed place. Therefore, it was of paramount importance for me to find that assigned place because being in God's will was the safest place to be.

As we strolled through the parking lot, we stopped at a curious van, and my brother announced that my mom had bought a practical vehicle to transport large paintings from her Art Gallery. The van had heart-shaped windows and was named "Love Machine." As my brother slid the door open to deposit my bags, there was a water bed atop a shaggy carpet. I climbed in, sat cross-legged on the water bed, and sloshed mindlessly through the city, heading to the French Quarter.

My brother was a great prankster - I swallowed the van story hook, line, and sinker. I thought, how cool is that for my mom to buy a "Love Mobile" to transport art? It seems a finance company had just repossessed the van, and it was in limbo for a few days in their sales lot, so he borrowed it for the airport run. I had become immune to his antics during my three years of non-stop travel and unlimited readjustments.

However, I looked forward to my visit to the Crescent City with anticipation! Crossing Canal Street, we rolled into the French Quarter on Bourbon St., then right onto Iberville St. for a few blocks, and down Chartres Street. Within minutes we were in mom's townhouse and art gallery. The *Vieux Carre* (Old Quarter) is actually of Spanish design, even though it is referred to as the French Quarter. The balconies display hand-crafted wrought iron railings, while inner patios are flooded with flowers, allowing light into the interior rooms. The spacious patios also separate the master's house from the workers' quarters.

Less than half a block from my mom's Art Gallery is the famed Jackson Square with the venerable St. Louis Cathedral that opened in 1794. It is flanked on one side by the historical *Cabildo* (Spanish for town council) looking onto the green square. On the other side is the Presbytère, built initially on the site of the residence of Capuchin monks. It then became a courthouse and ended part of the Louisiana State Museum.

Center stage in the landscaped square stands a bronze equestrian statue of Andrew Jackson, the General commanding US troops during the victorious Battle of New Orleans in the War of 1812.

A mere hop, skip, and a jump away is the mighty Mississippi and why the original site for New Orleans was chosen by the Sieur de Bienville in the early seventeen hundreds. He wisely chose the river's sharp curve with deep waters, and by 1840 New Orleans port was the fourth largest in the world! Nearby are the famed Café du Monde and the open French Market with fresh produce.

Due to the historical architecture, curious culture, the birthplace of jazz, and the fame of grandiose Mardi Gras parades, New Orleans reigns as a top tourist destination. With the stunning ambiance of the French Quarter, let's take a close-up view.

Jackson Square has become a multi-colored carnival of artistic artists, con artists, musicians, street performers, hobos, derelicts, and multi-national eccentrics who can't afford to leave. The horse-drawn carriages are bumper to bumper on Decatur St, emitting the aroma of sweat and horse manure mingled with the perfume of chicory coffee. However, the city has not only charisma and charm but lots of soul – so let the good times roll . . . !

In the old quarter, infamous Bourbon Street has a string of vintage burlesque shows and is now littered with t-shirt shops and other souvenir dives. Regal Royal Street is lined with art galleries, bars, and classy restaurants. However, peeping between commercial sites are stately, nostalgic apartment buildings, with Blanche DuBois-style ladies lounging on the verandas. Tennessee Williams, the famous playwright, was inspired by New Orleans when he wrote *The Streetcar named Desire* from his French Quarter apartment just around the corner.

Despite the litter and rowdy tourists, the atmosphere was electrifying. Young Afro-American boys, truant from school, were tap-dancing on every street corner while exquisite "live" jazz and blues streamed from opened doors of all the bars. For the meager price of a beer, your return on investment was a hundredfold. Aspiring musicians poured into the city from every nook and cranny of the US and abroad to soak up the sound and glean from aging maestros who were now on the rebound.

* * *

New Orleans is a 'convention city,' and everyone wants to return home with an original work of art. My mother's art gallery, Adventures in Art, is in a commercial spot. Removed from the tourist center's hustle and bustle, it's a stone's throw from Jackson Square and easily spotted from a distance.

Mom's goal was to birth a gallery to accommodate the first showing for university art professors and their graduating students. Unless you're Picasso, it's hard to get your toe into the art world. Most Fine Arts graduates work in frame shops, become art teachers, or attempt to marry well.

The *Times-Picayune* newspaper liked mom's approach and covered all her openings with rave reviews in their *Lagniappe* column. She adored becoming a patron of the arts and lifted up many gifted artists with her savvy promo skills and polished sales pitch.

After stacking my suitcases in the revamped servants' quarters, my mom (Peggy) kindly asked, "Honey, what would you like to eat?" . . . . "Okra gumbo" rolled off my tongue. We went to a simple neighborhood restaurant where a lady called Maw-maw Boudreaux, who could single-handedly wrestle an alligator while reciting the Rosary in Cajun French, created the best seafood gumbo this side of Lafayette.

We caught up with all the latest news, then reminisced about our month spent together at Safari Camps in Kenya, cycling around Mombasa and Lamu, and then boating to Zanzibar with an amazing crew.

It was fun having a mom who allowed me to choose our vacation destinations and agreed on my choice of funky accommodation. I could hear the tssss, tssss hissing sound of her Lysol spray as she disinfected toilet seats, hand basins, and nearly everything. I thought it was normal to have a mom with the same energy level and enthusiasm, even though she was double my age. Peggy was petite and elegant but a resilient ball of fire.

My brother made me laugh so hard that I could hardly breathe as I slurped my seafood gumbo and sipped my freshly brewed iced tea. Bananas Foster flamed with rum and served with homemade ice cream boosted my energy so I could boogie around the Quarter, visit friends, and soak up raw jazz in Preservation Hall. Yes!

Christmas was only a week away, and festive décor was strung everywhere. So were the bums and hobos camped out on the benches in Jackson Square. They were usually docile, so I'd buy them a hot dog and a cold drink from the Luck Dog pushcart.

The duck girl Ruthie was an eccentric who wandered around the Quarter with her feathered friend waddling behind. By now, she was nearing forty but still referred to as the 'duck girl' since she was about five feet tall and weighed in wet at 90 lbs. Posing for photos with her duck pal became so lucrative she exchanged her office job for an outdoor, sociable existence and enjoyed being unusual. She wore long, frilly dresses and a flashy bonnet secured with a fancy ribbon, tied in a big bow under her small chin. Her voice blended perfectly with her quack talk, surpassing that of Disney's Daisy Duck.

New Orleans was a fun city except for the violent criminal element. My brother explained how he jogged around the French Quarter after work with a Mace can in his hand, ready to spray any would-be attackers. As kids, we lived in the ultra-safe lakefront zone where our most formidable enemy was the DDT truck that sprayed the mosquitoes (and us) every afternoon.

Our folks made the wise decision of buying a property in an ozone forest forty miles north of New Orleans. The causeway, a twenty-four-mile bridge that crossed Lake Pontchartrain, converted the north shore of the lake into a suburb, and my dad commuted to work in New Orleans.

We were brainwashed into believing that rural life in the country with horses, dogs, and a river would be a step up from life in the metropolis. My mother adored gardening, my dad loved fishing, and my brother was a cross between Huckleberry Finn and Davy Crockett. I longed for asphalt, cement, and window shopping. I bid my time until I was fourteen and passed my driver's license so I could sneak into the French Quarter scene.

Feeling isolated in the beautiful snake-ridden *San Souci* (without care) forest, I imported friends to sleep over on the weekends. We'd ride horses, swim in the river, play tetherball, shuffleboard, pool, ping pong, dance around our game room with the jukebox blaring and talk all night long. Looking back, it was a paradise; it just goes to show you what an insufferable brat I was.

However, being a people-pleaser, I pretended all was hunky-dory. After a decade in Covington, my brother and I headed off to Universities, and our mom opened an art gallery in one of her French Quarter properties. Voilà! New Orleanians love their city, and most never think of leaving . . . .for good. The ambiance of independent thinkers, creative spirits, and non-conformists is unique and something I could appreciate.

My mom had already retrieved the sturdy suitcase I shipped her, chock-full of silver belts and ivory bangles. It seems she outwitted the customs officer with charm and logic and already had a display set up in her gallery. She decided that "Adventures in Art" covered hand-crafted silver belts as well as etchings, sculptures, and paintings. Having sold several belts already, I acquired instant pocket money for my journey to South America.

Mardi Gras was synonymous with New Orleans and world-renowned, but I was headed to THE Carnival in Rio de Janeiro in mid-February. I'd be shoving off on the 3rd of January.

Parades, floats, music, and dance are deeply etched into my eight generations of French ancestry. *Mardi Gras* (French for Fat Tuesday) is celebrated the day before Ash Wednesday and the beginning of Lent - with the first grand parade (Mystic Krewe of Comus) commencing in 1856.

However, this Catholic observance had long since mutated into an unrivaled revelry of krewes and floats. The themes, borrowed from Greek mythology, are transformed into opulent floats manned by a King and his court.

Glass-beaded necklaces and doubloons are tossed from these moving extravaganzas, all the while crowds scream in unison, "Throw me somethin', mister!" By now, there were about thirty-five different parades. A krewe is a social organization that puts on a parade or ball for the Carnival season. This year's top parades are pegged to be Bacchus and Endymion, both with celebrity guests.

There's no neat way to connect the dots between ancient pagan festivals and the modern pre-Lenten revels that explode in different guises around the globe. Mardi Gras was transported from Europe to the New World during the colonial era. In New Orleans, the grand gala has evolved from a celebration for locals into an iconic, internationally recognized spectacle.

There's even unique Mardi Gras lingo and a parade aristocracy. Your social standing depended on how long your ancestors had been involved in a prestigious krewe. Your status was hiked higher if a family member had been elected king of a parade and crowned at the ensuing ball. My mother displayed acute discernment by boarding up her home and gallery and fleeing to a nearby state during the week of wild debauchery, described by many as the highlight of the year.

* * *

We would have Christmas lunch with my mom's brother, Uncle Clay, my Aunt Joei, and our well-behaved, morally-conscious cousins, Clay III and Dodie. Their uptown mansion was located in the Garden District - just blocks off the famed St. Charles Ave, where the streetcars run and the Mardi Gras parades roll by.

My Uncle Clay and Aunt Joei were a "nothing is impossible" couple. My Aunt Joei was a California girl who embraced not only my uncle but the New Orleans lifestyle. They loved to entertain and Aunt Joei was an excellent cook, a gracious hostess, and a genuine beauty.

They owned a string of business schools and crisscrossed the US in their private Mooney, single-engine piston-powered aircraft, selling business, motivation, and self-improvement courses. On weekends, they sped around in their classic Chris-Craft wooden speedboat, moored at the lakefront yacht club. Our cousins excelled at school and everything else.

The Spencers were a fun family, and my uncle was a kind, practical joker, but we couldn't help feeling like country bumpkins when we joined them for a Christmas soiree. Our laid-back country life lacked a dress code or structure.

I would have had to buy a green velvet Christmas gown with dressy pumps and a handbag to obey the proper protocol. I opted for something in my suitcase. My choice was a turquoise catsuit that matched my ethnic Tibetan jewelry, bell-bottom jeans and a tie-dye t-shirt, or my Roberto Cavalli suede, hand-printed designer ensemble. I decided on the Cavalli suede since it was more appropriate for a swank banquet.

We had a rustic luxurious lifestyle in the country. My folks built a replica of the family plantation from the actual blueprints, and we had a boat in our backyard on a deep river. Nevertheless, I felt like a gate crasher when we entered my aunt and uncle's elegant Victorian three-floor, immaculately decorated home filled with rare antiques.

Fearful of sitting on their white silk sofa, I opted for a brown leather chair to avoid leaving a suede imprint of my derrière. My brother sported a smart-looking suit but plastic dress shoes from Wal-Mart. We tried hard but missed the mark. Never mind, we had exciting travel stories to compensate for being late and slightly out of sync.

My mom was conservative with class and wore a petite Pierre Cardin ensemble that fit both her and the occasion. Turkey with oyster dressing, homemade cranberry sauce, and sweet potato pure with sautéed vegetables comprised the mouth-watering main course. The meal was topped off with pecan pie, pralines, and homemade Hungarian Christmas cookies for a sweet ending.

Aunt Joei was in her element and excelled at entertaining. Rather than appearing drained, she was pumped and radiant. Everything was perfect until the background Christmas Carols were interrupted by what sounded like a Broadway Musical.

I liked musicals, but this number didn't blend with the Yuletide spirit. It started off okay, and then the singer seemed to wander off-key, trying to reach C above high C. There was a painful screech as the singer hung on for dear life, trying to keep it together. We looked around in disbelief, and my brother started to snicker. My aunt was perplexed." How did *that* get into my Christmas Carols?"

BAM, it was like someone had pulled the rug from under my feet when I realized it was my prank present to Spike for Christmas. I discovered a tourist trap recording studio and took the bait by recording a tape with a karaoke background. Their version of "It's Summertime" was written for an opera star, not me. There was no way to lower the key, so I kept singing to get my money's worth.

My dilemma was, what do I do with the tragic tape? My lightning-fast mind came to the conclusion of giving it to my brother for Christmas. Oh no, my bro had converted my warped joke into his own, and I was force-fed some humble pie.

Being immensely proud of my singing abilities made the farce a more significant blow to my ego. There was no way of back-pedaling or denying it was me. I was attempting to transmit the image of a local girl who makes it big in Europe and returns home a success. So I just gave in and laughed hysterically while trying to figure out a just retaliation.

That evening we went together to sing Christmas Carols in Jackson Square, and I felt absolute joy, even euphoria, in singing about the birth of Yeshua. But I longed to spend quality time alone with my Lord and opted for the St. Louis Cathedral. I realize that Jesus doesn't live in church buildings, but I felt a hallowed atmosphere there.

* * *

New Year's Eve would be a blast with my extraordinary ex-roommates. I stayed with Joey and David in Morocco and then again in Switzerland. I was amazed to discover they could reintegrate into a semi-normal lifestyle after years of travel. I couldn't. They had cuisine genes and whatever they created was five-star Michelin quality. However, rather than cook professionally, David irrationally opened a specialty pet shop. They had purchased a huge home in an uptown residential area with a business license. What a rare find. With three floors, they converted the ground floor into "Wings and Things" unique pet shop and enjoyed spacious living above.

It was clever to have peculiar pets, less competition, and more compensation. I wondered what David's turnover was in tarantulas, toucans, reticulated pythons, blue cockatoos, grand electus parrots, and snapping turtles. Joey was a realist and snapped up a secure job as a registered sanitarian. Soon after, she was appointed head of the New Orleans Sanitation Department – a natural-born stickler for hygiene. Her passion was entertaining, and New Year's Eve would be a memorable food fest.

I arrived early to help. With astute wisdom, Joey assigned me menial tasks such as making sandwiches while she and David whipped up amazing dips, casseroles, seafood extravaganzas, and prime rib. Perhaps I was assigned to simple sandwiches to tactfully keep me from underfoot.

New Year's Eve was the perfect occasion to wear my turquoise bell-bottom catsuit and Tibetan tribal silver. I planned on bumping and grinding my way into the New Year with some salsa and disco moves that would devour any excess calories. Even the klutzy wallflowers were rockin', and I clucked my way towards the New Year doing the Funky Chicken Dance. David was the in-house DJ, knew the tunes to get people moving, and was an amazing dancer. "Go, David, go!"

David's dad was an in-demand doctor, and his mother was a high-society southern belle. However, David resembled Joe Cocker unrestrained. Joey was tall with Bette Davis-sized eyes and lips that stood out, colored with Revlon's famous fire-engine red. Her dark hair dangled past her waist, and she wore a parrot on her left shoulder that Long John Silver would have envied. She had on an embroidered blouse and vest she'd discovered in Afghanistan and some of my prized Indian silver. Cool as a cucumber, Joey revealed zero stress despite dozens of dancers rocking around ruthlessly in between the priceless antiques.

I felt like the belle of the ball until some guy walked up and said, "Well, Tyke and Spike, the world travelers - are y'all really related?"

"Yep, we're only a year apart," I bragged.

"Oh, I thought you were more than a year older than your brother." I could see Spike smiling. OUCH, I'll never fall into that trap again. The guy shuffled away, having met the infamous Spike and Tyke combo. My brother grinned, "Got ya' good that time." Lesson learned. I'd have to be more specific in how I worded my replies.

The party was a hit, and the firecrackers and rockets shot from the roof at midnight soared through the neighborhood without incident. New Orleans didn't have rules; instead, it was accepted that rules were rejected. I was invited to spend the night, so I popped my toothbrush into my bag. It was nearly 4 am when I succumbed to my four-poster bed in the gargantuan guest room. The heirlooms from their family plantation, Shadows-on-the-Teche, wedged in well with the extra high ceilings. I drifted to sleep mid-prayers in my antebellum canopied bed and dreamed sweet dreams until noon.

* * *

I was getting itchy to experience new lands, brush up on my Spanish, and also the salsa. I'd learn the tango plus glean from the vibrating moves of the street-strutting Samba Queens. I had the right anatomy for that Brazilian dance; I was a beanpole whose innate ability to dance and mimic hip-shaking rhythms was certainly not from the proper, sensible Spencer side of my family.

With only two days until my flight to Bogota, I borrowed my mom's car to zip over the causeway to Covington and catch up with some childhood school pals. I was eight when we moved across the Lake into a rented house while my parents built their dream home in the depths of a snake-infested forest. As fortune would have it, the girl next door was conveniently my age, and we became bosom buddies. Her name is Becky, and her large family became my extended kin. Becky and I were inseparable for a decade. We eventually ended up in distinct Universities, then different states, and now separate continents.

As kids, we dressed alike, and people often asked if we were sisters. Meanwhile, Becky looked like a child star from the TV Mickey Mouse Club or perhaps the lead role in a Walt Disney film. People stopped us on the street to comment on her beauty. I looked like a child version of Carol Burnett, but I could tap dance and sing. Never mind, Becky was my best friend, so I took on her beauty, and she absorbed my camouflaged X-Factor. Becky was a champion at every sport, and I was a polite people-pleaser, so together, we were individually complete.

We decided to visit a mutual friend who had married her Southeastern football beau and had three toddlers under the age of five. "Hi Tyke, what have y'all been up to? I haven't seen ya' since high school graduation. Wow, you've improved . . . . .who would have ever imagined you'd become sorta attractive?"

"Sarah, I can't believe you have three children already – they're so cute and well-behaved." On that note, two kids started to scream while the third threw up.

"Tell me where you've been. I heard you went to Europe."

"Yes, I've been gone for three years, traveling to the Far East, India, Nepal, the Middle East, Africa, and most of Europe."

"Oh, how scary! How can you travel alone? You are so brave!" Our conversation was sandwiched between baby wipes and shrieks, but Sarah was obviously in heaven.

"On the contrary," I replied, "You're the outrageously courageous one - getting married right out of school and having a trio of kids!"

"But I want a few more; I'm missing some girls."

I realized early on that most former friends blanked out if I spoke about my travels and would rapidly return to safe ground chatting about diaper rash, recipes, measles, and the best burping techniques. If someone sincerely wanted to hear about my Odyssey, they'd have to beg me—different strokes for different folks. God has a unique plan for each of us, and the key is to discover His plan and try to stay in step without tripping.

My mother casually primed me, "Honey, don't feel pressured into getting married. Not everyone needs to marry, and there is such an overpopulation problem. There are SO many children in the world already, no need to add any more." I felt comforted that my mom wasn't harping on me to get serious, settle down, and have offspring. It certainly gave me a sense of freedom. (On the other hand, I wondered if she lost sleep, fretting about having a few kids dumped on her if I divorced and decided to take off to Timbuktu. Something to contemplate . . . . . later.)

I wanted to breeze around Covington to our old stomping grounds and take in the changes of the past decade. Claiborne Hill referred to as 'The Hill,' was more of a bump. It boasted the title of the "in" Dairy Queen and was our favorite hang-out to connect with friends and flirt with wild Catholic guys from St. Paul's High. In an attempt to cultivate some curves, I inhaled a banana split daily, but the calories evaporated, and I considered contoured padded pants and the oomph of a Wonderbra. I wanted to live the American dream and not the gangly girl nightmare.

We then sped by our alma mater, Covington High. I had mixed memories. Some were sublime, and others I am still trying to forget. They called me 'teacher's pet' when I was named one of the thirty students selected from Louisiana to attend a Space Seminar headed up by Wernher von Braun, the aerospace engineer and leading figure in the development of rocket technology.

We were bused to New Mexico and taken in by families who jumped at the chance to rub shoulders with a future astronaut or engineer. Hopefuls from all fifty states were given an aptitude exam. I achieved a perfect score on the multiple-choice questions by my bullet-proof method of eeny-meeny-miny-mo, placing my X in the adjacent box. Bingo!

For two days, I thought Mr. Braun was speaking in his native tongue - German. When I realized that all my companions were taking notes and he was indeed speaking my language with an accent, I wisely skipped classes and discovered the charming city of Albuquerque. The family I was housed with felt honored to sponsor me and imagined they were conscientious citizens supporting our expanding space program. I didn't want to disappoint them and tried to appear intelligent, which took a lot of time and effort.

Becky broke into my daydream, "Come on, Tyke, let's whiz up Lee Road and find your old house in San Souci Forest." I had mixed memories of my forest years. Spike, my slightly older brother, had an affinity with nature and an innate love of flora and fauna. He was in hog-heaven camping out, suspended between sturdy pine trees in a canvas hammock, draped with a mosquito net and some captured lighting bugs to combat a moonless night.

I was basically a city girl but loved having dogs and horses. I made friends with Spike's raccoon, Bonnie, Billy the goat, three tamed squirrels (Huey, Duey, and Louie), bottle-fed into adulthood, plus the chickens, ducks, geese and other critters. I kept my distance from the vicious pair of peacocks that prowled around our property, aggressively guarding our house. Tyrone, the spider monkey, swung from the exposed rafters of our vast salon, and a few "safe" snakes slithered around the house.

My brother would advise me to keep some plant fertilizer in my bag to toss at the roots of struggling trees. Obviously, we had different priorities, and looking back on it, I wish I had paid more attention to what he was saying. He was an authority on country things. It was great having a river next to our house, a huge pond and rowing boats, and a game room full of entertainment, but I quietly bid my time until I passed my driver's license at fourteen and could escape that paradise. I appeared to be a good kid. I didn't have fits or tantrums and was rarely rude, but I'd politely stretched the truth with a sweet ear-to-ear smile.

My mother would invite my entire school class for an end-of-the-year bash at our country Disney Land, and I thought that was normal. I guess people didn't worry about liability and lawsuits in those days. Friends who'd never mounted a horse were galloping into the woods shrieking, while others were rowing around the deep pond without lifejackets, smacking each other in the head with the oars. Yet others were swimming in the river down the hill, and I could hear someone screaming, "Snake, snake, HELP!" My mother was in perfect peace, chatting with the teacher. Her fearless nature enabled her to encourage me to travel the world, and she was right; I needed a master's degree in *life* before I could think about settling down.

My mother also encouraged us to have weekend parties in our well-equipped 'playroom.' We could dance around the ping pong and pool tables to the blaring sounds of our art deco jukebox. She figured it was safer than the drive-in movie off Causeway Boulevard. She was right. When my cousin Fran came to visit, I planned a grand soiree in her honor and invited my entire class.

Fran was a sixteen-year-old cross between Marilyn Monroe and Gina Lollobrigida. Hailing from the capital, Baton Rouge, she dazzled us country kids. The Twist was the rage, and when Chubby Checker belted out his top of the pops hit, Fran mobilized into action. She had us mesmerized, and we gathered around in awe. However, she executed The Twist with such exuberance her knee jumped out of joint. Her damsel in distress display ended the soiree since every guy rushed to her aid – but I forgave her 'cause she was my cousin.

We had tapped danced together at Tony Di Benedetto's Studio since we were four. Then we camped together at Windywood and fished up a storm at our family escape in Mississippi. She inspired me to walk, run, ride, bicycle, and swim the extra mile, so she had a free ticket to steal my boyfriend. She'd return home to Baton Rouge in a few days anyway.

Becky broke into my daydreaming, "Hey Tyke, let's go; it's getting late." We ended the day by swinging past Marsolan's Feed and Seed Store. Becky's dad built up the business and worked hard. He was solid and disciplined, having grown up on a farm. Her beautiful mom, a descendant of the Destrehan Clan with their antebellum plantation nearby, did the bookkeeping and multitasked as a working mom. Covington was rural, and business boomed – the store was a pivotal part of the community.

We returned in time for Becky to collect her kids from school, and I had a chance to visit Noel, her serene, graceful, well-grounded mom, and then catch up with her stunning sister. Jeanie was the head football half-time flag-bearer. All eyes were on her at all times. Flag-bearers were chosen not only for their beauty but also their stately stature and endless legs.

Jeanie was open, friendly, and natural. She was unaware of her allure, allowing her to be spontaneous and easy-going, thus very popular. She wasn't a competitor or a predator and found humor in everything, so you felt well and accepted in her company. Although our lives and goals had taken different twists and turns, what we three had in common was powerful - our newfound faith in the "King of kings and Lord of lords" – YESHUA! Our deep-rooted bond defies description, so I won't attempt to describe it.

3. COLOMBIA

I had a two-hour layover in Miami but would arrive in Bogotá before nightfall. My Avianca flight was on time, and I had an assigned seat. Therefore, I wouldn't have to ruthlessly elbow my way to the front and then make a mad dash to the rickety staircase. Assured of a window seat near the front, I needn't worry about being smoked to a frazzle in the rear section.

There was definitely no hippie trail in South America, and I was advised to try becoming invisible or at least dress conservatively. I wore my designer jeans, a long-sleeved burgundy-colored t-shirt, and a well-cut jean jacket. I hiked my long hair up into a ponytail, but I still stood out like a sore thumb. I had a problem with blending into crowds. First of all, I was a head taller than the rest of the passengers on the plane. Never mind, I was going to have the time of my life in Colombia, known as "The Land of a Thousand Rhythms."

Surprisingly, the second largest carnival celebration in the world is in Barranquilla, on Colombia's northern Caribbean Coast – evidently influenced by the beat of the nearby islands. But my destination was the *numero uno* Carnival in Rio de Janeiro! I was wired to dance and couldn't wait to experience the extravaganza. For professional travelers, dancing barefoot on the beach of Copacabana was a prerequisite.

As I thumbed through the in-flight magazine, I discovered there were 1,025 rhythms in Colombia. The best-known genres were cumbia, vallenato, and the highly celebrated salsa – even though it was initially Cuban. I couldn't wait to boogie! Meanwhile, I took a mental note of the 'must-see' museums. It seems that Colombia is the largest producer of emeralds and one of the biggest producers of quality coffee beans. I wondered if the businessman sitting next to me was into emeralds and coffee or if he was a drug baron returning from a mission. He obviously was not a salsa instructor.

We were descending rapidly and my ears were popping, so I started to smack some bubble gum and yawn. My ear canals opened in time to catch the question from my seatmate. "First trip to Bogotá?" I thought, here it comes; now he wants to invite me for dinner or sell me something. I nodded my head and continued reading. It wasn't my style to be so rude, but I didn't want to egg the guy on into thinking I might consider a date.

Mr. Colombia continued in his swarthy accent, "I advise you to put anything of value into your boots, including your gold earrings and the sunglasses on the top of your head. If not, the street kids will jump up and steal them." I wasn't keen on listening to his lecture, but he rambled on, "Every back pocket of my suit trousers has been slit open several times with a razor blade, so my wallet will fall out. My wife kept sewing them up but finally insisted I use a body pouch. Pickpockets were fairly harmless compared to the gunpoint robberies in my natal city.

I was becoming slightly offended that the guy didn't ask me out to eat or offer to show me around the capital. Naturally, I would have refused; however, this man's motives were clearly to warn me, nothing more. I thanked him profusely and followed his advice. I decided that I must be intimidating, or men thought I was an undercover agent or a karate expert….or all three. Whatever the case, I was convinced I had a guardian angel, or perhaps two.

Feeling pumped and ready to discover a new country, I could feel a buzz as we screeched down the runway to an abrupt halt at *El Dorado* (The Golden) International airport. There was no jet bridge to the terminal, so we waited ten minutes for two decrepit but shiny buses to transport us to 'arrivals.' I traveled light and had only my hand luggage with essentials since I planned on buying specialty items from each country.

I was in the mood to dance and did the salsa to the airport's piped-in music as I waited my turn to pick the brain of the hotel service agent. In my best high school Spanish, I explained, "*Quiero un hotel limpio, barato y central.*" (I'd like a clean, cheap, central hotel.) The problem with speaking a smidgen of Spanish is that, in turn, you receive a full-throttle reply that you can never follow. I inspected a faded picture of Hotel *Plata* (Silver) and thought $5 was a fair price for the small, tarnished lodging. They even boasted a shuttle bus. I figured if it was too crummy, I could handle one night and then look around.

Feeling a bit whacked and starved, as soon as I checked in, I threw my bag into my room and zoomed across the minuscule lobby to hit the lamp-lit streets of Bogotá. "*Espera señorita!*" (Wait, miss!) The receptionist explained that he would not let me exit into the inky night alone without a chaperone. In all my reckless travels, no one had ever barred me from leaving my hotel. I asked the guy in Spanglish, "Do you really care about my safety?"

His reply was blunt; "No, not really. I just don't want the police taking up my time with reports of a stabbing, kidnapping, or theft. I must keep all my clients' passports in case they disappear."

"But I'm starving."

"Too bad," he replied. "I will only let you leave, accompanied by a man."

"UGH," I thought – welcome to South America.

* * *

After about twenty minutes, which seemed like an eternity, two guys rambled through the lobby and headed toward the door. I politely screamed, "Wait! Where are you going?" They looked at me bewildered and said, "We are going to eat. Why?"

"Great! Can I come along?" How embarrassing is that? After years of traveling alone, I felt humiliated to ask some strange guys if they would take me out. They looked like football-tackling backpackers. They were fair and foreign, perhaps northern Europeans in their Gap year before starting their college studies. At least they were polite. "Hello, my name is Sven, and this is my friend Lars." They shook my hand with an iron grip, and I figured I would at least be well protected. "Hi, I'm Marie France from New Orleans."

I had to take giant steps to keep up with the Vikings. They were in deep conversation in a Nordic language. Since Danish, Norwegian and Swedish are similar, I used my eeny, meeny, miney, moe method and asked, "Norwegian?" They looked at me with slack jaws and asked, "How can you tell?" They were only missing horned metal helmets and long blond braids. Their scraggly beards betrayed their youth – I could tell they were not more than twenty years old.

"You guys must be mountaineers heading to *Pico Cristóbal Colón* (Christopher Columbus Peak)." The in-flight magazine had an article about the highest peak in Colombia, which was part of the Sierra Nevada de Santa Maria. The Viking boys stopped and looked at me with worried expressions, "Who are you?" was their next question.

Maybe they thought I was a troll or a sorcerer. Clearly, they weren't into cocaine, they were too young to be teachers, and they didn't fit the bill of your stereotype missionaries. I had the uncanny ability to figure people out. The only category they slotted into was that of extreme sports fanatics and, most likely, mountain climbers with their apparent stamina and well-worn trekking boots.

"People tell me I'm intuitive," was my casual reply to their question. They seemed to have a new respect for me, or maybe it was apprehension. Even though we were in the historical center, they explained that the place we were going to was frequented by locals. We entered an inconspicuous door that opened up to a lively eatery. There was a buzz of activity and laughter.

The guys asked if I liked the place and where we should sit. They had changed their tune and become attentive. They probably thought I'd cast a spell on them if they didn't cater to my every need. *La Puerta False* (The Fake Door) was cozy but stylish and undoubtedly lived up to its reputation as one of the best eateries in town. It first opened for business in 1816, making it one of the oldest *restaurantes* in the country.

On my own, I would have eaten a few tamales from a street vendor or looked around for a small, simple, unpretentious place. The Fake Door was chic, but the prices were fair. The Nordics insisted I try the specialty, *ajiaco* soup. From what I could see, it was an entire meal. A nearby table revealed oversized soup bowls filled with chicken, potatoes, carrots, egg, and onion. The room was vaporized with a perfume of oregano and cumin.

We all had the 'house soup,' and the boys each ordered a *Bandeja Paisa* (regional platter) – the national dish. The quantity of food was obscene - two types of Colombian sausage, ground beef, rice, red beans, a fried pork rind, *arepa* (cornbread), a *plantain* (cooking banana), a slice of avocado, and a fried egg to top it off. I swiveled around to have another focal point and dug into my *dulce de leche* dessert. The Vikings inhaled their trays of food as if it were an hors d'oeuvre. Perhaps all the high carb and grease would propel the guys up the mountain. I was impressed that these young Nordics spoke Spanish with the servers.

Walking back to the hotel at 11 pm was eerie, and the lack of noise was deafening. Northern Europeans rarely asked personal questions, so I figured I had a free ticket to be intrusive as an American.

"So, are you two heading directly to the Cristóbal Colómbus Peak? Then what, back to Norway?"

"NO," they laughed, "It's just the beginning of our trip in Colombia. We have to meet up with the rest of our group in the Caribbean Port of Santa Maria, where there are pure white sand beaches and exceptional seafood. When everyone arrives, we'll drive through the rich tropical forest, considered one of the most biologically diverse places on the planet. The starting point is surrounded by pre-Colombian ruins, only twenty-six miles from the sea."

Lars continued, "First, we'll visit with the Kogi tribe, who permit access to their land and the sacred grounds of the 'high peaks.' Our mission has been building relations with the Kogi people for the past eight years. We supply them with agricultural tools, medical supplies, and Bibles in their Chibchan language, Sánha. After our six-day expedition to the 18,800-foot summit, we'll help build more thatched roof huts if conditions permit."

Sven turned to me and said, "Do you know Jesus?"

All I could muster was, "Uh-huh." I was dumbfounded and had to catch my breath. "Yes, but I know Jesus by his real name, Yeshua."

Sven looked perplexed, "Do you speak Hebrew? Are you a Messianic Jew?"

"No, but Jesus told me to call him Yeshua."

"Oh, a personal encounter. I guess you're here to spread the Gospel, then?"

"Not really; I'm working my way down to Rio de Janeiro for the Carnival. My next stop is Machu Picchu. Then I'm bussing around Lake Titicaca and over to La Paz, Bolivia. From there, I'll fly to Santiago, Chile, then Buenos Aires, Argentina, and on to Rio by mid-February."

"You've got a lot of ground to cover. I can give you the address of our good friends who live in Cuzco, the Inca Empire's belly button. They'll clue you in on all you need to know about getting to Machu Picchu, and you can join in with their revival. God is working amazing miracles in South America these days."

I tried to digest everything Sven told me, but my brain was scrambling. I felt like screaming, doing cartwheels, and then jogging, but I remained breathless and had to stop. "Hey guys, I have to catch my breath. I don't know if I'm in a digestive stupor or if the mind-blowing stuff you've told me is affecting my metabolism."

"How long have you been in Bogotá?"

"I arrived four hours ago from New Orleans. I left at 9 am and had a layover in Miami."

Lars laughed, "Bogotá is 8,530 feet above sea level, so you have to acclimatize. Take it easy for the next few days. Drink lots of water and eat bananas and avocados for potassium."

"By the way, how old are you two?" I asked. You sound too wise and experienced for 'gap year' guys."

"Ha! I'm thirty-one," said Lars, "And Sven is twenty-nine. I guess the Norwegian climate has conserved us. Not much sun damage this time of the year, when night lasts eighteen hours. That's why we chose this month to volunteer with the mission."

I tried to keep up with the Jesus Vikings. I was still panting and found it impossible to walk and talk simultaneously. We finally arrived at our nondescript *Plata* Hotel, and Lars asked me to wait in the lobby. He said he'd bring me their friends' address in Cuzco and a book I could use to guide me along the way. Lars was back in a flash and handed me a slim book entitled *Smith Wigglesworth*. He quizzed me on the version of my Bible.

"Uh, dunno, old-ish English, pocket-sized Gideon Bible."

"It must be the KJV version. Might I suggest NKJV? (New King James version). It's easier to read."

"Thanks, I'll look into that. Smith Wigglesworth sounded like a peculiar name for a person or even a cartoon character. I was hoping it would be a travel guide.

"Good night Miss Marie France from New Orleans. We're off tomorrow for Santa Maria, which means an eighteen-hour bus trip, so I'll say goodnight and goodbye. I feel our Lord will use you mightily in South America. Be prepared!"

"Thanks for the book and the address Lars. God bless you two and your mission." I felt like I was speaking another language. I was curious why such a sanctified salutation rolled off my tongue as if I hobnobbed with missionaries all the time. But they were cool, normal, sportive guys who evidently had some kind of calling on their lives. Phew, I'm glad I didn't have a calling to build mud huts in a tropical forest. I was so happy to escape the sticky humidity of New Orleans.

With too much food, not enough oxygen, and travel fatigue, I was ready to hit the sack and dream about my upcoming adventures. I needed time to process the events of this evening. My intuition is usually flawless, but Lars and Sven defied being defined. They were fathoms deeper, multi-faceted, and surprisingly more spiritual than what came across at first glance. I decided to think about it later – after all, as Scarlet O'Hara would say, "tomorrow is another day."

* * *

I have an obsessive-compulsive disorder when it comes to museums. Attempting to be invisible, I wore my airplane outfit and braided my hair in indigenous style, then headed to the renowned Gold Museum, passing dozens of shoe shiners and pushcarts along the way. Shiny shoes were clearly a sign of prestige since all the shoeshine stands were filled with customers waiting. I only passed one band of pesky boys who checked me head to toe, shrugged, and walked on. I took my seatmate's advice on the plane to Bogotá and had all my possessions tucked into my boots.

They say all that glitters is not gold. However, the artifacts in this museum were a glittering exception to the rule. Bright spotlights ricocheted rays of light off each of the 35,000 golden works of art on display, so I was obliged to stifle the glare with my signature sunglasses.

The museum boasted the most extensive pre-Colombian collection of gold items and works of art worldwide. Many were religious objects, such as Inti, the sun god. His warmth embraced the Andean earth and matured crops, so the local farmers loved him. The display was impressive if you were drawn to gold, but I was basically a silver lady. Chunky pieces of tribal silver were my delight. However, the diverse display gave a history lesson on the different pre-Colombian regions of the country.

The riverbeds on the Pacific Coast were chocked full of gold nuggets. The yellow color attracted indigenous inhabitants who worshiped the golden sun and considered 'yellow' corn a major mainstay for survival. They melted the nuggets and poured them into intricate forms. A solid gold helmet was displayed, elegant nose rings covering the lower facial features, and extended ear to ear. A wide variety of earrings and earlobe plugs were also on display. Stuff I would wear, in silver, of course.

The legend of *El Dorado* (the golden one) was inspired by a tribal king supposedly covered in gold dust. He drifted out on a raft into Lake Guatavite, near present-day Bogotá. There he threw massive amounts of emeralds and golden objects into the lake to appease the goddess, then emerged radiant and fearless. As legends go, the story mutated from El Dorado being a king into being a city, then a kingdom, and finally into an empire.

Spanish conquistadores had noticed the native people's awesome gold artifacts long before any legend of lost cities had appeared. The quantity of such valuable items and the natives' apparent ignorance of the value inspired speculation as to the existence of a plentiful source. In 1535, triggered by the accounts of the mythical "City of Gold," two groups of conquistadors set foot toward the inner highlands of the Colombian Andes. They were ruthless, determined, and driven by their lust for gold. The collection was laid out in logical thematic rooms over three floors, and I didn't miss a nugget!

I then headed to the nearby Emerald Museum, literally a two-minute hop along Santander Park. Upon entering, I was engulfed by emeralds, my favorite gem. There were fist-sized emeralds and large sections of sedimentary rock walls with emeralds embedded in them, just waiting to be chiseled out and polished into perfection. Colombia is the country that mines and produces the most emeralds worldwide. I subtly leaned into a guided tour in English to pick up more details about the mining process.

The guide spoke fluent Spanglish, and the group was made up of a patchwork of nationalities, ages, sizes, and shapes. "If the stone sparkles and has intense 'fire,' it is probably a fake. Hold the stone up to the light, and it will shine, but with a dull fire."

José, the guide, continued, "The most productive mine, Muzo Mine, is in the mountains northwest of Bogotá." I was glad to pick up that tidbit since I wanted an emerald souvenir from Colombia. "The miners are lowered down 1,300 feet into a 115-degree furnace with horizontal passages that extended nearly eighty miles." I thought what a brutal way to earn a living unless there were some perks to compensate for it. I guess the miners had to swallow stones to smuggle them out.

Professional scavengers are allowed to scour the shale debris from the mine dumped into valleys. Many men work twelve-hour shifts for decades, hoping to uncover overlooked gems. Go-betweens buy emeralds from these scavengers at rock-bottom prices and then hawk them in the historical gem quarter near the cobbled stone Candelaria neighborhood. I'm sure I could spot a fake. It would be worth the effort to find a cut-priced gem.

Colombia has a bad rap due to the drug cartel, but little is said about the emerald mafia. It was common knowledge that illegal mining was more profitable than dealing cocaine. Perhaps at this very moment, an emerald war is still raging among the gem Tsars of the region.

Oh well, on to The National Museum. The brochure from Tourist Information described it as a world-class museum housed in the old Bogota prison. That should have been a warning. Yes, it housed collections of history, art, culture, and more, but the dark, dismal prison vibes forced me to jog from one apparent prison chamber to the next. I was ready to make a break and escape into the glorious daylight as soon as possible.

* * *

Passing multi-hued street art covering buildings like mammoth murals, I continued jogging to Bolivia Square – drawn by the music and lively atmosphere of that prismatic hub oozing with activity. The Ringling Brothers Circus paled in comparison to what was offered here. I was on sensory overload, caught by the salsa beat vibrating from the conga drums and double bass. Yeah, now the brass blared its way into the beat, and I joined a swinging group of dancers in full motion. OK, salsa is a partner dance, but there were a bunch of singles that I tried to blend in by bending my knees to appear shorter.

Meanwhile, a man was weaving around the square with a llama. He was dressed in an explosion of color and wearing a Peruvian hat - hoping to catch a tourist for a photo or a lopsided llama ride. A cartwheel of colored umbrellas shaded artists and produce laid out on carpets covering the ancient stones. There were loads of food tables, and corn on the cob was being grilled on portable pits.

I lunged towards the table with *empanadas & arepas*. The quintessential and ubiquitous street food in Colombia, the humble *arepa*, is made of deep-fried sweet cornmeal dough. *Empanadas* are also a mainstay in Ibiza, my Spanish island. They're similar to pie crust wrapped around savory meat, fish, or spinach with pine nuts and raisins. I found a half-empty bench, sat down to devour my lunch, and sipped my double portion of fresh pomegranate juice.

Aware that leaving my hotel after dark was out of the question, I decided to buy more of everything to eat in my hotel room rather than hang out in the lobby, ready to pounce on an unsuspecting male exiting the hotel, begging him to take me out to eat. It worked out well with Sven and Lars, but I didn't want to press my luck.

Similar to southern European countries, life was celebrated on the street, and cafes were filled from daybreak to midnight. Before leaving Bolivar Square, I went to pay my respects to General Simon Bolivar, the mighty hero who liberated Colombia from Spanish rule in 1822.

The most prominent structure bordering the square was the Sacred Holy Cathedral, one of the largest churches in South America. However, convinced that God was omnipresent and didn't stay cooped up in a church building, I pursued a beer hall that included the well-loved game of Tejo, the national sport.

This popular game was imported from the countryside and became a success in beer halls since it kept players drinking. For the price of a local Craft beer, you could hurl stones at a large target covered with clay, aiming for a triangle of gunpowder. I guess it's the same objective as darts at pubs or bar pool tables. However, Tejo required a huge hall since the stones were thrown from twenty yards. I wondered if I had the power to hit the target.

I was told to look for a famous beer hall called Tejo *La Embajada* (The Embassy). After accosting several people on the street, a local lady led me to a shed. I could hear gunpowder exploding as I entered and marveled at the size of the hall and the number of lanes – a Colombian-style bowling alley. I was glad to see a group of ladies on a lane having a ball, laughing, and chugging their bottled beer. I'd observe for a while to get the hang of the game before making a move.

How convenient, I noticed an empty lane half the length. I knew I could hit the bull's eye from ten yards. My brother and I knocked cans off the wall at that distance with rocks until we graduated to guns. Easy peasy! Ugh, I missed the first one, then POW. I hit the gunpowder with enough force to ignite it. POW! POW! I was on a roll. They had to replace the pellets of gunpowder. I ordered another beer, so I could continue playing. A few kids gathered around me, laughing and clapping. Perhaps I was in the kiddie lane.

I gave my puck to a little guy about ten years old, and he launched it into a sunken niche encircled by the gunpowder as if to say, 'Lady, aim for the center and not the noisy powder.' You got more points for lodging the puck into the dead center than for setting off the ammunition. I was happier without the brat's demonstration, but to be fair, I took him on.

The kid won by a landslide, but I was enraptured by the national sport. I abandoned my two full bottles of warm beer, shook hands with my mini-opponent, invited him and his entourage for a round of soft drinks and snacks, then moved on.

It was the right time to head for the gem quarter, where the hawkers would gather to haggle with customers. Aware that they would consider me a gullible gringo, I was prepared to offer a fourth of their price, then work my way up to half. I felt confident that I could identify the best genuine emeralds and snatch 'em up for a fair price - that's what I was good at. My innate ability to wheel and deal has kept me funded thus far.

An assortment of twenty men gathered on a busy street corner of the historic center. Some were dressed in ill-fitting suits and others in t-shirts and jeans, but what they had in common was their evident desperation.

Each man carried two to ten gems in a sheet of paper tucked into their pocket. They didn't have to pay rent or employees, so it stood to reason that their prices would be lower than shops. I had checked out a few jewelers selling emeralds to get an idea of prices. I was ready to settle for half a carat with some minor inclusions.

Of the five guys who approached me, I decided on a few gems from an owlish-looking man with muddy shoes – a tell-tale sign he'd been to the mountains in the morning to buy gems from the shale debris scavengers. The Colombian men were adamant about having polished shoes, but this guy didn't have the time or money to do so. I felt good about the price and quality and skipped back to my Hotel Plata singing, "I've got plenty of nothin' and nothin's plenty for me … …."

* * *

It was still daylight when I ducked into my hotel, and I was glad to have an early evening to catch up with my journal and look at the Smith Wigglesworth guidebook that Lars had given me the night before. As I flipped through some pages, I was disappointed that it was not a guidebook for traveling through South America. However, three hours later, I understood that the Wigglesworth book was, more importantly, a guide for life.

Every word I read resonated with my spirit and soul. I was like a dry sponge soaking up a life-giving message. Smith's life, saturated in the Holy Spirit of God, demonstrated the love and power of Jesus. I was thirsting to hear those empowering words from such a dedicated and humble servant. Smith Wigglesworth was a faith giant who simply obeyed the commands of Jesus and walked in his compassion.

I desperately needed that book. I needed to know that it was humanly possible and that Jesus IS the same yesterday, today, and forever! How could Lars discern that I needed this book? Was it so evident that my soul needed a realignment to synchronize with the Spirit of God? I hoped not.

Mr. Wigglesworth was a humble, illiterate plumber who received the baptism of the Holy Spirit and was transformed into a powerhouse of faith. He dared to believe the promises of God. His wife, Polly - a preacher from the Salvation Army, taught him to read and write. Shortly afterward, he began to lead revivals not only in his natal Yorkshire but all over the UK, then worldwide.

He merely acted on the Word of God. His heart's desire was to win souls for Jesus. At least 25 percent of the ministry of Jesus included healing and deliverance – so Smith followed in the footsteps of Jesus with childlike faith, and amazing miracles ensued. His unwavering faith in God characterized his ministry.

Smith believed for the impossible, yet his primary concern was that God should receive the glory, not himself. I wondered if God was using Lars and Sven to heal the Kogi tribe they were ministering to in the foothills of the Andes of northwest Colombia. I found the prospect of miraculous healing uplifting. How awesome to be used to help alleviate suffering and sickness.

Wigglesworth had performed the same signs, wonders, and miracles that the Apostles and disciples did in the Book of Acts. Why not? When did believers lose their God-given authority? Jesus validated His words through his actions and commanded his disciples to do likewise. As a teen, I didn't even hear about the Holy Spirit in church. He certainly didn't have a co-starring role with Jesus or even a walk-on cameo role. He seemed to be the postscript of the Trinity.

There was a brief mention of a Holy Ghost, and it gave me the jitters. I hoped the ghost was more like *Casper the Friendly Ghost* rather than the ghoulish variety at Halloween or the scary, dark ride at Pontchartrain Beach. I wondered when and why they evicted the Holy Spirit from church. Wrong dress code? Too spooky? Too challenging? It seems like people are afraid of the supernatural. Jesus clearly stated that when he ascended, his Father would send another Guide, a Comforter, and the Spirit of truth, to live within believers and empower them to do what he did.

In the pocket-sized Bible that Jonathan had given me in Jerusalem several years ago, there was a key verse highlighting the words of Jesus: *"Most certainly I tell you, he who believes in Me, the works that I do, he will do also; and he will do greater works than these because I am going to my Father."* John 14:14

No doubt about it, Jesus didn't mince his words. He gave the disciples his authority and sent them out to do what He did. What went wrong along the way? Why have believers deviated from the New Testament teachings? Fear of failure? Fear of rejection? Fear of looking foolish? Had Christianity morphed into a course in ethics? Was religion replacing relationship?

After studying and participating in the mystical Eastern religions on the hippie trail, I decided that following Yeshua (Jesus) was the logical choice. It was the only belief system that extended GRACE and the ONLY one including a SAVIOR.

So, why do I need a Savior? My Gideon Bible says we have all sinned and fallen short of the glory of God. I couldn't argue that point. Growing up in predominantly Catholic Louisiana, my playmates pointed out that nearly everything I did was a sin. So naturally, I grew up fully aware of my tarnished condition. However, God, in his infinite love, devised a rescue plan. An amazing plan that would enable our broken relationship with Him to be restored.

Wigglesworth explained that God Almighty, pure Holiness, could not accept our fallen nature and shortcomings because they separated us from Him. Therefore, He placed our waywardness onto an innocent substitute. Jesus took our muck upon Himself at the cross, and in exchange, we took on His goodness. Not logical and not even fair - that is *grace*, totally underserved favor. I hung onto Jesus' words, *"about sin, because people do not believe in me. . "* (John 16:9). I realized that was *the* ultimate sin of separation.

Our part is faith in this too-good-to-be-true news. Out of love and gratitude for this earth-shattering good news, I seemed to have lost the desire to do many of the undesirable things I was accustomed to doing. However, I realized I was a work in progress and had the Holy Spirit to advise me when I went off the rails, and He would help me to get back on track.

In other religions, you must earn your way to heaven through self-effort. Sometimes that entails being reborn repeatedly until you get it right, which seems impossible. Meanwhile, Jesus was a rebel – a revolutionary! He hung out with the wrong people and broke the social norms. He was someone I could relate to. I was drawn to His boldness and charisma. I decided to become a follower of Jesus because I was convinced only He had the words of eternal life.

* * *

I awoke with the first rays of sunlight and wanted to get to the bus station early in hopes of experiencing the Muisca people in full regalia. The Muisca were the indigenous inhabitants of Colombia who thrived until the Spanish colonialists staked their claim on the land in hopes of expanding the Spanish Empire. I read that the Muisca people were decimated by the weapon-wielding Spaniards who generously shared the common cold and measles. The holy conversions weren't very hallowed, and many Muiscas sadly disappeared during that misplaced fervor.

I was told by a guy outside of Tourist Information that there was a remote tribe living in a dense forest outside a village three hours from Bogota by bus. They wore red body paint, perhaps mud, and the witch doctor diagnosed and treated ailments with smoking herbs. I couldn't wait – how quaint is that?

When I worked my way to the bus stop, only two seats were left on the rickety old school bus. I chose the window seat only to discover I didn't fit. The bus was clearly built for indigenous children. Still, I could comfortably twist into an angle that positioned me to aim for the window, so I was guaranteed a perfect view. If I developed a cramp, I could always dangle my legs out of the window. Looking around, I noticed I was the only gringo and celebrated my good fortune with a candy bar.

It looked like all the locals were weighed down with city supplies and the overhead racks were packed. I was surprised by how well-behaved the kids were as they sat quietly without whining or crying. It occurred to me that perhaps they were scared of the string bean gringo with the unruly hair and local fashion.

I was advised to travel incognito throughout South America, so I tried blending in with the local 'look.' I had on my faded bell bottoms and a red t-shirt. However, I couldn't resist wearing a sassy black and red striped poncho and a typical wide-brimmed hat I purchased in the Bogota street market.

Bogota is one of the world's highest capitals, and we were heading further into the Andes, careening around valleys with serpentine hairpin loops. The roads had no guard rails, and when I gazed over the edge of the sharp turns, there was always a pile of rusty cars and buses that spoke of dramatic mishaps. Either their brakes failed, or maybe they met head-on traffic. La-la-la "Over hill, over dale, as we hit the dusty trail…..as those caissons keep rolling along." My dad always sang old army songs when we traveled, so I followed suit.

Colombia is a land of extremes. We were in the central northwest spine of the Andes, where snow-covered volcanoes decorated the landscape. Not far away were the tropical beaches on the Caribbean coast and the Amazon rainforests were due south.

I grew up in the rainforests of sticky Louisiana and was pleased to be high and dry. Bogota boasts the largest condors in the world with a ten-foot wingspan and weighing in at thirty-three pounds. I had seen two scavengers gliding through the valleys scouting out lifeless prey. I hoped they weren't following us in hopes of a snack.

We were nearing our destination, and people were walking along the edge of the road leading llamas and alpacas. Their presence was not a tourist gimmick – there were no tourists. The bus stopped at a small *tienda* (shop), and everyone fell out of the over-packed bus with their city treasures. I scanned the village for a taxi, but not one was in sight.

When I asked where I could find a taxi, tuk-tuk, or even a bicycle, the scrawny, sun-ripened *señora* stared at me with saucer-shaped eyes without uttering a word. Was I the first foreigner in her *pueblo*? A slender man spoke up, "Me taxi." I hoped he didn't mean piggyback style. He then pointed to an antique Chevy parked out front. What luck, I congratulated myself on such good fortune.

Using sign language and Spanglish, I muttered while pointing to the forest, "Tribe, red paint, witch doctor, smoke."

The young man replied, "Sí, I know where shaman live."

"How far, how much cost?" I don't know why I was speaking broken English.

"One dollar," he pointed into the forest. "One dollar," he motioned return trip.

"Muchos pesos," I replied. "One dollar into the forest and return."

He shook his head and held up two fingers, "Two dollars."

I agreed. What was I thinking? This waif of a guy had the auto monopoly in town. I wasn't prepared to go by llama, and it would be nightfall by the time I got back, thus missing the afternoon bus. He opened the back door with a closed-mouth grin and motioned for me to enter with a gallant swoosh of his thin arm. "My name Miguel."

After about seven miles of a potholed, mud-splattering dirt track, we arrived at a small settlement. The chief was not disappointing, nor were the two ladies seated on a mat, stone grinding cornmeal. I felt like I was flipping pages in a National Geographic magazine.

I explained that I had neck pain and needed healing. My taxi driver explained something in the local dialect, and the chief nodded. He explained to my chauffeur that it would cost me a bottle of whiskey and two cartons of Marlborough cigarettes.

"Whoah, too much, buddy!" I explained that the pain in my neck had disappeared and I'd be on my way. The men babbled a bit more, and Miguel said, "Only one carton Marlborough." I wondered if I had to pay another two-dollar taxi fare to return to the village for the purchase.

Meanwhile, Miguel popped open his trunk and pulled out the black market items. I realized this was a racket, but I was in over my head and wondered if the guy outside Tourist Information with the "red tribe" tip was also getting a cut. I sighed and paid up.

I was then instructed to lie down on a bamboo mat with bumps. Ouch! I would have called off the charade, but I figured this ordeal would make a good story or perhaps a paragraph in my future book. Meanwhile, a young maiden was building up clumps of dried grass, weeds, and tiny branches about a yard from my body. The chief then splashed a bit of water (or gasoline?) onto each clump. He then whisked out his cigarette lighter and clicked away. Rather than blaze into flame, the dampened herbs began to smoke. I began to pray and hoped my guardian angels were on duty.

Oh well, I thought, why not just go with the flow? The smoke was actually pleasant and smelled like rosemary and thyme. I hoped this was not a cannibal tribe, but it didn't seem to matter. I was in la-la-land and felt as if I was levitating. I didn't do drugs or even drink alcohol because I despised the sensation of being in an altered state. A childhood tune began to surface, and I heard myself singing, "Run rabbit, run rabbit, run, run, run . . . . ." on that note, I got up and started running. I guess it was a subliminal message to get out of there.

Since I was paid up in liquor and tobacco and didn't want to hang around for an encore, whatever that might be. I desperately needed to get back to the village. The smoke made me wobbly, but I kept my eyes focused on the trees in the distance to help my balance. On a positive note, the pain in my neck was gone. I heard a car behind me and wondered if I should dash into the woods, never to be found again. The car caught up with me and stopped. Miguel jumped out, and I was convinced I could restrain him if necessary.

"Señorita, señorita, I take you pueblo." I prayed he wasn't speaking with a forked tongue. I reluctantly hopped into his car but held my fingernail clippers in the palm of my hand as a defense weapon. Then I started to laugh hysterically. I guess it was a well-needed release from built-up tension. I began to see the funny side of getting smoked, but I hated that out-of-control feeling brought on by whatever I inhaled. I had to own up to not having a go-with-the-flow personality when it comes to hallucinogens or whatever I was breathing that got me so ga-ga goofy.

The three-hour serpentine bus ride back to Bogotá was uneventful. Without a camera to distract me, I tried to file the breathtaking views into my memory bank to retrieve them at will. The condors were still gliding and searching, but I tried not to take it personally. Our driver was young, but he seemed to have school bus skills. I would continue to follow the Andes from Colombia to Ecuador, Peru, Bolivia, Chile, and Argentina. Therefore, I decided to make friends with the varied terrain that always included curves, loops, and dizzying heights. Although I would fly to the capitals, I would then discover the glaciers, volcanoes, grassland, desert, lakes, and forests by local bus. God willing.

4. ECUADOR

The flight from Bogotá to Quito, the historical capital of Ecuador, was a mere two hours. My early afternoon arrival was perfect for taking in the city sights before nightfall when I'd be hotel-bound. I would have preferred an unlimited time frame for exploring so much mind-boggling beauty and radical contrasts. Still, I decided a "taster" of South America would whet my insatiable appetite for more. I had commitments with Roberto Cavallini for the mid-March Fashion Weeks in Milan and Paris, presenting his Fall collection – then again in September for his Spring designs.

With the earnings from modeling in March, I'd head back to Nepal and India to scoop up more tribal jewelry and search for some gemstones while in Jaipur. Best of all, I'd reconnect with Mahesh, my precious orphan boy in Kathmandu. He lived in the newly built orphanage and went to school each morning, but his afternoons were free to visit with his rotating "aunts and uncles" from abroad. Everyone hooked on Nepal returned faithfully, and the local children were never forgotten.

As the plane taxied into Quito's Mariscal Sucre International Airport, I felt the usual drum roll in my soul as I anticipated with excitement an unknown country. Even though Quito was 1,000 feet higher than Bogotá, I had acclimatized to the thin air and refused to feel altitude sickness. I made my way to the bus stop with long strides to beat the rush.

My Andes poncho and hat were a success, Some people stared shamelessly, and children pointed at me. I felt honored to receive so much attention. I wondered if they confused me with my look-a-like, Carly Simon, the superstar singer, and songwriter married to James Taylor. Strangely, no one asked me for an autograph. Oh well, perhaps they were too shy.

I bussed into the center of Quito so I could ramble around the historic center and choose a modest hotel rather than depend on the airport hotel clerk, who probably got a kickback anyway. I decided on a small hotel several blocks from the *Plaza Grande.* It looked simple, clean, and affordable. I checked in, left my over-stuffed bag, and hit the streets.

After only a few blocks, the soul-embracing call of a mellow Andes flute beckoned me onward as if the Pied Piper was hypnotizing me. A crowd of people surrounded a single man of about thirty who wore long dark hair, a leather headband, and a silver feather earring. The serenity of his melancholic melody was like a deep massage that relaxed every fiber of my being. I had the urge to interpret that mood with modern dramatic dance but refrained.

The main square, *Plaza Grande,* was the center of the Old City and artistic creativity. It was similar to the main square in Bogotá but void of the usual pesky pigeons. Whoosh, within seconds, there was a thunder of hundreds of flapping wings, and a Hitchcock-type onslaught of pigeons engulfed me. I stunned them with a Navajo war cry, broke loose, dodging coca leaf vendors, and came to a standstill near a classical guitarist whose cultured sound was divine.

Further down was a sole saxophonist who held court with some hard-core sax fanatics. There was something for everyone, and with such altitude, it was comfortably cool to mosey around the bright, naïve paintings on display and check out the food stands. I snapped up some tasty-looking tortillas, potato patties, yucca and fried plantain. I found an empty bench with a view of the centuries-old volcanic stone Baroque Cathedral, *La Compania de Jesús* (The Society of Jesus).

It was still early, so I visited the vast baroque Cathedral. This Jesuit church's large central nave was profusely decorated with ornate gold leaf, gilded plaster, and wood carvings. It seemed lavishly out-of-place in proportion with the country's economy, but that's how it is. Being the most extravagant and impressive church I had visited in South America, I couldn't help but cringe while contemplating the "holy" conversions.

I decided to return the following morning for the changing of the guard in front of the Presidential Palace and then take a short bus ride bus to the middle of the world. After all, Ecuador is Spanish for *equator,* and Quito was situated at zero degrees latitude.

Meanwhile, I read that this lofty capital had many significant historical buildings, so I would try to find them. I had a city map from my hotel, but it didn't work, so I just quizzed people en route. Maps rarely worked for me.

As night was falling, I rewound my way back to my meager hotel for an early evening. I had some dragon fruit and local chocolate to dine on and was happy to have some downtime. However, I was intercepted in the lobby by a couple desperately trying to sell a ticket to a football (soccer) game in the famed Atahualpa Olympic Stadium. I knew that women weren't encouraged to venture out alone at night, so I'd try to swing a deal and a ticket to freedom.

"Hey, how much is the ticket?" I inquired.

"Cost price – our friend is sick with Montezuma's revenge, and we just want to get him his money back."

"So, how much is the cost price?"

"It's equivalent to three US dollars, and it's a great seat."

"Yeah, okay, I'll buy it if I can go with you since I don't know the area."

"Sure, meet us in the lobby in half an hour."

I decided to push my noise tolerance perimeter to the limit. Soccer was the *numero uno* passion of the Ecuadorian population, and the cheering racket reached one hundred decibels easily. It gave zest to their existence and hope for many young boys trying to kick their way out of poverty and into the national league. I knew some rowdy chants so that I could join in. After a quick shower, I grabbed my alpaca shawl and dashed to the lobby.

"Hi there, I'm Michael, and this is my wife, Lidia."

"Great to meet y'all, my name is Marie France, but my friends call me Tyke.

"What mission are you with?" Michael inquired matter-of-factly.

"Mission impossible," I replied. "How about you two?" I was lost for words. Ugh, did I look like a missionary?

"We're with World Vision," answered Lidia. "Presently, we're working with impoverished children in a village two hours northwest of Quito. Michael and José are football fanatics and insisted on coming to Quito for the playoffs tonight. However, José is out of commission. He was feeling invincible and drank the hotel tap water. Poor guy."

Lidia and Michael sounded American, even though Lidia looked Ecuadorian. I'd try not to pry but give them a chance to tell their story - Americans always do. Michael led the way to the bus stop and explained that he was a third-generation missionary on his father's side and was born in Ecuador. He and his family returned to the US when he was sixteen, but he said he left his heart in Ecuador with Lidia. "Lidia's folks were my parent's best friends, and they ran the mission together, so I've known Lidia since we were knee-high to a grasshopper."

I felt like a heathen. I didn't know missionary lingo, so I remained silent for a change. How could I explain to this holy couple who were sacrificing their lives to make this world a better place that my destination was Rio, and my goal was to dance with Samba Queens for Carnival? I wondered if my eight generations of Mardi Gras genes compelled me to head to Rio. Instead, I ventured to say, "Ah, what made you think I am here in Quito for a mission?"

Michael admitted, "Well, tourists come to South America on guided package tours. Occasionally they come independently in small groups, and once in a while, two or three students travel together. However, you rarely, if ever, encounter a young woman traveling on her own. It seemed logical that you flew into Quito to join a mission team. Revival has been erupting all over South America. You look like a typical 1970s Jesus Freak or perhaps someone involved in the 1971 Bario Revival.

I explained, "Um, I'm not really a team player. I'm more of a one-on-one type of person."

"Oh, you're into relational evangelism," commented Lidia. "That is a key ministry."

"Some Norwegian missionaries in Bogota gave me a book about the supernatural life of Smith Wigglesworth. I'm getting grounded in the Holy Spirit. To tell you the truth, I'm a rather new follower of Jesus, and since I travel non-stop, I haven't had time to join a Bible group."

"Well, you know what they say, a chapter a day keeps the doctor away. Actually, you could pass for a Bario Revivalist - spontaneous, dynamic, Holy Spirit led and well fed," offered Lidia, "You've definitely got a gifting."

"I was a serious 'seeker' before I found Jesus, or rather He found me. I followed the hippie trail throughout Nepal and India, searching for the Truth, and like Mahatma Gandhi, I found it in the person of *Yeshua* (Jesus). Several believers have told me, 'God has a special plan for your life.' I must admit, I'm not good at making mud bricks and thatched roofs or most other practical things, so I'm just traveling along waiting for a revelation."

"Oh yes, God will use you! You are bold. Don't worry; availability is more important than ability." Lidia and Michael were very kind and caring people, so I tried to take Lidia's backhanded compliment with a positive, optimistic attitude. But, I couldn't help but reflect on what made me appear unable to have ability. I knew I didn't have much common sense. However, I had uncommon sense, which was head-over-heels more intriguing.

Our bus, number 101, came screeching to a halt. We hopped in and backed away from the door so that it could close. The bus was stuffed, and we still had about six miles to the stadium. With each ensuing stop, more people worked their way into the mass, finding loopholes to squeeze into. I was praying I wouldn't suffocate, but fortunately, my height lifted me above the hordes, up into some tainted oxygen.

My fellow passengers were toting flags and wearing their team's colors. Michael explained that people traveled hundreds of miles to attend this playoff, and the stadium was constructed to hold nearly thirty-six thousand people. I was not fond of crowds, so I was counting on getting caught up in the distracting mass hysteria that would be rippling through the stands.

A mob was already waiting at the entrance, but my missionary guide knew enough to buy tickets that would fast-track our access into the stadium. Wow! We made it in and had seats near mid-field in the second tier. Music was blaring, and I had to admit there was more raw emotion bouncing around this coliseum than anywhere I had experienced before. It was somewhat scary. Like animals, people are capable of anything when they are in packs.

I gazed around at the sea of humanity and realized I was being swept up into the electricity of the mega event. Our Ecuadorian boys made a point early on, and we all went berserk. I waved my flag non-stop while eating a plate of mystery meat and lapping ice cream. I treated the kids on my row to the flavor of their choice and ordered a pitcher of beer for my peers. Chile was not too hot, and their team only scored a last-minute point, ending the game three to one for Ecuador.

Fireworks were blasted into the sky, fights broke out, and police were harassed, but overall, everyone seemed well-behaved. Michael shouted, "Let's hold hands and head for the exit before the masses decide to leave." If you tripped or fell, you were a goner, so I prayed for the speed needed to outrun the crowd nipping at my heels.

Phew, out of the gate into a taxi in one smooth leap. We made it! Hallelujah! I insisted on paying for the cab. I was pumped and laughing so hard that I was gasping for air. Even though I was euphoric, I was exhausted. After all, it was only day one in Quito, and I drifted off to sleep the second my head hit the lumpy pillow.

* * *

Changing of the guard was only once a week, each Monday at 11 am, so I rose bright and early. I skipped to the *Plaza Grande* to locate an optimal spot to view the spectacle. The pomp and ceremony of paying respects to Ecuador's president on his Palace balcony seemed what you might expect in South America. President Guillermo Rodriguez Lara rose to power in 1972 and dug his heels in to remain the leader despite opposition. He was a former military dictator, which says a lot. Nevertheless, his regime kept the populous from getting too far out of step.

I loved parades. Perhaps it was a combination of the thrill of Mardi Gras processions plus the frequent parades my father performed in while I was growing up. Since my dad voluntarily participated in the National Guard, I learned to adore the drama of bands playing and men marching around in uniform with whistles blowing and commands being shouted. Precision drilling with intricate formations and rifles flung around in unison was and still is startling.

However, executing the changing of the guard, these marching soldiers resembled the toy soldiers from the Nutcracker Suite who fought The Rat King's mice. Their diminutive stature made them appear to be masquerading pre-teens in a junior high play. Their jackets were electric blue, and their golden-fringed epaulets coordinated with the gold buttons and braid that crossed their chests and glistened in the sun.

The marchers thrust their nation's flag, attached to long sugarcane poles, into the backs of the soldiers preceding them, and the band played on. Their hats were a cross between Jackie Kennedy's pillbox and a mini Shriner's hat worn by an organ grinder's monkey.

The rhythm of the regal band wavered, and the Cavalry's horses, in dire need of grooming, clippity-clopped along the cobblestones. Nevertheless, when the anthem was played with pride, hundreds of voices sang off-key in harmony, *"Salve Oh Patria"* (We Salute you, Our Homeland). Meanwhile, a semi-peaceful demonstration was happening nearby, so I hit the jackpot with a double feature on which I hadn't planned.

I tried slouching to appear shorter and blend in with the crowd. I wore my red poncho and Andes hat with my hair in two indigenous braids and exited the square with bent knees, Groucho Marx-style, not to draw attention. No matter how hard I tried, I didn't seem to blend in. However, no one was outright rude to me. They were only somewhat indifferent. "La-la-la, oh, what a beautiful morning, oh what a beautiful day . . . ."

I grabbed some tortillas and my favorite soda pop, Inca Kola, and headed to the bus stop. The trip to zero latitude was about sixteen miles north of Quito through the Andean countryside. Supposedly, conflicting gravitational forces pull both North and South on the equator, making it difficult to walk a straight line. I find it difficult to walk a straight line anywhere, so this will be an amusing challenge. I think it's because my arches are too high. It's like walking around on stiletto heels when I'm barefoot.

Due to the earth's tilt at the equator, there are two summers, two winters, two springs, and two autumns. Multiple seasons are practical in varying your wardrobe and not getting bored with your winter wools. Another advantage of living on the equator is that you weigh less than at the North or South Pole due to the force of gravity. I noticed in developing countries, they have to milk their tourist attractions with as much hype as possible.

We tumbled out of the bus and looked around, only to discover a red line painted on a strip of pavement. We were told there would be an impressive monument placed there in the future, plus a museum, shops, eateries, and other attractions. Everyone wanted photos straddling the red line with one foot on the northern hemisphere and the other foot securely on the southern hemisphere. It was sheer excitement. We were informed that scientists in 1736 had made precise calculations.

A local lady stood on the Northern Hemisphere with a second-hand portable sink and a bucket. As soon as everyone calmed down, she started to give a demonstration of the Coriolis Effect. She placed a stopper in the drain with pizzazz and poured the bucket of water into the basin. First, setting the bucket under the drain, she pulled the plug, threw in four small pebbles, and motioned that little stones were swirling down the drain clockwise.

She then crossed over to the Southern Hemisphere and repeated the same demonstration. The water swirled counterclockwise. We all cheered, and she beamed. She was clearly in her element.

Then for an encore, our nimble demonstrator placed the sink directly on the equator, and the water and pebbles drained straight down without swirling. We applauded wildly.

A lady with a German accent and a fascist mustache asked what would happen if a typhoon crossed the equator. A school teacher from Idaho responded, "Tropical storms and hurricanes would spin down, disorganize and cease to be." No one had the knowledge to refute her theory. So we nodded in agreement and made hmm, hum noises and returned to the bus enlightened.

A guy with a Galapagos t-shirt sat down beside me and asked what languages I spoke. I tossed the question back to him, and he replied, "Mainly American, some Yiddish, and a bit of English."

"Ditto," I responded. I knew at least ten Yiddish words, so that qualified my response.

"Hi, I'm Larry from New York City." He then offered me his knuckles in a 'fist bump,' which I thought was less personal and more hygienic than a handshake.

"Hi there, I'm Marie France from New Orleans." Larry's greeting appealed to my idiosyncratic personality and seemed to break the ice. Europeans would never introduce themselves on a bus or anywhere else. You waited to be introduced or produced a book or newspaper when entering a mode of transport to avoid anything as personal as eye contact.

"So, what's your story?" asked Larry.

I couldn't help but laugh. This guy was so over-confident and brazen.

"You first, Mr. Galapagos," I quipped.

"I'm a New Yorker, a CPA, single, and just returned from an awesome cruise around the Galapagos Islands. Your turn."

"I'm a professional traveler working my way down to Rio for Carnival."

Larry cocked his head and said, "Has anyone ever told you you're a Carly Simon look-alike?"

I smiled, "Yep, plenty."

"But how can you afford to travel? Travel ain't cheap, sister!" He winked as if he was sharing a secret with me.

"Actually, I buy stuff in one place and sell it in another. I'm a nomad."

"Yeah, you avoid the nine-to-five workday drudge - smart cookie."

"Enough about me - I can't picture you working as an accountant. Such a straight-lace, tedious occupation for a guy like you?"

Larry admitted, "You should see my clientele. I have the entire staff of airline stewardesses from TWA and United Airlines. When word gets around, I'll also scoop up on the Delta gals." Grinning, Larry punctuated his credentials with a wink.

Okay, this guy was attractive and charming but not my type. He had an athletic build, about five foot eleven, huge pale eyes, and sandy hair. He wore faded jeans, a blue tourist t-shirt, a gold Star of David on a long chain, a golden Rolex, and an insignia ring.

I couldn't resist, "You certainly don't look Jewish; you look about as Aryan as they come."

"My grandparents emigrated from Germany at the turn of the century, but we still speak Yiddish at home. How about you? I'm surprised New Orleans has a Jewish population. By the way, you look as Semitic as an Israeli-born Jew - with lots of *chutzpah* (audacity)."

"Thanks!" I took Larry's remarks about me looking Jewish as a compliment. I was fascinated with anything Jewish. Jesus was Jewish, and as a matter of fact, He still is. It was the race God chose to reveal himself to the world.

Larry explained that he was on a two-week package tour, including a ten-day cruise of the Galapagos Islands and a few days around Quito. He raved about the islands and the out-a-sight wildlife. With wild enthusiastic gestures, he explained the mysterious, bio-diverse nature. His eyes widened as he spoke of the endemic species developed in isolation, such as the giant tortoises, flightless cormorants, and marine iguanas. The downside, he explained, was that he was stuck with a bunch of boring middle-aged tourists from New Jersey.

Appearing to be about thirty-five, Larry said he was a tennis ace and a great dancer and to call him when I was next in New York. He handed me his business card, offered another fist bump, and exited into his waiting tour bus that would whisk him off to the five-star Hotel Plaza Grande. I was glad to have a quiet evening. Larry's intensity and exaggerated enthusiasm were exhausting. He outdid me on both counts.

* * *

The receptionist called me over and handed me a message. Michael and Lidia, my missionary soccer buddies, had checked out early to return to their village. Cool of them to leave me a message. Their message was mystifying.

"God does not call those who are equipped. He equips those whom He has called." 1 Corinthians 1:26-27

Come to think of it, they had previously mentioned something similar – "It's not about your ability; it's about your availability." I couldn't wait to see what the Bible verse had to say. I always carried my special little Gideon Bible with me since 'Jerusalem Jonathan' highlighted many vital verses. I dashed to my room, sat on my lumpy bed, and thumbed to the passage.

"Brothers and sisters, think of what you were when you were called. Not many of you were wise by human standards; not many of you were influential; not many were of noble birth. "But God chose the foolish things of the world to shame the wise; God chose the weak things of the world to shame the strong." 1 Cor. 1:26-27

It took me a while to digest all the derogatory insinuations, swallow my pride and allow the dots to connect. I was nailed. No matter what illusions of grandeur I possessed, I knew that it wasn't logical that God Almighty might call me into His service because of my wisdom and talents.

Okay, I was a misfit, but what better way could the Creator of the Universe demonstrate His grace? It started to make sense. I just might be usable. And even if God, heaven forbid, called me to build mud huts with thatch roofs in the Andes, He would equip me. Amen! Why was I singled out for the extraordinary encounters in the belly of the Great Pyramid of Giza, then on Golgotha and in the Sahara Desert? Why was I enveloped in liquid love from above? I now had the answer – because I didn't deserve it! God could demonstrate His amazing Grace!

"Amazing grace, how sweet the sound that saved a wretch like me; I once was lost but now am found, was blind but now I see . . . . . ." I drifted off to sleep humming that grace-saturated hymn and awoke the following morning in the same exact position, refreshed and raring to go.

5. LIMA, PERU

As we descended through thick marshmallow clouds, the Jorge Cháves International Airport suddenly emerged into view. I realized from the size of the terminal. Lima must be a bustling metropolis. It was. Surrounding villages had merged, becoming the outskirts of the sprawling city. I was a city girl and boasted about my addiction to noise, concrete, and asphalt.

However, I needed peace to ponder my mission friends' message, meditate on the highlighted verses in my Gideon guide, study the supernatural life of Smith Wigglesworth, and look for signs of the elusive Holy Spirit. After all, Jesus told his disciples that they would be far better off when He went away, then He would send the Comforter (Holy Spirit) to them. What could be better than Jesus in person? What a mystery.

As I waited patiently at the information desk, I studied the faded map of Peru suspended behind the counter. There were some interesting red dots south of Lima. When I inquired about a peaceful pueblo on the sea, the agent suggested the second dot, Pucusana. He said it was a quiet, quaint fishing village with a few modest hotels. Bingo! Pu-cu-sa-na, Pu-cu-sa-na, yep, it had a catchy four-syllable rhythm. I did a Pu-cu-sa-na soft shoe while waiting for the bus. There were mainly locals waiting in line, so that was a good omen.

We piled into a dusty bus and slowly rolled out of the grimy haze that hung over Lima's southern suburbs. Following the Peruvian coastline southward along the Pacific for an hour and a half, the bus screeched to a halt at a protected harbor. That natural bay housed about a hundred brightly painted fishing boats that bobbed up and down in the water. Although Pucusana appeared to be a shabby fishing settlement, it had an innate soulfulness. Perfect, a few days to chill out here, then I'd head to Cuzco and wrap up my time in Peru discovering Machu Picchu – considered one of the Eight Wonders of the World.

I found a small hotel from the 60s with a superb view of the bay where I could watch the seals frolicking around the boats, hoping to catch a free snack. There were fishing skiffs with single outboard motors that you pulled manually and fed diesel. Most village inhabitants fished, gutted, and packed the day's catch in dry ice to be trucked into Lima. Others owned simple seafood huts. I also noticed net fishermen and a deepwater fleet bringing in tuna, swordfish, and sharks.

There was non-stop activity swirling around, but the village maintained an uncanny calm. I asked for a tour boat and was directed to a small handmade skiff called *Los Tiburoncitos* (The Little Sharks). On the boat's stern were written Moises and Aaron (Moses and Aaron), the Jewish patriarchs and brothers of Old Testament fame.

The Spanish Conquistadores had imposed their form of Christianity on the indigenous population. However, the Peruvians retained their ancient beliefs and devised their own version of Catholicism. Evangelical missionaries were now pouring in to present the undiluted truth, along with Bibles translated into local dialects. I'd heard that revivals and miracles were rippling across the continent. Fascinating! I hoped to connect with the Holy Spirit during my time in Pucusana.

My boat captain explained in battered Spanglish that the best time to push off was at 7 am. I reluctantly gave a 'thumbs up' and decided to stroll on the beach and feast on an early seafood supper. I ordered the national dish of Peru, *ceviche* (Chita fish marinated in lemon), served with a sliver of red onion, fiery *rocoto* pepper, and sweet potato. For dessert, I indulged in a *crema volteada* (Peruvian flan), topped with whip cream and nuts - washing it down with a fluorescent yellow Inca Kola.

As I ate up, the sun sank, illuminating the horizon with a multi-hued blaze reflecting red-hot fire onto the cold Pacific. Another long walk in the water-softened sand relaxed my muscles. It stretched each tendon and ligament so I could artfully perform brazen leaps similar to a startled gazelle. A few puzzled seagulls kept their eyes on me but followed cautiously at a distance.

I was happy to spend my evening reading and anticipating a full day of sightseeing. I drifted to sleep with the comforting sound of waves gently rocking boats and awoke with the roar of motors as fishermen sped away at dawn.

After splashing some frigid water in my face, I jumped into my jeans, pulled on my long-sleeved red t-shirt, and then hiked my hair up into a high ponytail. By the way, the captain, who was waiting in the boat with three other passengers, looked like a dead-ringer for Popeye the Sailor Man. His forearms were the most significant part of his body. In addition, he had an anchor tattoo, smoked a corncob pipe, and wore a white captain's cap.

The most annoying part was that I looked like Olive Oyl, his curveless fiancée, with my beanpole body and oversized hands and feet. I'm unsure if my hands and feet were too big for my body or if it was an optical illusion since they were attached to my rail-thin limbs. Two Japanese passengers were taking photos of us and laughing. Had they noticed the resemblance?

Our Captain Diego made the sign of the cross twice and then started up the motor on his first power pull. You could tell he was weaned on a boat. We zipped through the calm, protected waters of the crescent-shaped harbor southbound toward the open waters. We then followed the coastline until we arrived at a rocky bluff that housed a nesting area for Incan Terns with their bright red beaks. Bonanza! Unbelievable! Diego stalled the boat so we could 'ooh and ahh' while snapping photos.

I was good at imitating accents and bird calls, so I had an intimate chat with a Tern before Diego continued south. After about thirty minutes, he pointed to some beige boulders that turned out to be sea lions sunning themselves on slabs of rock, oblivious to our intrusion. I wondered if this was the real deal or if they were planted there by the tourist board.

Our captain announced, "Next stop - Humboldt Penguin colony." I laughed, impressed with his sense of humor. One of my Japanese boatmates stuck a tattered brochure under my nose with a photo of a Peruvian Penguin. In choppy English, he explained that the Peruvian Penguins' habitat is highly influenced by the cold, nutrient-rich Humboldt current, which flows northward from Antarctica.

Why was Pucusana merely a faded dot on the map at the airport information counter? This fishing village was an accessible, bargain-priced goldmine! It was not only a vibrant ecosystem but included some endangered species. Yet, with all the Galapagos Islands' promotion, nothing was advertised about Peru's coastline being home to some of the world's greatest natural spectacles - where the desert meets the sea and the seabirds reign. There was no mention of the Guanay cormorants, boobies, and Peruvian pelicans, much less the petite PENGUINS!

Peru was synonymous with Machu Picchu. There was some talk about Colca Canyon, Rainbow Mountains, and the Amazon jungle but no mention of the explosion of marine wildlife and amazing seabirds. Diego cut the motor as we approached the small colony of penguins. He said they were timid and didn't want to scare them out of sight. Although the penguins were flightless, they were underwater torpedoes chasing after krill, squid, hake, and herring. We drifted and rocked in the waves, absorbed with every move of these bird-type fish mammals who flew underwater.

Diego finally started up the motor, and we returned to Pucusana feeling like part of a Jacques Cousteau documentary. It turned out that the Asians, being ornithologists, brought their penguin brochure from Japan. However, they primarily came to visit family in Lima who had opened the city's first Sushi Bar and were thinking of joining forces. Okay, I ask a lot of questions, but I'm curious to know what makes people tick.

Without being consciously aware, I felt that the Holy Spirit (being dove-like in nature) had accompanied us on our tour. In times like this, I understood my brother's oneness with creation and envied his awareness and concern for it. I was starting to wake up to more wonders of our universe!

While we headed back to Pucusana, I let my hand drag in the icy water, causing a mini wake. I belted out in honor of our captain, "He's Popeye, the sailor man, he's Popeye, the sailor man . . . . ." Diego broke into my tune to warn me about the school of sharks circling our boat and to get my hand out of the water. I took his advice as I watched the hungry 'blue fins' cut through the water on the prowl.

As we entered the harbor, the backdrop of colossal sand dunes starkly contrasted with the vibrant blue Pacific's natural cove. Giant pelicans circled overhead, spying out fish bits while Diego announced, "Ahoy, ahoy," as he motored up to the dock with expertise, tied up his pride and joy, and leaped out with a smile. The half-day tour of a lifetime cost a mere five bucks, so I paid him double for his trouble and felt blessed.

A bit jittery from a drop in blood sugar, I dashed to the hut where I had dined the evening before and pointed to a weather-worn photo of a bowl of orange soup filled with seafood – *Chupa de Camarones*. The thatched-roof one-person operation was perfect, and it had to be fresh with only one dish of the day. I was the sole customer since most people had lunch after 1 pm.

The magic soup was a cross between shrimp chowder and seafood gumbo. I became comfortably aware that the chef/owner watched me, with adoration, slurp every last spoonful. The delicacy comprised a perfectly spiced mixture of a ton of shrimp, with slivers of corn off the cob, potatoes, fresh fish stock, garlic, eggs, milk, and cheese. Power food for pennies!

I noticed the proprietor wore a simple gold cross and had a small shrine in the corner of his hut. Although professing Catholics, the indigenous Peruvians seemed to have a nearly synonymous association with Pacha Mama (Mother Earth) and the Virgin Mother. However, they *were* devout – not an hour-a-week faith but a lifestyle of devotion.

As I sat there digesting and catching my breath, something unusual happened. I felt intense compassion toward this somewhat older man. He was obviously limping from pain, and I knew God wanted to heal him. I wondered if the faith giant, Smith Wigglesworth, and his many testimonies of healing had influenced me. I had read his amazing book twice and was now pouring over it slowly. My Gideon Bible stated that all you needed was a mustard seed of faith to see miracles happen. I had at least a mustard seed, and the limping man seemed to have more.

I became self-conscious and cleared my throat. "*Perdoname Señor*" (Excuse me Sir). I then placed my hands into a prayer position and pointed to his leg. The man smiled and nodded his head. I decided to go for it – "In the name of Jesus, leg be healed." Well, I did it, but I wanted to pay up and high-tail it out of there before we both discovered it didn't work. I thought to myself, 'Oh ye of little faith.' So I got the courage to point to the guy's leg, raised my eyebrows, and said, "Leg better?"

The man paced up and down the hut with a big grin and said, "*Pierna – no dolor*" (Leg – no pain). He then started jumping up and down and running in circles. I was startled and surprised. Lars told me back in Bogota that God had a mission for me. Maybe this was my mission? I was so glad I might not have to build huts in a jungle. I was laughing and pointed to the sky. "God healed you," to ensure he didn't think it was me. I wanted to remain humble. I paid my bill, left a large tip, and floated out of the rustic restaurant.

Walking down to the beach, I glanced back and saw the chef limping around again. Was his healing so short-lived? Had he staged a show to please me or to prompt a tip? Was I one of the many hopefuls who had prayed for the man, wanting to be used by God Almighty to alleviate pain and suffering? I blushed and hoped I didn't damage the man's faith. I meant well. The food was exquisite, so nothing lost, even if nothing was gained. But just maybe he was healed, or perhaps there would be progressive healing? God works in mysterious ways.

* * *

It was only a ten-minute walk to Nymph beach, located to the left of the fishing boat terminal. The water was crystal clear, but the Antarctic current flowing northward from the South Pacific Ocean prevented me from plunging in for an afternoon swim. Instead, I walked for miles, blissfully singing and reflecting on the mind-boggling events of the past few weeks and wondering about the upcoming episodes that would soon unfold.

One quick stop by the market for some prickly pears, passion fruit, maracuya, tuna fruit, and fried pastries. I wanted to read on my hotel balcony and watch the sublime sunset since I had to rise early to catch the bus back to the airport in Lima.

I felt cocooned and secure, wrapped in the cozy but lightweight alpaca blanket. With the abundance of boating, fresh air, and beach gallivanting, I was whacked and ready for a slow-wave sleep. You know, the kind of solid sleep where you awake in the same position you fell asleep.

Whoa . . . . who had the nerve to knock on my door in the middle of the night? "Get out of the hotel, NOW!" The command was screeched with a thick accent. What nerve? Was this a funky fire drill? When I stood up, I felt like I was on a surfboard. I spread my arms for balance. As I worked my way to the wall and switched on the light, I saw my fruit dancing on the table, and then a framed poster fell off the wall. Finally, I heard someone screaming, "*TERREMOTO!*" (EARTHQUAKE!). I jumped into my jeans and t-shirt, grabbed my body pouch with my tickets, passport, and money, and raced down the hotel steps barefoot into the cold sand.

My only experience with earthquakes was one faint tremor in Kashmir several years ago. I remember everyone in the carpet factory disappeared from the building while I casually lolled around inspecting the rugs. I had oodles of experience with hurricanes. You either left town or stood your ground. Perhaps God was trying to tell me something. I recall reading that The Almighty often woke people up in the night to give them a verse or a message. However, this was a bit radical.

Meanwhile, a Dutch-looking couple with matching wooden shoes clunked over to chat. "I guess you realize Peru lies on The Ring of Fire, and there are at least two hundred tremors a year and lots of volcanic eruptions."

"Why no, I didn't. How intriguing!"

"The interface between the Nazca and South American tectonic plate is near the Peruvian Coast. The South American Plate is moving three inches every year."

"Wow, three inches. Is that a lot?"

"Well, it's enough to cause earthquakes and occasionally a tsunami."

After an hour of waiting with eager anticipation – nothing happened. A handful of us, fed up and cold, returned to bed. I realized it was good timing to move inland and further away from that unpredictable tectonic plate.

6. CUZCO, PERU

Yea, I was on my way to Machu Picchu! So what if I had to share the plane with a few rowdy tour groups – I'd merely tune them out. I suppose they were also entitled to experience this eighth wonder of the world. We would soon be landing in Cuzco, the famed Inca capital and pivotal point for day tours. I was armed with the address given to me by Lars, the Norwegian Viking in Bogotá, but I would first find a quaint old hotel and get settled.

The Velasco Astete International Airport was nothing to write home about but adequate to accommodate year-round Inca seekers. The huge historic Plaza de Armas and center of the city was only about five miles from the airport, so I jumped on the bus raring to discover the navel of the Inca empire, belting out Jimmy Durante's famed "Inka, Dinka, Doo" hit.

Wow, the town square was vast, so I started skipping to cover more ground. Yikes, I couldn't catch my breath, so I staggered to a bench covered with pigeon poop and sat on the corner to recoup. I'd forgotten that I had flown from sea level up to 11,154 feet within an hour and a half, and my lungs were still in Lima. I thrashed through my bottomless bag to find some glucose candy lifesavers. Phew, just in the nick of time. After about ten minutes, I restarted at a slower pace.

It seems that this small city of Cuzco unfurled one of the most pre-eminent empires in the history of humanity. The Incas expanded their frontiers in less than a century from the North of Quito, Ecuador, southward to Santiago, Chile, and eastward to Argentina.

Cunningly, Cuzco was built in the shape of a giant puma. The sacred puma's body incorporated the palaces, temples, and governmental buildings, while the fortress outside the city formed this animal's head. I was standing in the square between the legs of the puma. What an optimal point of view.

The zealous Spaniards who arrived in 1533 were also gob-smacked by this beautiful city of gold but, sadly enough, plundered its treasures and destroyed most of the temples. However, there are still remnants of the temples dedicated to lightning, rain, moon, sun, wind, and other natural phenomena. This city of contrasts was the most captivating city I'd seen thus far. I could understand why Lars' and Sven's friends had established a permanent mission here.

I scanned the city's strange mix of Inca architecture and Spanish-Moorish colonial style for a central but cheap lodging. Then, on the other side of the main square, I spotted Selina Plaza de Armas Hotel - olé, a typical colonial-style building. Their rooms were monastery modest but had a hand basin, toilet, and the right price. The vibrant Incan zig-zag bedspread made my eyes cross, but it wouldn't matter while I was asleep.

It was low season, and I had high hopes. I felt centered in this city of gold. What remained of the Incan architecture gave an inkling of the empire's grandeur. The gargantuan boulders were put together without mortar and with such precision not even a knife blade could fit between them. I had never seen such perfectly shaped megaliths anywhere. Their dimensions and weight often exceeded the boulders used in The Great Pyramid of Giza, and the engineering skills of the Incans were unequaled.

The first stop was fuel – I needed carbohydrates every few hours to combat the altitude! The receptionist suggested San Pedro Market, about an eight-minute walk from the main square. Go where the locals go was my motto. What a wild conglomeration of everything!

Four aisles of smoothie stands with jovial women were trying to snatch my attention. Peruvian fruit, cultivated in the Andes, was unique in texture and taste. I chose a combo of Grenadelle, Cherimoya, and dragon fruit mixed with carrots, papaya, pineapple, and banana. It was a power drink that would keep me going for hours. I'd return for the main course after sunset. The chicken noodle soup caught my eye, so I sketched a map to find my way back to the stand.

My body still needed time to acclimatize, so I did some slow-motion sightseeing. The famed Sun Temple, Qorikancha, was a short walk from the main square and at the top of my must-see list. Cuzco was a techno color town, so I coordinated well with my newly purchased electric-hued poncho, locally woven by the nimble-fingered Andes maidens. With my black fedora, I still appeared subdued compared to some locals.

Boom! As I turned the corner, the Sun Temple came into full view, and I could imagine the massive structure in its past glory glimmering with gold. Typically the entrance was through an attached cathedral, demonstrating the mix of deities. The temple stones were seamless, and the carved-out niches accommodated mummies and offerings to the sun god, Inti.

Naturally, the southern hemisphere's longest day of the year, the 21st of December, was the super celebration known as Solstice and initiated by the Incans. They were big on astrology and had provided an opening in the thick wall to allow the sun to flood in on the exact day of solstice.

Still hyperventilating while climbing the precarious stone steps, I decided to retire to a comfy chair in the main square and indulge in people-watching. Clever ladies from the nearby hills captured the art of marketing by wearing colorful handiwork and carrying a baby lamb with matching knitted garments. Tots were tossed on their backs papoose style, and they more often led a llama around the square to draw attention. I never carried a camera but gladly donated to their innovative enterprise.

I was ready for a big bowl of chicken noodle soup and a good night's sleep. However, I wasn't prepared to slurp around intimidating chicken claws attached to plump legs! So I had to shut my eyes while lapping up that "soup with an attitude."

The cook laid out three types of chili peppers for me to experience. I could sense all eyes were on me, hoping I wouldn't be the tourist victim of the day, but I thwarted their expectations by actually enjoying the lethal hot stuff. "Hmmm, perfecto!" I wondered if smoke was steaming from my ears. I had a refreshing smoothie and retired back to my convent-style hotel.

* * *

A new day, a new adventure! I was curious about Lar's mission field friends and their impact on this Andes sun-worshiping culture. I found their street in a flash. Santa Clara was part of the ancient Inca road, and I could still see details of the preserved original walls. Awesome! I wore my faded bell bottoms and a blue t-shirt with my grey alpaca shawl, not wanting to frighten them. My hair looked less electric with the arid climate, and I could pass for a nice, normal person.

A pretty young woman opened the door on my third knock. "Hi, I'm Marie France. I met Lars and Sven in Bogotá about three weeks ago, and they gave me your address. They told me God has a mission for me."

"Welcome, how wonderful; please come in. My name is Jessica, and my husband, James, will return in a jiffy. What mission are you with?"

"None yet. I'm touring the continent and feeling out the land and what God has prepared in advance for me to do." I was quite impressed with my response. It was not a lie and not too committal.

"What great timing! We're experiencing a wave of revival in Peru and throughout South America."

Being polite, I returned the question, "What mission are you with?"

"We're with the South American Mission. It was founded in 1914 and kicked off in Paraguay by an American couple from New York. SAM first sent Protestant missionaries to Peru in 1929."

"Cool," I commented.

"Even though Peru was assigned as the Catholic headquarters from Chile to Nicaragua and Catholicism was declared the state religion in 1845, the Peruvians have remained Christo-pagans. However, the land reforms of 1968 have brought a significant change in the Gospel's receptivity among the indigenous Quechuas. Now we are reaping the harvest."

I didn't follow Jessica's spiel very well and was unsure why she started discussing the harvest. Perhaps they were teaching avant-garde agricultural techniques. She said, "There are large areas of the country, especially in the highlands, the jungle, and the Amazon, where the message of the Gospel had not yet been reached."

It seemed the right moment to mention that I had commitments in Europe within several months, not to mislead this sweet young lady into thinking Jesus sent me here to spread the Gospel in one of those god-forsaken places. I envied her faith, commitment, and sacrifice, but I wasn't prepared for that kind of total surrender.

James burst into the living room and announced that José (Yiye) Ávila would have a crusade in Lima during March and might extend his stay to include Cuzco. Then he noticed me and offered his hand with a smile, "Hi, I'm James." It didn't surprise him that a strange woman was sitting on his sofa. I could tell they had open house and were used to people dropping by.

"Hi, I'm Marie France. Lars and Sven gave me your address."

"How are those Vikings? I sure miss them. They have hearts of gold and hands of steel. They're building a village single-handedly on the Caribbean Coast of Colombia. Have you come to help us bring in the harvest? It's ripe and waiting to be gathered."

Did I look like a farm girl? I hoped not. "Sorry, but I can't stay long in Cuzco. I'm going to visit Machu Picchu, Bolivia, and southbound. I have too many obligations in Europe, but I love Cuzco and will pray for your mission work here."

"Well, I hope you have at least some time to plant a few seeds with us."

"Absolutely, I'd adore planting some seeds!" I hoped it was Johnny Appleseed style, where you walked through the fields and tossed seeds to the left and right without getting down on your knees and digging a hole for each one. I noticed they had precisely the same book I had. "Are you into Smith Wigglesworth also? Lars gave me a copy in Bogotá."

"Without a doubt, he's a faith heavyweight who believed God's Word and followed the instructions to a T. We have a healing ministry, and Wigglesworth encourages us with his 'Nothing is impossible with God' attitude. After all, Jesus IS the same yesterday, today and forever. Jesus gave his disciples authority to do what He did - spread the Gospel with signs, wonders, and miracles. Then He poured out His Holy Spirit to empower them."

"Awesome, so what about this Yiye Ávila you mentioned? He must be someone special. What kind of crusade will he be leading? I don't guess it's the medieval military version."

"Far from it," James laughed. "He's an evangelist from Puerto Rico and one of the most influential Protestant preachers of the Spanish language – the Hispanic Billy Graham. Yiye had a personal encounter with Jesus in the early 60s and a miraculous healing. He then felt called to preach the good news of Jesus, so he left his job of twenty-two years as a science and chemistry professor and started holding large revival meetings intending to reawaken interest in Jesus and His imminent return. Simultaneously people were being healed."

"He sounds like a present-day Wigglesworth," I confirmed.

"Exactly, that's why I was so ecstatic when I heard he was coming to Peru. Yiye Ávila has been holding huge rallies throughout Central America, where there has been an awakening accompanied by healings and transformation of cities and villages. Crime had ebbed, and souls were saved, so now church leaders and even politicians have invited him to Colombia, Peru, and Chile."

"Aw, how disappointing. I won't be here," I replied with regret.

"Hey, why don't you join our Bible study and healing service this afternoon at five?"

"Yeah, awesome, I'd like nothing better!" I knew that would give me time to cover more sights of Cuzco, return to the San Pedro Market for lunch, freshen up at my hotel, grab my mini Bible and be back at Jessica and James' place on time.

* * *

I arrived at 5 pm, and three shy Peruvians were waiting at the door. With her brilliant smile, Jessica greeted us graciously, "*Bienvenido, por favor ven*" (Welcome, please come in). There were nine other people already seated in their spacious living room. I was the only other gringo besides the host and hostess, but we were a group of twelve, like the apostles - how apropos.

James introduced Carlos, an indigenous believer, who would translate the teaching into the local dialect and convey the group's comments back into English. Carlos commented that the group was speaking about how Jesus had healed them.

"Today's topic is *Sozo*," announced James. He explained the meaning of the Greek word *Sozo*: to save, deliver, heal, and be made whole. James continued, "The word *Sozo,* translated into English, is used over one hundred times in the New Testament. It is the word applied especially when Jesus heals someone, be it physically, emotionally, or spiritually."

James informed us that Salvation, over the centuries, has come to be referred to as forgiveness of sins and life eternal only. I thought, "ONLY?" It sounded like a massive reward for putting my faith in Jesus. But James pointed out that at the cross, the sacrifice of Jesus provided not only salvation but healing and wholeness as well. He then went on to quote verses that illustrated and confirmed his teaching.

I was amazed that two-thirds of Jesus' earthly ministry involved healing. James said that after Jesus ascended to heaven, the Holy Spirit was sent to earth in His place and empowered the disciples to continue the works He did. These works are recorded in the Book of Acts – seven healings, six miracles, and two raised from the dead.

Okay, Jesus is Jesus, and everything is possible for Him. But it's a stretch to fathom His disciples, ordinary guys, were performing the same healings and miracles. I wonder why the Church kept the empowerment of the Holy Spirit a secret for so many centuries. Perhaps they feared losing control? Some believers were martyred for translating the Bible from Greek into English and other languages. What a major overreaction, but now I understand why.

After James wrapped up the study by resuming, "We have a loving, passionate God who is on a relentless quest to rescue his people," Jessica invited members of the group to share their experiences or ask questions. The rather introverted gathering became wild with excitement. After being prayed for, one man of about fifty jumped up and started raving about how he could hear from his deaf ear. A woman started laughing because the pain in her leg had gone after eight long years, and she started running around the house.

One by one, each person explained the recent life-changing healing that had taken place. I didn't want to be the odd one out, so I prayed a 'help me Lord' prayer, and words began to flow from my XL lips in melodious song . . . *"Amazing Grace, how sweet the sound that saved a wretch like me, I once was lost, but now am found, was blind but now I see . . . ."*

Carlos didn't even have time to translate my words. The group knew the tune and what the words meant - they started to cheer and applaud wildly. I considered myself a talented singer but didn't expect such an overwhelming response. As far as I knew, I was singing the folk ballad made famous by Joan Baez.

In response to my microwaved prayer, perhaps the words flowed from my heart, betraying what I had so cleverly blocked out. I felt choked up and needed an emotional release. I didn't want to lose control and sob, so I asked Jessica if I could wash the cups or take out the garbage – so unlike me. After hugs and handshakes, I lingered on to quiz James and Jessica about the mass hysteria I had just witnessed.

"Oh, that was pure joy you saw," explained James.

"But how can it be that everyone here today has had a miraculous healing?"

"Faith, my dear friend, these lovely indigenous believers don't have a plan B. Our faith has become diluted with options. If we're ill, we've been conditioned to start looking for a specialist instead of starting with God's Word. Jesus said, '*By my wounds, you have been healed.*' (1 Peter 2:24)

"The new disciples in this study believe every word of the Bible. They embrace the Holy Spirit because they are aware of a spiritual world. When they read Scripture, it speaks to them, and they accept it one hundred percent. Only the Holy Spirit can reveal God's Word to these precious uneducated believers."

"Okay, I believe what you're saying – it echoes the Acts of the Apostles and disciples played out in the New Testament. The Bible states that 'the Truth' will set you free, but clearly, it's the Truth you know."

"Some people have the mistaken idea that all illnesses have a stamp of approval from God since He is sovereign. They think He must be trying to teach them a lesson. However, the Lord's Prayer clearly says – '*Our Father who art in heaven, hallowed be thy name, thy kingdom come thy will be done on earth as it is in heaven ....*' So what's God's will in heaven? '*He will wipe every tear from our eyes. There will be no more death or mourning or crying or pain, for the old order of things has passed away.*'" (Revelation 21:4)

"Yeah, it rings true. The Lord's Prayer should, without a doubt, convey the Lord's will," I deducted.

James added, "Just keep in mind John 10:10 and the words of Jesus, 'The thief comes only to steal and kill and destroy. I (Jesus) came that they may have life and have it abundantly.'"

I knew what James said was on the level, but I felt a heart-cry surfacing, so I changed the subject. "Oh, by the way, what's the best route to Machu Picchu?" I needed time alone to reflect on the events of this evening. It was like climbing into Wigglesworth's book. What occurred in the book of Acts and the ministry of Smith Wigglesworth happened this evening. I needed time to digest it all.

* * *

Jessica kindly handed James a notebook and pen. "The easiest way to get from Cuzco to Machu Picchu is to take the train to *Aguas Calientes* (hot waters), which is named for its natural hot springs. The train ride is a glorious three-and-a-half-hour trip along tracks that run parallel to the Urubamba River in the Sacred Valley, with dramatic canyon walls on either side. There are lots of little hostels and hotels, and there's not much tourism this time of the year, so you won't have to book." I couldn't wait!

"From *Aguas Calientes*, it's a two-hour hike up to the Citadel of Machu Picchu or a forty-minute ride by shuttle bus. But, of course, once you get to the ruins, you'll have plenty of hiking up and down the original stone Inca trail discovering the multi-leveled ancient city. Then, when you get back to *Aguas Calientes,* you'll be ready for a long soak in the hot springs."

"Great, thanks. I've gotten my bearings and am forming a strategy for discovering the majestic Machu Picchu." I gave Jessica and James a grateful hug, thanked them for the life-changing afternoon, and headed back to my colonial convent cell. I had so many thoughts swirling around my mind, and I didn't know how to sort them out. Finally, I realized the jumble in my brain and my rattled peace was due to the day's challenging but marvelous events. After years of dabbling in other religions and everything else, I now knew that only Jesus had the words of eternal life.

My lack of peace stemmed from the uncertainty of my place in God's scheme of things. Heaven forbid I should be called into full-time ministry. After all, the Lord Almighty needed followers to support the missionaries living in marginal conditions and risking their lives.

Wheeling and dealing was my comfort zone – I found it gratifying to earn money. It gave me freedom and purpose and seemed to validate my existence. Yes, I could help support the missions. Better I remained in the background since I was concerned about the image I might project as a PR agent for Jesus. My idiosyncrasies were limitless. After all, I was known as the Queen of Quirk.

The words of Mahatma Gandhi reverberated in my mind, "If it weren't for Christians, I'd be a Christian." What skills did I need to draw people *to* Yeshua and not away? Perhaps God wanted me to quietly write a book. But that would be a cop-out and too tedious.

What drew me to Jesus was His unconditional love and GRACE. He hung out with the misfits, and that stirred my faith. However, I seemed to be going through performance anxiety. Although I embraced His grace, I could feel I was trying to impress Jesus rather than relax and let Him work through me. I could feel a battle raging within. How do I become humble? Is there a course 101 on humility?

Maybe I'm being called into a traveling-healing ministry? I've been on the move for the past three years, so now I could include healing. The answer slowly dawned on me. I needed to pray about it and discover God Almighty's plan. I was so used to plowing forward with my own ideas.

Wigglesworth said he never prayed longer than half an hour, but he never went longer than half an hour without praying. That was it. I needed to spend more time in prayer and perhaps learn to listen. I'd start soon. Tomorrow, I'd get up bright and early for a new adventure.

My decision to leave for *Aguas Calientes* at daybreak was a wise one. That way, I'd have time to see Machu Picchu the same afternoon, then I could return for a second dose the next day before heading around Lake Titicaca to Bolivia.

* * *

My hotel receptionist suggested I share a taxi to Poroy, where the train station to Machu Picchu was located - thirty minutes from Cuzco's center. A small crowd of international tourists was waiting in the terminal with anticipation. There was a background chatter of at least seven different languages. I wore my red and black Colombian cape and fedora, not to be mistaken for a backpacker or a package-tour traveler.

I could wear my hair wild and free since Peruvians weren't familiar with the negative hype from ghetto hippies. Their desire for the US dollar blurred any prejudice against unusual-looking travelers. I guess I resembled an odd-ball traveler or an eccentric-looking missionary.

The journey on Peru Rail was only three and a half hours to *Aquas Calientes*, and I was advised that I didn't need to pack a lunch since there would be food vendors wandering up and down the train cars. I wasn't informed that there would also be entertainment, but it was a welcomed element in the overall experience.

Especially the guy who jumped on at a village station, wearing a suit of iridescent rainbow colors from head to toe and a headdress that bobbed around to the rhythm of Andes pop music blaring from his hand-held radio. The Peruvian flute, carrying the melody, got me up onto my feet.

I found the sound of the *quena* cane flute irresistible and mimicked the guy's folkloric jig with expertise since I'd observed local dancers on the main square of Cuzco. I could hear cameras clicking, so when we finished, I passed my hat up and down the aisle to collect funds for the petite music man. We could have passed for the South American version of Sonny and Cher. Instead, I declined when Mr. Music motioned for me to join him in the next car. I realized he'd do better as a solo act.

The scenery that whizzed past was awesome. We were accompanied by a lazy river that became ferocious. Then we passed fields of corn, potatoes, squash, tomatoes, and other New World foods first introduced to Europe by Christopher Columbus. There were other vast fields with which I was unfamiliar. I overheard the backpacker across the aisle explaining that the coca plant was the top cash crop in Peru and best grown on the lower slopes of the Andes.

Leaning nearer, I pretended to be fascinated with the landscape on my left to glean what this knowledgeable traveler had to say. "Chewing coca leaves acts as a mild stimulant, suppressing hunger, thirst, pain, and fatigue. Almost all Andean people indulge in chewing leaves or sipping coca tea." I couldn't remain anonymous any longer.

"Do you think they get high on coca leaves?" The backpacker was American, so he didn't mind my intrusion.

"Not really, the effects are more or less like drinking an espresso," he replied. "The leaves are actually beneficial for good health and keep teeth sparkling white. The coca plant is sacred within indigenous cultures." I didn't look naïve, but maybe this guy was pulling my leg.

"You must be joking!" I exclaimed.

"No, it's a fact. Cocaine is another story," the guy replied.

"What about Coca-Cola? Do you think coca is its main ingredient," I asked?

"Coca-Cola is not just a catchy name. When it was first launched, coca leaves were key ingredients. However, the company removed the coca over one hundred years ago, but the leaves are still used to flavor coke."

"How fascinating!" I was sure this American know-it-all was trying to pull the wool over my eyes, but I wasn't going to take the bait. Did he think I was born yesterday? "Have you thought about chewing some leaves?" I inquired.

The guy pulled a few leaves from the pocket of his jean shirt and asked if I'd like to try some. I couldn't believe he'd do that in broad daylight in front of everyone. I started to wonder if he was a narcotics agent.

"Thanks, but no thanks," was my curt reply. I then gazed out the opposite window and pretended to be absorbed by the river splashing over some rocks that had fallen from a landslide.

I was told to look out for the spectacled bear near the river. This smallish, flat-faced bear was unique to northern and western South America. Its white muzzle and forehead with circles of dark fur around its eyes gave the bear a bespectacled intellectual appearance.

We chugged along the Sacred Valley, in awe of the dramatic canyon walls on either side of the track and snowcapped mountains perforating windswept clouds. It was the rainy season, and the constant drizzle kept the countryside green and my cascade of hair frizzy.

As we neared the town of *Aguas Calientes*, the familiar drum roll in my soul started to rumble, and my heart began to tap dance. We were only miles from Machu Picchu as the crow flies, but I was told that the shuttle bus would take thirty minutes to climb the steep, narrow zigzagging dirt road that connected the town with the ancient Citadel.

I bolted out of the train to scan the colorful hot springs city for a decent hotel. Wanting to ditch my hand luggage as quickly as possible, I'd then race to the bus station to buy a ticket for the next trip up the mountain. Hotel Inca had the right name and the luxury of a bright room with a toilet en suite and a clean hand basin.

The receptionist explained that the bus depot was only five minutes from the train station, so I jogged there in three minutes flat. The following bus would be leaving in less than half an hour, so I retraced my steps to the market to buy some fruit and a Kola. It was 1 pm, so I'd have at least four hours to discover the world's eighth wonder. I'd bought a return ticket for 6 pm, so I'd have a good 'taster' and tomorrow I'd return for more!

7. MACHU PICCHU, PERU

The rickety adventure bus was packed, and I recognized a lackluster group of tourists from the train. But, at least they were well-behaved, and we somehow bonded in our mutual allure to discover the lost city, the mystical Machu Picchu. I was feeling immune to scary bus rides until I gazed over to our driver, who was chewing coca leaves, reading a comic book, and changing the station of his portable radio – all at the same time.

I imagined that grabbing the front seat opposite the driver was a clever idea for an unobstructed view. I didn't count on having a kamikaze chauffeur with attention deficit disorder. All the wooden crosses with artificial flowers that dotted the side of the steep potholed road didn't contribute to my peace of mind. I shot a desperate prayer towards heaven and started to sing Kris Kristofferson's country gospel hit, "Why Me Lord."

We dodged backpackers trudging up the steep incline and out-of-control oncoming traffic heading downward. There were no guardrails, and peering down into the bottomless valley would have been awesome if it wasn't so spooky. It was a mere ten minutes before we arrived at the imperial city. Phew, I had survived a dozen switchbacks, a dramatic rock slide, and a mindless driver.

When the famous fifteenth-century citadel came into full view, I realized the trip up was worth the death-defying risk. I took a deep breath and decided to walk down and forfeit my return trip ticket. Meanwhile, looming before me was Machu Picchu! I was reeling in the glory of the moment.

I had seen so many photos and postcards, but NOTHING could have prepared me for this moment. It wasn't just the ruins and mysticism of the city being 'lost' for five hundred years; it was the lofty grandeur of the majestic setting. I was aware that this moment would become future nostalgia.

The remote Incan city was built in 1450 and abandoned a century later during the Spanish conquest. When it was rediscovered in 1911 by an American archeologist, the city was barely visible through the tons of overgrowth. The Incans made sure their path to the mountain was obliterated so the Inca Emperor Pachacuti's estate would be preserved for a later date. Little did they know their empire would be decimated by the Conquistadors and the diseases they transported with them.

I was now standing on the mountain ridge, eight thousand feet above the Sacred Valley, deciphering my sightseeing strategy. Of course, there were directional arrows, for what that's worth. Ah, I spotted the mundane group from my bus being led by a guide. I decided to subtly merge into the group for some basic info, and then I'd wander off on my own. It was hard to sneak in with my cape and hat, but I'd just hang in there until I was asked to leave.

The American guide bellowed out details in a mid-western twang, "It is believed that the Incan aristocracy inhabited Machu Picchu, likely nobles, priests, and 'aqlias' (Virgins of the Sun). We will visit the Temple of the Sun, Temple of the Three Windows, Temple of Condor, Sacred Rock, and the Moon Temple. Then you can make your way to the best viewpoints, Huayna Picchu and Puyupatamarca. There are sixteen hundred original Incan steps, so we will attempt to leave our footprints on each one."

I got the layout in a nutshell, so now I could lag behind unnoticed and trail them unobtrusively. At that moment, I heard the guide shouting in his Midwestern accent, "Hey, you in the red cloak and hat, you're welcome to join us." Ugh, how embarrassing. Everyone turned around and motioned for me to come. I didn't want to insult them by refusing, so I nonchalantly swaggered up to the crowd.

As Americans do, they all wanted to introduce themselves to me and added pleasantries like, "You needn't be alone. We'd really enjoy your company." That's what I was afraid of. How could I explain that I preferred to be on my own? I guess it was too late to try and speak with a foreign accent and say, "No understand."

I was caught at my game of getting a gratuity-guided tour. Now I had to pay my dues. "Where are you from, and what do you do? Why are you traveling alone? How can you afford to travel the way you do at your age?" One lady insisted I see photos of her plump grandchildren. I would politely continue for three temples and then explain that I was going to a viewpoint to meditate.

It just dawned on me that perhaps this encounter was God-ordained. Lars the Viking told me God had a mission for me in South America. Was this it? Was I to be an ambassador for Jesus with this package tour group? Nah, no way. I bailed out at the Temple of Condor, thanked Gary, the guide, profusely, and blew kisses to the group.

Huayna Picchu Peak lookout was my destination. It was the dramatic peak pictured behind the legendary ruins, seen on every postcard. As I sashayed through the ruins, I spotted no less than one hundred and fifty buildings, ranging from palaces to baths to temples and fountains. I imagined thousands of Incas pushing the massive stones up the steep mountain. Gary said they had no wheels to aid in the transport; therefore, sheer blood, sweat, and tears built the imperial city.

As clever and advanced as the Incas were, they had no written language. Instead, they tied knots in a rope to convey messages. As a result, so much of their history was transmitted from one generation to the next via traditional stories, ceremonies, and hearsay. They also constructed an infrastructure of roads, walls, and irrigation systems that are still in use today. Little did they know they had created the top tourist attraction in Peru and, for that matter, all of South America.

After crossing a sketchy bridge and working my way up and down thousands of steps, I arrived at the lookout point of Huayna Picchu Peak. I pulled in a deep breath of pristine mountain air and burst into song, "Climb every mountain . . . . . 'til you find your dream." I needed an emotional release and concluded that an ear-shattering song was an optimal choice over a blood-curdling scream. Ruins are ruins, but Machu Picchu was all about the setting. These royal ruins were nestled amongst jungled mountains in the high Andes plateau that rises steeply from the Urubamba River Valley.

I was immersed in fifty shades of serene green. Two Andean Condors soared on a thermal updraft, and a small herd of llamas was grazing on an ancient cultivated terrace. I thought, "Is there more to life than this?" I received a resounding "YES!" It's about the Creator of this paradise. I guess I was having an ah-ha nature-creation awakening. I felt I had to claim this pagan wonderland for the King of Kings and Lord of Lords. So I shouted toward the heavens, "Y-E-S-H-U-A, King of Machu Picchu!"

Reveling in another realm, I contemplated doing an interpretive dance in the spirit. I was interrupted by a sharp rap on my right shoulder. "Lady, enough is enough! We've been patiently waiting twenty minutes for you to wrap up your euphoria and move on so we could get some unobstructed photos of the peak."

I swung around and faced a group of about thirty dour faces. I wish I could have taken off in flight or merely disappeared. Instead, I placed my hands in a prayer formation under my chin, bowed my head, and whispered Namaste. The Indian custom simply means "Hello" and shows respect. There was no one there from the Indian sub-continent, but at least I could blame my narcissistic behavior on a hippie influence.

To soften my crime, one tourist asked me for my autograph. "Oh, Carly, what a surprise! I love your latest hit, 'Mockingbird.'" I smiled and said, "I'm so glad you like it." To explain that I wasn't Carly Simon would have made her look foolish and ruined her day. I signed and sauntered off towards the Sun Gate without looking back.

I gallivanted around the ruins for an uninterrupted hour, circling counter-clockwise to the directional signs and coming face to face with other anomalies on the narrow path. As the sun was hovering over the mountain peaks, ready to sink without warning, I decided to hightail it down the hikers' route with a batch of aging boy scouts who resembled professional trekkers. I'd heard that the hike up the steep mountain was at least an hour and a half of pure agony, but I knew I could descend in less than half an hour since running down mountains was my specialty. I was born with shock absorbers in my otherwise bony knees.

Arriving at Aguas Calientes in record time, I had a generic tourist meal before hitting the hay. The following morning, I planned on catching the first bus at 5 am to have a sunrise view of Machu Picchu.

It was an eye-opener to see such a long line of half-asleep tourists waiting for the bus to pull up. Finally, I broke rank and wiggled my way into the bus. Braving the reckless, nauseous bus trip, we jackknifed our way up to the citadel through low-lying clouds. But it was worth it! After several hours of absorbing the riveting beauty and serenity from the viewpoints, I did my mountain goat descent hopping from one Incan stone step to another, dodging grimacing hikers heading upwards.

* * *

I looked forward to a super soak in the thermo-medicinal waters that gave the Andean rainforest *pueblo* its descriptive name - *Aguas Calientes.* Stopping by my hotel, I first slipped on my Olympic-type Speedo one-piece bathing suit, threw my clothes on top, and headed out to search for the hot springs. The town was small but contained a confusing labyrinth without taxis or tuk-tuks.

Instructed to follow the river that goes down the middle of the city, I was assured that it would lead to the path going to the baths. The directions were typically scrambled; however, I saw three muscle-bound intrepid travelers toting towels, so I followed them. After a fifteen-minute walk tailing the trailblazers, we came to five round outdoor pools. I decided to do the American thing and introduced myself to the hikers so they wouldn't think I was a weirdo following them. But, on the other hand, that's what I was.

"Hi, I'm Marie France from New Orleans." They looked at me as if they were thinking . . . who asked?

Reluctantly, a Dudly Do-Right-looking guy offered his calloused hand, "Hi, I'm Don from Burnaby, British Columbia."

"Ah, that explains your demeanor – rugged country, I've heard. Isn't that where the Canadian Mounties keep law and order?" I love their ensembles with fire engine red jackets, black Jodhpurs with a bright yellow stripe, Nazi knee boots, and cute Smoky the Bear hats." Don glanced over at his friends, who were chuckling.

"Well, you fit the bill for a Yank. Cajun, by any chance?"

"Nope, wish I was."

"This is Matt and his wife, Michelle. We *are* RCMP."

"Oh yeah? Sounds fascinating. What does RCMP stand for?"

"Royal Canadian Mounted Police."

"Well, there you go, I'm very intuitive. I can see you're serious hikers. Did you climb up to the Michu Picchu ruins?"

"We did the six-day track from Cuzco to *Aguas Calientes*. Then, after the beginners' walk up to the ruins, we climbed Huayna Picchu mountain - one thousand feet straight up."

"You Canadians *are* invincible! Michelle, what's it like being married to a Mountie?"

"Ask my husband. He's married to one, also. We met at work, and this is our honeymoon. I was the first female to pass the requirements since they changed the law nine months ago. So the 8th of May, 1974 is our victory day for equal rights."

"Well done. Congratulations! Sounds so romantic." They looked like TV body-slamming pro-wrestlers. I guess they'll shine in their swimsuits.

Matt explained, "These hot springs come from a natural source of volcanic origin and may have been used by the Incas. It emerges from underground channels and springs up onto rocks at high temperatures. Then they transport the water to these five outdoor pools."

"How interesting, but it looks like an entire kindergarten class had a pee in the middle pool."

Matt shook his head and sighed, "The water is opaque yellow due to the sulfur. The temps range from 100 to 115 degrees, and the chemical composition has healing properties. Good for bones, joints, and skin. It also releases toxins. Relax and heal."

I wondered how often they changed the pool water. I wasn't too keen on relaxing in sweaty people's toxins. With those temps, my synthetic Speedo would melt. So I chose a cooler pool and let the three jumbo trekkers have the boiling yellow one. They deserved it after all their mountaineering.

My pool was bathwater warm and felt luxurious after a month of tepid showers. I couldn't resist singing Nelson Eddy and Jeanette Mac Donald's love-lorn musical hit, "Indian Love Call." Nelson Eddy was such a romantic Canadian Mountie. I sang both parts bouncing from baritone to soprano and back. I hoped it helped the Hulks relax.

After half an hour of marinating in hot minerals and who knows what, I hoisted myself out of the pool and had a cool shower.

I brought my bar of soap and shampoo, just in case, and decided to scrub off the residue that lingered on my limbs. "Yoohoo," I shouted to the zonked-out Mounties, "I'm heading back to town. It was nice meeting y'all. Enjoy soaking in all that sulfur." The trio waved without muttering a word but displayed ear-to-ear smiles as if they were in la-la-land and unaware of my departure.

Back in town, I had a typical mouth-watering Peruvian meal of *rocoto relleno* (stuffed spicy peppers) and decided to have a peaceful evening jotting down all my impressions of Machu Picchu, the hot springs, and everything. I then caught up with a few more chapters of Wigglesworth and sang some Psalms to a mysterious melody that welled up from my innermost being and exited through my lips like a free-flowing Artesian well. I was in awe of it all until I heard what sounded like a shoe being whacked against the wall, *"Baja el volumen!"* (Lower the volume!)

Perhaps my neighbor wasn't on the same wavelength. What a pity. I believe I had a divine download. Oh well, to each his own - I decided not to take offense. Instead, I would anonymously place some delicious fruit in front of the complainer's door and pray for him. I read in my Gideon guide, *"If your enemy is hungry, feed him; if he is thirsty, give him a drink. Doing this will be like heaping fiery coals on his head."* (Romans 12:20). It was a puzzling verse, but I'd give it a try.

I reviewed my options for the best way to get to Puno – the Peruvian City at the tip-top of Lake Titicaca. I'd first needed to return to Cuzco, a three-and-a-half-hour ride full of breathtaking scenery with rambling musicians and food vendors. It seemed to be the optimal choice for returning from Aquas Calientes to Cuzco.

I'd go back to my convent-style hotel on the main square for one night and leave early the following morning on the local bus for an eight-hour trip to Puno, including a few scenic stops.

* * *

The scrawny bus driver made the sign of the cross three times before cranking up the battered bus. Finally, we were on our way to Lake Titicaca – another legendary landmark that would soon become a notch in my extended travel belt. Besides having a catchy name, Lake Titicaca was not your run-of-the-mill lake – it was the largest lake in South America and the highest navigable lake on earth! The elevation of the lofty lake in the Andean Altiplano boasted 12,507 feet.

I was pleased to discover that nearly seventy percent of the passengers were indigenous. They somberly displayed an explosion of color without looking self-conscious about the multi-layered brash hues and varied patterns that defied any known fashion etiquette. I adored their reckless combinations. These mountain people were proud to sport the identifying hand-woven fabrics of their villages, so you knew where they were coming from without prying.

The overhead racks were filled with their bargain hunting from Cuzco, including live chickens and guinea pigs – a delicacy in that region. The tourists on board were taking a plethora of photos of the dazzling mountain people. I was indignant that no one had asked permission or even offered a tip. I'd soon change that. Feeling like the union boss, I took off my Colombian fedora, shoved it under the noses of the photo snappers, and said, "Thank you," very politely, and no one dared refuse. I then went from row to row to distribute the offerings to the Andean passengers.

We passed shantytowns that had sprung up beside the road while the background landscape had remained the same for millenniums. Snowcapped mountains alternating with volcanoes held ancient secrets of past civilizations. As we rolled by the second major town, Raqchi, the bus driver pulled off onto the grassy shoulder. There was a string of locals with eager expressions and a menagerie of hand-woven fabrics, shawls, *chullos* (knitted hats with ear flaps), and everything imaginable to strip an alpaca of its fleece: so many hopefuls and only a handful of buyers. A large sign indicated that the *Templo de Sol* (Sun Temple) was nearby.

As everyone ran off to the Sun Temple, I bought packable items from the least commercially situated sellers. Perhaps the bus driver got a cut, but so what. It was a glorious day, and the temple's ruins beckoned me. Needing exercise and a good stretch, I incorporated a few ballet leaps into my long galloping stride. I slowed to a moderate trot to stop and read the bronze info plaque.

"Inca archaeological site in Peru – one thousand six hundred feet above sea level and sixty-eight miles from Cuzco - also known as the Temple of Wiracocha. This Sun Temple was built in the fourteen hundreds and destroyed by the conquistadors in the mid fifteen hundreds."

Looming before me were eight gigantic portions of 65 feet high walls. The stone stubs of eleven columns that once supported the roof were still visible. Behind the endless structure were one hundred fifty-two round stone huts that served as silos for storing grain. Initially, they had cone-shaped thatched roofs. Finally, our bus driver started to lean on the horn to announce our departure. Adios Raqchi ruins.

The bus had only one vacant seat by the time I boarded. My seatmate told me he and his trekking buddies were getting off at the pass to do some serious climbing. Only Americans give out such personal information. I had become accustomed to the European way of pretending other people on public transport were invisible. And if you did speak, it was about the weather. "Where are y'all from?"

"The Rockies, more precisely Boulder, Colorado. I've been climbing mountains since I could walk - how about you? My friends and I figured you must be from New York City."

I was amused that they had discussed me. "Why do you think I'm from New York?"

"Your brazen way of collecting money for people on the bus we photographed and your imitation of a condor trying to get off the ground. Getting a lift to glide is the hardest part for the Andean Condors. But, once they're up, they can soar for a hundred miles without flapping their wings. So we nicknamed you the Red Baron."

"Why the Red Baron?"

"Why do you think? It seemed appropriate when you were trying to get airborne, and your red cape was flapping in the breeze."

"Ah, you're referring to my ballet leaps. I didn't realize anyone was watching." I couldn't believe this guy was so brutal, but he wasn't malicious. Perhaps he had Asperger syndrome. He certainly lacked social skills. Most Americans are overly diplomatic, but this guy went for my jugular vein without mercy. Curious fellow. I decided not to take it personally. After all, you can't please everyone all the time. Amen.

I was glad we were nearing *La Raya* Mountain range and the pass, so my seatmate would exit, and hopefully, I'd get a better roll of the dice on the next passenger who entered. There was a hi-way marker indicating we were at 14,107 feet. I expected oxygen masks to plop down from the ceiling of the bus. No luck. The bus stopped for a break, and another street market along the road.

It looked like fifty Andes merchants had high hopes of selling an item or two. No tables - each vendor waved their wares with animated body language to attract attention. They were all shouting *allianmi* – pronounced, *Eye-eee-on-meee* (hello). Of course, the best response is *munay*, pronounced *moon-eye* (love), which can be the proper response for an item you want to buy. Unfortunately, there wasn't enough oxygen to bargain, so I purchased an ear-flap hat for the first price.

Our driver honked, and we filed back into the bus like trained geese. As good fortune would have it, one of the colorful salesladies plunked herself down in the seat next to me. I noticed she was chewing coca leaves and had a tell-tale wad stored in her cheek that bulged out. Of course, this was like a stiff espresso for the Andes people – no more, no less. We exchanged smiles every once in a while, and she pointed out distant volcanoes with enthusiasm.

I noticed the little lady kept rubbing her right wrist and bending it back and forth. I asked, *"Dolor?"* (Pain?) She responded with a nod of her head and then smiled. I noticed she had made the sign of

the cross when she sat down, just like the bus driver, so I felt a particular affinity with her. I clearly had a nudge from the Holy Spirit and tried to shake it off.

There was the familiar feeling of love and compassion for this lady in pain, and I knew God wanted to heal her. However, if I prayed for her and it didn't work, I couldn't get up and leave. Would I look like a fool? But, on the other hand, God chose the foolish things of this world to confound the wise. I fit the bill. I placed my hands together in a prayer position, then pointed to the lady's wrist. Lifting my eyebrows and tilting my head into a quizzical expression, she understood and offered her wrist.

I dove into the deep end with a command, "Pain, in the name of Jesus, I command you to go!" I opened my eyes slowly to discover the lady was wearing a big smile while waving and shaking her wrist. In Andean Spanish, she confirmed, *"El dolor se ha ido"* (the pain has gone). I had a mustard seed of faith, but she had an entire tree's worth. "Hallelujah!" jumped out of my mouth, "Thank you, God!" The lady then took my hand and held it in hers until the next stop. She got off, waved to me from the side of the road, and then headed towards the hills.

Our next brief break was in Pukara – a small town with a huge history. A bronze plaque enhanced the story of the settlement, dating as early as 1800 BC. The site spread over two miles and was the influencing culture north of the lake, dominating the region by 200 BC. I had seen bits and bobs from this area in the Cuzco Museum and was pleased to get the full picture of the empty landscape. More merchants waved their wares with faded enthusiasm. After seven dusty, bumpy hours, we were longing for Lake Titicaca.

8. LAKE TITICACA, PERU

Within two hours, we approached the outskirts of Puno. I was shocked to survey such a rambling metropolis. With only a two-mile flat stretch between the lake and the Andes, the city was forced to grow upward into the steep hills – obviously the low-rent district. There was no sign of electricity or running water. This rugged, innovative Andean race survived for thousands of years from their blessing of land, lakes, and herds, combined with no-nonsense hard work.

I quickly discovered that the best thing about Puno was its location on the north shore of the world's loftiest navigable lake. It was chilly at 12,500 feet, so I layered myself with three t-shirts, two ponchos, and the hand-knitted alpaca ear-flap cap. I kept my hair in braids to blend in with the local look and avoid being mistaken for a hippie. I thought of myself as 'nomad chic' and had succumbed to chewing coca leaves to combat altitude sickness. Do as the locals do - so I did. I also sipped coca tea with my meals.

My instinct was to attack the city – find the main square, colonial churches, best markets, and eateries and then sit back and people-gaze. However, I was feeling spaced out, bordering on delirium. I knew I'd have to take it easy for the next twenty-four hours to be fit for the bus trip around the lake and regain my vitality to visit the incredible hand-woven islands.

The name alone, 'Lake Titicaca,' has an air of intrigue attached to it – similar to other iconic places I had visited, such as Kathmandu, Timbuktu, Machu Picchu, Mt. Kilimanjaro, Cairo, Casa Blanca, Siam, Rangoon, and Bali. However, idle adventures can eventually run their course. Without a meaningful purpose involved, travel can become hopelessly egocentric. I needed to avoid that at all costs. My bartering, buying, and selling gave meaning to my travels, but they needed to be intertwined with a more significant motivation. I would try to stay in sync with the Holy Spirit.

First, I had to find a hostel near the main square to hobnob with some backpackers recently arriving from Bolivia. Hotel Condor stood out as bleak and affordable, with clean sheets and a large lobby. I overheard three southern accents enthusiastically planning their route to Machu Picchu. I chipped in with some valuable advice, and they asked a lot more. Sharing my experiences with them opened the door for a mutual exchange of travel tips. They had arrived from La Paz and explained that they were with YWAM (Youth with a Mission) and gave me their friend's address in that lofty Bolivian capital.

They were obviously fresh out of high school, using their gap year to enrich their lives by helping the needy – plus, a mission in Peru had the perk of a visit to Machu Picchu. They explained that they would help build a school on the outskirts of Lima. It sounded like a pie-in-the-sky project, but their hearts were in the right place. They told me the best local bus to take to La Paz that allowed a few stops for local snacks and then invited me to join them for a hike up to the Kuntur Wasi viewpoint, which has a large metal sculpture of a condor.

A hardy girl named Jane pointed to the distant sculpture and explained that there were seven hundred steps to climb to reach the metal condor, but the view across the city and Lake Titicaca would be breathtaking. That was my primary concern. I couldn't afford to have anything taking away what existing breath I had left. I explained that I was acclimatizing but would be fit as a fiddle after a rest and some fuel.

Man-made floating islands surrounded Puno's access to Lake Titicaca. For centuries the Uros escaped intruders by pushing their unique island homes off into the lake – out of reach. Using the totora reed that grows on the lake's edges, this ancient tribe of resourceful craftsmen weaves their homes, furniture, boats, and the islands on which they live. The indigenous Uros people birthed this ingenious idea when the Incas expanded onto their land in the 1400s.

It had been about four hundred years since the Inca Empire tumbled; however, the Uros continued their aquatic lifestyle as if they had no other option. Although their primary income is from fishing, tourism now runs a close second. Overland travelers from La Paz headed to Machu Picchu are obliged to travel on or around the lake and happily snap up the unique reed handicrafts and colorful hand-woven alpaca items.

The following day I dedicated myself to exploring some of the hand-woven Uros Islands - those ancient engineering marvels that lay a few miles offshore from Puno. I signed up for a taxi-type skiff that resembled a cross between a Viking long boat with a modified puma's head and a Moroccan shoe with a curled Aladdin toe. The picturesque boats were propelled by an oarsman – mostly inhabitants of the islands. Naturally, there was ongoing repair to these islands since the reeds deteriorated at an accelerated rate.

Our skiff had room for six passengers; luckily, an Englishman who boarded had done his history homework and had given us a guided tour. He explained that 'Titicaca' translates into 'Grey Puma' since the lake resembles the shape of that ferocious feline. Our self-appointed guide informed us that the puma symbolized power, strength, and life on earth. Incas considered it essential to replicate puma-like qualities, as the animal was considered the most significant predator and something to emulate.

The Incas even designed the city of Cusco in the shape of a puma. We all nodded in agreement as if we had known all along. I was glad I had worn my handmade shoulder bag with a puma motif embroidered on both sides. I was still layered with my two ponchos and glad to have my ear-flap cap snuggly pulled down over my frigid ears and frosty pigtails.

We visited several other floating islands, obviously the immediate family of the oarsman, since they all embraced one another and chatted like long-lost cousins. The island families were dynamic and had their hand-crafted wares laid out neatly on bright blankets. There was a food hut with quinoa vegetable soup piping hot, and we all dashed towards that steamy stand as if the music had abruptly ended during 'musical chairs.'

I admired the alternative lifestyle that the Uros clung to since the invasion of the Incas in 1450. I was tempted to stay longer in Puno but decided to stay on track and head to La Paz the following morning.

* * *

Finding my way to the local bus station, I booked the deluxe bus with cushioned seats and a brief narration 'en route.' The journey would take about four hours to Copacabana, Bolivia, near the border, then another four hours to La Paz - plus an hour or so for the frontier crossing and snack stops. I would wrap up my sightseeing of Puno and take off on the morning bus at daybreak, arriving in La Paz by nightfall.

When I arrived at the bus depot at dawn, I discovered a lengthy line of multi-hued travelers waiting to stake their claim on a seat and a portion of the overhead luggage rack. The contrast of anemic-looking backpackers was sprinkled with a handful of Asians but mostly petite, sun-baked locals.

Fortunately, I found a seat on the aisle to stretch out my lanky legs once the bus took off. *"Perdon, puedo?"* (Excuse me, may I?) I asked the lovely local lady, covered in a hand-woven shawl and thousands of wrinkles.

She smiled, *"Si, los extranjeras traen buena suerte."* (Yes, foreigners bring good luck.)

I quizzed the little lady, *"Que clase de buena suerte?"* (What kind of good luck?)

She replied with a grin, *"Siempre me compran mucho."* (They always buy a lot from me.) Oops, I'd been outwitted by a wheeling and dealing old lady. How could I refuse? I laughed and forked out tourist prices for several of her embroidered items.

A young indigenous guy, dressed in sync with the backpackers, stood up with a microphone and started to speak English with a thick local accent.

"My name is Luis, and I am your guide. To your left, you see Lake Titicaca. We will be traveling south the entire one-hundred-twenty-mile length of the lake - so I will explain its history and cover some interesting points."

I was amazed that the young man, not more than twenty-five, had such a knowledgeable grasp of my language and a cool demeanor. I was interested to learn more about this emblematic lake and its place in Andean history.

He continued, "Lake Titicaca is the sun's birthplace, in Andean belief. Situated between Peru and Bolivia, it's the largest lake in South America and the world's most navigable body of water. This enthralling, deep-blue lake is the unifying, longtime home of the mountain cultures steeped in the old, traditional ways. In this region, crops are still planted and harvested by hand. *Campesinos* (farmers) wear sandals recycled from truck tires and women work in bowler hats and petticoats, and llamas are tame as pets." He then sat down again and allowed us to chew on that well-presented information.

After about ten minutes of silence, I was relieved to discover that his 'talks' would be sporadic. I needed time to reflect and drink in what I was experiencing. The checkerboard fields were backed by rolling hills, while high Andean peaks towered from a distance, and a mist hovered over the lake, creating a mystical aura.

Both colorfully dressed women and soberly attired men dotted the fields, working shoulder to shoulder to ensure their families had food on the table and extra to sell. Every five miles or so, a small town flashed by with a shock of color that mimed the farm ladies' bright skirts and boleros. Impossible combinations of shocking mustard yellow, lime green, orange, or peacock blue facades livened up the otherwise bleak *pueblos.*

Our young guide stood up again, and someone screeched, "SHUSH!" All ears, we awaited the next slice of historical folklore. "Lake Titicaca is steeped in history, legends, and uncovered mysteries. According to Incan mythology, the creator god emerged from Lake Titicaca and created the sun, moon, and stars. Legend has it that there is a lost city under the face of the water. I believe - according to nearby ruins - that the remains of a temple attest to the previous existence of one of the oldest civilizations in the Americas." He sat down again and let us chew on those tidbits of data.

I was glad to have time to daydream and absorb my ethereal surroundings and spiritual relationship with El Shaddai, the mighty Creator of the beauty that embraced me. Wanting to express my thankfulness, I felt like belting out some Psalms in praise of The Almighty's handiwork. However, I sat there quietly and sang within my heart, la-la-la.

Our journey commenced at 6 am, and I felt like I was fainting from dehydration. I was pacing myself on liquid intake and snacking on nuts and bananas - keeping my coca leaves for an emergency. Spot on, our guide stood up and announced that the bus would be stopping briefly for a short break.

There was one dingy unisex bathroom we foreigners galloped to, and the locals wandered behind the nearest buildings. By chance, a few scrawny food vendors were selling grilled corn on the cob, potatoes with hot sauce, and souvenirs. I scooped up some lukewarm spicy potatoes wrapped in brown recycled paper and a cob of slightly charred corn. We remained at 12,500 feet altitude, so I didn't consider executing any pirouettes or jetés. I looked around for a handrail or ledge on which I could limber up my long legs and carry out some serious stretching.

Meanwhile, I did some lunges and squats to ensure my blood kept circulating during the long journey. Ah ha, I spotted a small shop under construction with a rusty, antique cement machine on which I could prop up a leg at a time. With finesse, I doubled over, stretching my fingertips to my toes and back up again, two-three-four. I gracefully repeated that ballet exercise until the bus driver blasted his horn, then everyone scrambled back to the bus, knocking each other down.

Being the last to enter our luxury bus, I was blessed to see our driver making the sign of the cross several times while drinking an ink-black coffee. I trusted he would get us safely to our destination. My petite seatmate, who had fallen into a deep sleep after coercing me into purchasing some of her handiwork, failed to return. I supposed her catnap gave her the zip she needed to help haul in the harvest.

After another half hour of intriguing landscape, our boy guide, Luis, stood up abruptly, cleared his throat, and announced with enthusiasm, "It is no surprise that a lake of this size boasts incredible biodiversity. Lake Titicaca is home to over five hundred aquatic species, including the spectacular Puno Ibis, the enchanting Chilean pink flamingo, and the not-so-charming Lake Titicaca frog – weighing up to ten pounds. The native fish that thrive in the lake serves as the mainstay source of protein for the local inhabitants, plus a major source of income."

Luis was a bright young man, and I wondered what his aspirations were - apart from being a prestigious, well-informed, slightly boring tourist guide. I had an inquisitive streak, bordering on nosey, with an analytical personality that longed to know what made people tick. I would gently corner Luis during the next 'rest stop' and politely pry some particulars from the bright young man. I wondered if this job was a stepping stone for him or if he was happy to remain near his beloved Lake for the rest of his sheltered life. I wondered if he believed in the sun god or if he knew Jesus.

Eavesdropping is an art. You gaze elsewhere while gleaning the juicy bits, and you never, under any circumstance, break into the ongoing conversation. I overheard a backpacker across the aisle telling his companion that we would be reaching Yunguyo in about an hour. The American-sounding backpacker then explained the process of entering Bolivia through the border town of Copacabana. I wondered how such a small town in landlocked Bolivia was given the name of Copacabana. A name that conjured up elite beach parties and the Carnival of Rio – my destination! What a curious coincidence.

After absorbing more of the compelling countryside and lofty Lake, guide Luis embarked upon a detailed account of what to expect while exiting Peru and the process of entering Bolivia via the customs/immigration office. My mind bounced back to Copacabana. 'Copa' in Spanish is slang for 'alcoholic drink,' and *cabana* is often referred to as a simple hut usually made of cane. More often, beaches had cabanas where you could change into a swim suit. We exited Peru without a hitch.

As we rolled into the town of *Copacabana,* the imagery did not match its rambunctious name - no, not by a long shot. Menacing customs officers, resembling hit-men from Al Capone's crime squad, belched a sinister air to our otherwise pleasant journey. Crossing borders always gave me the heebie-jeebies. I had nothing to worry about - my passport and papers were in order. I was not smuggling anything and was not 'on the run.' I relaxed and took a deep breath until I remembered I had a bunch of coca leaves tucked away in my top pocket. Like the natives, I needed them for altitude sickness.

A startling image flashed through my erratic brain at breakneck speed. There I was, languishing away in a rat-infested Bolivian jail. The thought sent shivers down my spine and interrupted my laid-back composure. I tried to envision a plan of action. Should I toss the leaves out of the window or onto the floor of the bus, perhaps eat them, or simply keep them in my pocket? I chose plan B and tossed the leaves onto the floor across the aisle while gazing out of the window. I decided that was the least conspicuous option.

We all filed out of the bus, through customs without incident, and on our merry way. The process took about an hour, so I had time to gulp an Incan Kola and munch on a corn cob. There was a plaque in Spanish and English; *Copacabana is the main Bolivian town on the shore of Lake Titicaca. The town has a sizeable 16th-century church dedicated to Our Lady of Copacabana, the patron saint of Bolivia. Pop. 5,000.*

In the local dialect, the words Kota Kahuana (view of the lake) somehow morphed into the name Copacabana, and Our Lady of Copacabana refers to Mary, the mother of Jesus. Meanwhile, the hottest showgirl club in New York City is called *The Copacabana,* and the most famous 'party beach' in Rio claims the same name. Strangely enough, it seems that life includes a series of contradictions.

9. LA PAZ, BOLIVIA

We were now in the country named after its fearless liberator, Simón Bolívar. Landlocked, Bolivia boasted an erratic terrain that spanned the Andes Mountains, the Atacama Desert, and Amazon tropical rainforest. However, I would be majoring on La Paz - a mere four and a half hours away.

As we skirted the southernmost leg of the lake, our bus came to a screeching halt! The road ended at a narrow span of the lake, and I wondered if we would have to swim across or wait until low tide. A long wooden raft that looked like it would buckle under the weight of a motorbike was strategically maneuvered in front of us, and the bus creaked onto the weathered planks.

I wondered if I should open my window for an escape route. The bus driver, along with the indigenous passengers, were making the sign of the cross and reciting "Hail Mary, full of grace … … …." There was applause as we rolled off onto the other side. I was disappointed that the melodramatic adventure was so short-lived.

Our next stop was at the Tiquina mirador, where we gazed back at the length of Lake Titicaca, disappearing into infinity, and looked forward to new, titillating wonders that loomed ahead. I had soaked up so many panoramic views that I was becoming waterlogged. Having spent six crucial years of my childhood in San Souci Forest, just forty-one miles north of New Orleans, you would think I was a nature lover, wouldn't you?

On the contrary, I longed to live smack dab in the middle of the nearby rural town of Covington. There I could hobnob with friends at the Dairy Queen or zip around town on my Schwinn Sting-Ray super bike, accompanied by my buddy Becky.

I patiently bid my time in the isolated countryside, a true paradise of flora and fauna. Waiting until I was old enough to pass my driver's license, I would travel at the speed of light to the frenzied French Quarter in New Orleans. Looking back, fourteen years of age seems premature for a driver's license; however, rural Louisiana teemed with farm kids who needed to get their family's produce to town, dead or alive.

On the contrary, my brother Spike was a nature connoisseur and would have joined the Lewis and Clark expedition had he been born several centuries earlier. His love for nature included all living creatures (venomous or not), all vegetation, and even rocks and minerals. My latent longing for nature had awakened on my travels to the Far East, Middle East, and Africa. By now, my oneness with God's creation was in full swing! However, saturated with so many exquisite landscapes, I was ready for a boisterous, big city.

Ironically enough, I was looking forward to discovering *La Paz* (The Peace) within the clamor of the largest Andean city in Bolivia. "The city was built atop the ancient settlement of Laja in 1548 by the Spanish conquistadors," quipped our whiz kid guide, Luis. He informed us that the population of the rambling city totaled more than 700,000 inhabitants, of which forty-two percent lived in extreme poverty – lacking clean water and sanitation. No wonder the *Youth with a Mission* students I met in Puno said they had been working with street children – it seems the kids comprised at least ten percent of the entire population.

I could feel the Lord expanding my somewhat desensitized heart towards the supposedly rough street children I was soon to encounter. I thought back fondly of Mahesh, the orphaned boy in Kathmandu with whom I would be reunited in several months.

Even though La Paz is at a dizzying twelve thousand feet above sea level, those traveling overland had the advantage of being acclimatized en route. Sitting in a lofty bowl surrounded by snow-capped mountains, the city reminded me of Kathmandu Valley. However, the lush green valley of Nepal seemed to be replaced with a desert-type atmosphere, but magical snow-capped mountains encircled both cities.

Never mind - I wanted to discover whatever La Paz had to offer! I'd also try out some tasty local dishes - excluding the furry delicacy of guinea pigs.

It was nearly dusk when the bus pulled into the terminal and screeched to a halt. I let everyone pile out first, so I could linger behind and ask the guide, Luis, for tips on an inexpensive pension and a restaurant with home cooking.

Yes, this young man would succeed at whatever he did – he graciously gave more of himself than was required. He was overly polite and even jotted down the names and addresses on a scrap of paper. When I gave him a US five dollar tip, he gazed at the ground and blushed until his ears became scarlet. Luis advised me to eat at the *puestos callejeros* (street vendors' stalls). "That's where the locals eat, so it is fresh at a fair price," offered Luis. "They have the best *anticucho* (grilled beef or lamb heart) and *tripa* (fried beef intestine)."

"Mouth-watering," I replied. Fishing with my dad off Grand Isle and in the bayous of Louisiana prepared me for unusual eatables.

Chitlins were a classic soul food consisting of fried pork intestines. Breaded, fried Catfish and Cajun *boudin* (spicy blood sausage) were the norm, accompanied by hush puppies – golden fritters made from a thick cornmeal-based batter deep-fried until crisp outside and tender-chewy inside. I was a fan of Tabasco sauce, and nothing could be too spicy. I made a beeline to the street vendors with my stomach growling!

My travel bag was lightweight since I wore everything I had purchased along the way. With the high altitude and low temperature, the nights became downright icy. In my haphazard attempt to blend in with the local culture, I kept my unruly hair in two sober pigtails. I alternated wearing my Andean alpaca poncho and my multicolored hand-woven shawl; however, this evening, I wore both.

I hoped I wasn't too conspicuous and wouldn't be charged tourist prices. I used to practice the Groucho Marx stooped walk to strengthen my leg muscles, so I could bend my knees for extended intervals in an attempt to appear shorter. Since girls had to wear below-the-knee skirts in my school days, I could knock a few inches off my height unnoticed.....but that awkward position was a challenge while slow dancing with guys a head shorter.

After hearing so much about the street children of La Paz, I was curious why there were none in sight. It was a far cry from the masses of street kids draped themselves all over me in India. I followed the initial instructions while descending into El Dorado airport in Bogota, Columbia. "Don't wear a watch, earrings, sunglasses, or anything visible that might tempt a robber. No matter how small a child is, he can spring up and snatch it from you."

My valuables were in my knee-high boots under my jeans, in my body pouch, or beneath my ton of clothing. I felt safe – I had never had a problem with thieves, not even in New Orleans.

Eenie, meeny, miny, moe – I chose a tiny lady with a big smile and got in line behind the local people waiting to eat at her stall. My cape was long enough that I could bend my knees and blend in. I learned it was better to wait than to chance a rancid, inedible meal. I followed suit with the two customers ahead of me and ordered *anticucho* (grilled beef or lamb heart).

I pointed to the skewered morsels sizzling on the grill and exclaimed, "Moo or b-a-a-a-h?" She b-a-a-a-h-ed back at me, and I was happy to savor charbroiled lamb heart. It was a bit gamey but offset by chili pepper and local spices. I then had a scoop of something unidentifiable and a *salteña* - a baked dough pastry filled with a gelatinous mixture of vegetables and other stuff. I stumbled away in a digestive stupor feeling satisfied and sleepy.

I found the Pension San José that my guide Luis recommended. It was near the main square and the boardwalk, but above all, it fit my budget. There was even a hand basin in the room. Of course, the sink was built in extra low to accommodate the Andean anatomy, thus serving as a multi-purpose fixture for us travelers. Although the room was basic and the bed had a few painful springs, I was lulled to sleep by the constant roar of traffic and sheer travel fatigue that commenced at daybreak.

Without curtains in my room, I awoke with the sun and wandered around the main square, looking for a breakfast stand. The locals gathered around a lady dishing out tall glasses of a purple shake. In pidgin English, a young guy commented, "Good breakfast, Api, *probar* (try it)?" I nodded 'yes' and sipped the thick purple mixture that tasted of corn, cinnamon, and cane sugar. It was addictive, so I slurped down several more.

I'd try to locate the couple the students had told me about back in Puno. They suggested I connect with them to help with their 'street children' ministry. I wondered how I could best contribute. Having no younger siblings, I had zero experience with youngsters. However, I felt like an oversized kid and was sure I could relate to them at some level.

I skipped through the square, Plaza Murillo, singing, "I've got plenty of nothin' and nothin's plenty for me . . . .oh . . . " until I nearly fainted from lack of oxygen. I slowed my pace to a slink and made my way down the tree-lined main street, El Prado.

The YWAM leaders, Mark and Mandy Maffin, lived in a neighborhood called San Pedro. According to my map, I was on track. After a short stroll, I arrived at Plaza del Estudiante (Student Square) and found their street, *Calle Conchitas*.

It was a mild miracle since I had been advised that the region in my brain, a structure called the hippocampus, was not functioning. It is also known as the 'map reader' of the brain. It enables individuals to determine where they are, how they got there, and how to navigate to the next destination. Perhaps my guardian angel led me to their street –that's it.

I located the couple's semi-modern building and the buzzer with their name and apartment number. It was only 9 am, and I wondered if they were up yet. I thought about waiting but decided to give them a short buzz. A youngish lady with long brown hair appeared on the third-floor balcony and called down, "*Quién es?*" (Who is it?).

"Hi there, I'm Marie France. I met your YWAM friends near Lake Titicaca, and they gave me your address. They said maybe I can help you with the street children."

Mandy replied, "We'll be right down."

* * *

Mandy was an attractive lady of about thirty-five, and her husband, Mark, was tall, fair, and wiry with a genuinely kind but crooked smile. I guess he was about forty but well-preserved. Mandy had a cultured English accent and exclaimed that they had been praying for help with the children, so I was an absolute godsend. I doubted that, but I nodded, "If you say so." I was slightly embarrassed to clarify that I was only in La Paz for three days. I hoped they hadn't thought I was staying permanently.

I noticed Mandy was wearing quite a trendy outfit that would have been a hit on King's Road, and Mark was wearing Levis with an army-colored, quilted jacket. Mandy said sweetly, "Oh, your rural, folkloric outfit is intriguing!" I read between the lines; according to our bus guide's dress code, European gear was more appropriate. That is unless you were a farmer in the Andes. The next time I'd wear the sober outfit I wore when I flew into Colombia. I'd also purchase a boring, solid-colored knit cap to replace my electric-colored Peruvian ear-flap cap.

"We were just going to walk over to the center of the old town, where many street kids hang out with their make-shift shoe-shine kits or scrub the store fronts. Others simply beg. The minimum age for child labor in Bolivia is ten years old – lower than in the rest of South America."

"How tragic," I replied with concern.

"Please join us and get to know some of the children." I accepted Mandy's offer and turned on my heels, heading back with them to the center where I was staying. Mark added, "We've lived in the San Pedro area for the past three years and chose our middle-class neighborhood because it was untouched by tourism and foreign influence. That way, we integrated quite well, perfecting our semi-fluent Spanish. We've even made a few close, local friends."

Mandy explained, "San Pedro is situated between the center and Sopocachi – a trendy bohemian neighborhood and the 'in' place for the city's elite and sociable youth. Upscale cafes, bars, and clubs are sprouting up daily. It's a mishmash of grand colonial mansions sandwiched between towering modern apartment blocks." I thought to myself, sounds like the place I'd rather be.

As a somewhat 'new believer' and not totally committed, I remembered what Lars, the Viking, told me; "The goal to having a heart for mission is to remember to remain *in* this world, without becoming worldly." I guess he meant I should try to look and act normal but allow the love of Jesus to shine through me. I'd try not to get caught by the glitter of the world. I realized it would be impossible without the Holy Spirit's guidance and grace (undeserved favor). Staying in sync with the Holy Spirit was my challenge.

After all, I was an authentic product of the 'me' generation. I was a legitimate baby boomer with all the proper credentials. The 'me' in me was relentless – always seeking center stage. I could sing "I Surrender All" with pure passion, but did I really mean it? No, I wasn't ready to surrender all. I would try to submit bit by bit, at my own pace.

God must have known about my quirky persona when He revealed Himself to me. I wonder what His purpose is for my life. If The Almighty wanted all believers to become missionaries, who would support the missions? God must have allotted a hefty chunk of believers to become money-makers to pay the bills . . . .right? I felt better suited for group B.

With genuine compassion, Mandy explained to me the situation of the street kids; "You will notice the harsh expressions of the children since they are products of physical abuse and abandonment, plus many of them have been orphaned. They also suffer from malnutrition." I asked Mandy why the street children weren't seen on the streets. "Oh, that's because the policemen here are quite brutal with them," replied Mandy.

"Many have to steal to eat, which is not acceptable here. The youngsters often wear ski masks to hide their identity and also stay warm in this icy climate. The police prevent the children from bothering the tourists, so the children have learned to remain low-key in order to remain in one piece."

"That is heartbreaking," I whispered, feeling the pain of such rejection.

"The children try to numb their pain through cheap drugs such as paint thinner or glue adhesive," added Mark. "Our approach is to emulate unconditional love towards these youngsters - the love of Jesus. Giving them material rewards would only set them up for bullying by fellow street children.

"Our long-time strategy is to develop a community center for year-round health and educational needs. It is their only way out - the only way they can realize their unique potential to become leaders and productive members of their communities. We are trying to rally churches back home in Brighton to invest in our sustainable dream for the street children's future."

I felt a lump forming in my throat as we approached the historical center of Las Paz, and I could spot a number of the kids on their little knees, cleaning and polishing the shoes of locals and tourists. Some tiny girls were scrubbing the sidewalks in front of tourist shops, and others were sweeping the streets. Instinctively I wanted to buy them a hot meal and shower them with gifts.

How wonderful it would be to see their hardened expressions transformed into happy smiles. They looked like bitter old people in children's bodies. It was haunting – unlike India or Nepal, where tourists adopted kids during their brief stay and were greeted with smiling, joyful faces.

Mark and Mandy won over my instant admiration. They were not searching for self-validation but longevity in their 'mission impossible' in a hard, hostile city. They were not enjoying the gratification of being able to give the kids a quick fix. They were in this 'street children mission work' for the long haul.

I noticed the kids' eyes darting over to my companions, and the tension in their tiny faces softened. Their dark eyes danced, even though their split, chapped lips and frosty faces revealed their inner pain.

"But how do you help these little urchins if you can't openly give them the basics they so badly need," I asked.

"We sit on a bench in the main square every day at 2 pm, when the shops are shut, and the moneyed masses are eating. You see," explained Mark, "We have a healing ministry, and the children come to us for a healing touch from Jesus - no tangible gift that would make them a target for the older, stronger children.

"When the youngsters thank us for their healing and bring their friends, we remind them, 'Jesus healed you.' Then they ask us about Jesus. As you know from the Bible, Jesus went from city to city healing people – it demonstrated his love and compassion for them. Rather than proactive evangelization that would disturb the local *religious*, we merely answer their questions."

"Brilliant! That's something I could do. That's right up my alley!"

"Yes, we thought so," said Mandy. "We were with Yiye Ávila, an evangelist from Puerto Rico, who had a miraculous encounter with Jesus and a miraculous healing in the 60s. He has been traveling around South America leading healing campaigns and spreading the 'good news' of Jesus."

"How amazing, I've run into other missionaries who've also attended conferences led by Yiye Ávila and witnessed the Holy Spirit working through him. They all say he's extremely anointed!"

"Yiye has the catalyst for healing," announced Mark.

"What sort of catalyst?" I inquired.

"Faith! Jesus nearly always told the miraculously healed people, '*Your faith has healed you.*' He put the ball back in their court. When these street children are healed and tell their friends, their companions come to us expecting to be healed. Simple as that, it is the pure faith of a trusting child.

"There has been a wave of miracles here in South America during the past decade, not just here, but also in most developing countries, where people don't have a medical specialist as an alternative. We have YWAM teams who join us periodically, and it always works. Children are healed! It's great that you can join us, as it convinces the children it is not our healing power but Jesus's. God is faithful!"

I was beginning to feel a bit apprehensive. What if it didn't work for me – of course, it had nothing to do with me. I would be a willing vessel. It will work because I'll let the Holy Spirit lead me. I tried to bolster my confidence that God would use me, not because of my ability or goodness, but because of His goodness and grace.

Mark and Mandy took me to *El Casco Antiguo* (the historical center). On every block, youngsters were diligently working at menial jobs. When their eyes shot over toward us, there was a subtle glimmer of recognition. However, they dared not take even a few seconds off from their full focus on their assigned work. Mandy assured me, "You will see a radical change when they meet us at the town square after the shops lock up for lunch.

"We have built up close, promising relationships with many of the children over the past few years. I guess you've heard the expression, *'Nobody cares how much you know until they know how much you care.'* They know, without a doubt, we want the best for them. Most have never previously experienced kindness, much less love. Some children have been challenging, but we continue loving them anyway."

Pointing toward a large fascinating market stall, Mandy explained, "This is *El Mercado de las Brujas* (The Witches Market)." Expecting to see potatoes in the vegetable market, Mandy clarified, "Those are dried llama embryos. To the right, you see a large variety of aromatic herbs for cooking. However, the fresh herbs are bottled and sold as aphrodisiac potions, beauty-enhancing mixtures, and others used for fertility. The vendors are said to cast spells and offer their services as fortune tellers."

"Do locals actually fall for witch trickery, or is this just a tourist trap?"

Mandy assured me, "Most of the products purchased here are offered as sacrifices to *Pachamama* (Mother Earth) in exchange for health, happiness, and prosperity. They also go as far as offering sacrifices to improve their studies or save their marriages. Over there are live serpents and dried tortoises.

Religion is very 'pick and mix' here. The locals enter the nearby Cathedral, Basilica of Our Lady of Peace, light some candles, then exit to the Witches Market to purchase something to appease *Pachamama*. I guess they're attempting to cover all their options."

"Yeah, sadly enough, I experienced a similar potpourri of beliefs in Colombia, Ecuador, and Peru. Many indigenous habitants meshed their ancestral beliefs into the Catholic teachings their Spanish and Portuguese conquerors introduced to them in the sixteenth century.

I've read that nearly forty percent of the world's Roman Catholics are said to reside in Central and South America. The *Holy Conversions* were made mainly by the sword since the Spaniards carried superior weapons, plus deadly viruses."

"However," added Mark, "The indigenous have clung to their belief in a master of all animals and frequently display faith in supernatural protectors of the different animal species. Such nature spirits exhibit powerful individualistic tendencies and are often considered evil.

Still and all, there has been an awakening to God's truth, displayed through Jesus, and there is a growing wave of believers who have been genuinely touched, healed, or have had personal revelations. The advantage the street youth possess is that they have no baggage. Since they've had no parental care, they've had no wrong teachings. God has called us to minister to the street children, knowing they are ready to receive."

"Who could have imagined that the street kids had any sort of advantage in their haphazard, precarious little lives," I admitted.

After a cozy, peaceful lunch under the warm winter sun, we moseyed over to the main square, scraped the pigeon poop off the wooden slats of the bench, and plopped down. Mark offered, "Why don't we pray together – there is such power when praying in agreement!"

"Why, of course!" I chimed in, "You pray, and I'll agree."

Phew, I got out of that sticky situation. I was uncomfortable praying out loud with other people. I didn't feel polished enough in their prayer jargon or familiar with their religious expressions. I discovered I was inept at squeezing in 'you are protected by the blood of the Lamb.' I found it awkward to interject prayerful phrase words such as behold, exalt, propitiate, redemption and righteousness. I felt like I would sound as if I was impersonating Lady Macbeth, Ophelia, or King Arthur of the Round Table.

I asked Mandy and Mark if I could pray for the kids in American English. They laughed out loud and decided it would work since the Bible says clearly, "*God chose the foolish things of the world to shame the wise; God chose the weak things of the world to shame the strong, and the despised things – to nullify the things that are, so that no one may boast before him.*" (1Cor.1:27)

Unsure whether my companions were referring to the kids or me, I took it as a 'yes.' American English would work just as well as the Shakespearean 'holier than thou' version. I was relieved since I could see a small group of children working their way toward us. A childhood tune emerged from my long-term memory bank, so I sang softly, "*What a friend we have in Jesus*," and was surprised that all the words surfaced.

I had highlighted Jesus' words in my Gideon Bible, "Let the little children come to me, and do not hinder them, for the kingdom of God belongs to such as these. Truly I tell you, anyone who will not receive the kingdom of God like a little child will never enter it." (Mat.19:14) Then Jesus took the children in his arms, placed his hands on them, and blessed them. I longed to hug some of the scruffy street children of our Lord.

Before I knew what hit me, two kids had craftily snuck up behind me, and each one grabbed a pigtail simultaneously and pulled with all their might. "YOW, LET GO!" I heard myself screaming. I wondered if I had been scalped – perhaps revenge for their ancestors' harsh 'holy' conversion.

"*Tranquilos muchachos*," (calm down boys), Mark spoke out sternly. I stood up when the kids unleashed my hair and towered over them; I glared down menacingly as they laughed and stuck their tongues out at me. I had every intention of loving these kids, but they made it difficult for me. They were tempting me to pray that they would disappear.

"I am so sorry, Marie France, these children have not yet developed people skills. They're making fun of you because they haven't seen a foreigner masquerading as an Andean farmer."

Mandy then picked up the toughest boy and hugged him, and he blushed.

It was clear that forgiveness was the crux of the Christian message, so I forgave the snotty-nosed brats. They were clearly victims of cruel injustices. They hadn't made a conscious choice to live on the streets – they were trying to survive, staying alive by working hard and running fast.

I'd have to ask the Holy Spirit to help me love these unlovable kids. After all, love is not an emotion; it's a decision. I made up my mind to love them because Jesus loved them. I just hoped that they'd be civilized to me in the future. And yes, I will wear my boring city clothes from now on.

In an attempt to make friends with the scruffy little group that had gathered around me, I did some of my double-jointed hand and knee tricks. Leaning back, propped up on my elbows, I bucked up one knee while spinning my other knee around like a helicopter's propeller. It worked! About five boys were trying to mimic me without success. I somehow escalated in their beady little eyes.

Then I pulled my thumb out of joint and wrapped it up over the back of my hand while doing a crab-crawl with my fingers. I quickly won the kids' respect and passed the initiation test with flying colors.

Mandy stood there with her mouth open, and Mark was doubled over, roaring. "If we'd only learned your tactics before arriving here, we'd have shaved off six months of the warming up process, trying to win the children's confidence. You have them eating right out of your hand."

My performances as a contortionist usually won over kids of all ages and flavors. I had a dozen more acts to impress them, but I would unleash my oddities little by little. Hey, that's it! I would teach the most flexible kids my craft and give them an alternative means of earning money.

I shared my enterprising idea with my companions, and they laughed in agreement. I'd have them doing backbends and splits within no time at all. Meanwhile, a few children had almost forgotten that they were in pain or had a nasty cold and had come for healing.

Bob Marley's words rattled around my mind: "Truth is, everybody is going to hurt you – you just gotta find the ones worth suffering for." Now I knew what he meant. These kids were worth it; they were surviving on the streets against all odds and weren't about to give up. With Jesus as their best friend, the sky would be the limit.

Mark popped the usual question, *"Alguien necesita ser sanado?"* (Does anyone need to be healed?) All eight boys looked up at Mark and nodded their heads, affirming their need. Most had scratches and bruises from fighting with other children. One little guy was hobbling with a swollen ankle, and another had his arm in a makeshift sling. Their faith had been ignited through previous healings, so they matter-of-factly waited their turn.

The kid with his arm in the ragged, filthy sling walked up to me and stood there waiting to be zapped. I screamed inwardly, "Help," placed my hands on the little fellow's shoulders, and commanded the boy's arm to "be healed in the name of Jesus." The kid took his sling off and skipped away, rotating his arms to try out his healing.

It was humbling to think God Almighty would use *me* as a vessel for His healing power. Ten minutes before, I contemplated the scraggly rascals' demise. I caught up with the little guy and asked him his name. "Javi," he replied, *"Tienes un chicle?"* (Do you have some gum?). "Yes," I replied, "I have some gum for all you boys," I shouted in pidgin Spanish. I figured that would be a safe treat since they could always swallow it if another kid tried to steal the wad out of their mouth.

These children needed at least two square meals a day. If a community center was the way, I would back Mandy and Mark's dream center and drum up support when I got back to the States and also Europe.

Mark explained to the kids that I would give an intensive flexibility workshop for those interested. I would continue the following two days between 2 – 4 pm when the kids were free from their taxing toil in the tourist center of the historic district. Their days often began at daybreak and ended after dark. Mandy admitted to me that she had studied dance as a teen, so I agreed to teach her the tricks of the trade for street entertaining. Mandy's eyes sparkled, and a new enthusiasm brightened her smile.

I had spent days in front of the Louvre Museum in Paris, soaking up street artists' ultimate fantasies. If only 'my' kids could dress up in Andean outfits to beg – the tourists would take their photos and drop some coins in their hats. I didn't have enough time to organize all the money-making schemes I had whirling around my fragmented mind. I left a list of ideas for my companions to share with the children.

Tourists would gladly tip kids for singing lively, familiar songs, carrying out simple magician's tricks, and performing acrobats. They needed a means of income more imaginative and innovative than shining shoes and scrubbing streets. They needed a boost for their self-esteem and hope for tomorrow.

Winging my way around four continents, I clung to Coco Chanel's advice, "Success is often achieved by those who don't know failure is inevitable." Besides, my Gideon Bible assures me, *"Nothing will be impossible with God."* I reassured the street kids that they would never be alone, and with Jesus by their side, there were no limitations.

I reminded Mandy to teach the youngsters some Beatles melodies and lyrics that the tourists could join in with if they wanted. I was hesitant to leave my newfound mission, but I vowed to stay in touch with Mark and Mandy, and hopefully, I'd make it back the following year.

My rather frivolous goal was to reach Rio for the week of Carnival – the world's biggest and most extravagant event of its kind. Too bad I'd have to zoom through Chile and Argentina to be in Rio for the pre-carnival parties leading up to the main spectacle.

Of course, my initial trip through South America would be a 'taster.' Then I'd return to zero in on my favorite spots, or rather where I felt the Holy Spirit was leading me. Sure, I'd have liked to experience the Bolivian Amazon, the infamous, death-defying hi-way (Carretera de la Muerte), and the *Valle de la Luna* with lunar landscapes. Oh well, I shouldn't be greedy. I'd leave some unseen phenomenon to whet my appetite for my next trip.

I gave Mandy and Mark heartfelt hugs and high-fived the kids heartily, thus avoiding the contamination of leaping lice.

10. CHILE AND BUENOS AIRES, ARGENTINA

I awoke bright and early for my 8 am flight to Santiago, Chile. I was advised to dress conservatively since Gen. Pinochet thought the "correct" dress code equated to having "correct" political views. He led the Military dictatorship of Chile since 1973. It seems the CIA actively supported the military junta after the overthrow of Allende but did not assist Gen. Pinochet to his liking. I wasn't involved in politics and would just mind my own business and explore the country's beauty.

Fascinated by the Atacama Desert, the driest place on earth, I had read it was also famous for the landscapes that inspired many of Salvador Dalí's surrealistic paintings. For example, the amazing melting watches draped over a naked branch and across a giant conch shell that jutted out of the desert. Near the top of my must-see list were the Osorno Volcano, the Petrohue Waterfalls, plus the San Pedro Geysers.

The flight from La Paz to Santiago's International Airport was just over five hours, and I couldn't wait until touchdown. I had heard the food was sumptuous, and the exchange rate was favorable, so I'd find a comfortable hotel and have a luxurious soak in a bathtub - an extravagance I hadn't indulged in since I arrived in South America.

I had become accustomed to a mildewed, leaky shower down the hallway in most of my pensions. I was singing "Somewhere Over the Rainbow" when the pilot announced, "The US Embassy in Santiago is advising all Americans aboard this flight to remain on the airplane due to the anti-Americanism sentiment of the Pinochet government."

It wasn't easy to digest this inopportune change of plans, and I discovered I was becoming less flexible to abrupt changes. On the other hand, Chile had a quake risk of 9.8. Another factor to take into consideration - I was seated next to a Stanford student from California whose Chilean leftist boyfriend was an anti-Pinochet poet.

Prior to the pilot's announcement, my owlish-looking pseudo-intellectual seatmate had been bragging to me about her communist philosophy. I wondered if I had already been documented as a left-wing sympathizer. Were there spies planted aboard my fight?

In Spain, where General Franco was the totalitarian dictator, people were hauled to jail for merely sitting next to a suspect at a café. The last time I was in Ibiza, dozens of innocent visitors were scooped up from the Montesol Café and incarcerated on the nearby island of Mallorca.

I recalculated my risk tolerance and decided to skip Chile, so I'd have more time to samba in Brazil. I dreamed about becoming a samba sensation, but it was so darn difficult to keep fluidity while holding the ever-changing rhythm....plus maintaining a natural smile! I'd learn from the best and try to impress someone at the Warehouse in New Orleans or Pacha club back in Ibiza.

No harm done, only a brief layover on a comfortable DC-10 from Chile's Latam Airline. As a perk, I was offered a lukewarm fizzless coke and some courtesy peanuts. Not the succulent meal I was expecting at the famous 'Central Market' of Santiago; however, something to calm my ravenous appetite until I arrived in Buenos Aires. Meanwhile, a stream of passengers entered the plane, and I wondered who would replace my high-risk commie seatmate.

A tall, dark, rather handsome man winked at me, shoved his hand luggage in the overhead compartment, and sat beside me. He smelled of classy after-shave lotion. *"Buenas tardes, Señorita Linda."* (Good afternoon Miss Linda). We both had assigned seats, so I couldn't just hop up and change rows – I'd have to grin and bear it. I nodded, *"Buenas tardes Señor. Mi nombre no es Linda.* (Good afternoon Mister, my name is not Linda)."

My reply provoked a peal of laughter from the playboy seated next to me. "Well, you look Argentinean, but you sound like a gringo," laughed Mr. Debonair, with a sing-song Spanish accent. "I could have sworn you were a compatriot. *Linda* means 'pretty,' but do not take offense. In Argentina, I call all the girls *Linda.*"

Actually, I felt offended that this slick guy lassoed me in with all the other females. I told him, "Well, you look and act Italian!" He shot back, "That's because I am Italian, the third generation on my mother's side and the fourth generation on my father's side."

"I thought you were Argentinean."

"Yes, I am one hundred percent Argentine and proud of it. Nearly seventy percent of my fellow countrymen are from an Italian background." Phew, I was glad to be prepared for the onslaught of meaningless compliments. Italian men seemed to tout their masculinity by verbally acknowledging a female's femininity. However, they were usually easy-going, affable, and wildly exaggerated. Actually, Italian men could be quite entertaining.

"So, what is your name, Miss Mystery, and where do you come from?"

"Marie France, but my friends call me Tyke, and I'm from New Orleans."

"Ty-ke, is there a Saint Ty-ke in New Orleans?

"No, why do you ask?"

"Because *everyone* in Argentina has a saint's name - we also have a saint's day that is more important than our birthday, and we have a huge celebration. My name is Santiago, but my friends and family call me Santi." I thought, how ironic, this guy looks far from a Santi.

"And there is a Saint Santiago in Argentina?"

Santi replied, "Of course, Santiago was a brother of *Jesucristo*. You would say Saint James in your country."

"Ah yes, I know lots of James', and also I adore the blues tune, 'Saint James Infirmary.'" I sang him the well-known chorus since it was one of my all-time favorites. My singing and his applause coincided with the engines revving up, conveniently drowning out our commotion.

I glanced over at Santi and took a quick inventory of his fascinating appearance. He resembled a young Dean Martin, with the same deep bronze tan, a prominent nose, curly dark hair that glistened like his warm chestnut-colored eyes, and brilliant white teeth flashing from his full-lipped smile.

Okay, the guy was attractive, but not to the extent to merit the self-confidence he oozed. He caught me glancing at the medal that hung on a heavy gold chain, dangling recklessly within view on his unbuttoned, white linen shirt.

"That's my Saint Benedict medal - blessed by the Pope when he was in Buenos Aires," confided Santi. "It brings me good luck. I always wear it when I travel."

"And do you travel a lot?" I pried.

"Yeah, I'm in sales," replied Santi.

"Hey, me too. What kind of sales do you deal with?"

Santi paused a moment and said, "Pharmaceutical."

I felt Santi was veering out of his comfort zone, so I changed the theme. "I have less than a week to discover Buenos Aires, and I was wondering if you could suggest the city's best and most interesting marvels!"

Santi's eyes widened, and mischief danced across his face. "The number one place you must experience is *Barrio* San Telmo! It is better known as *La Boca* (The Mouth). Of course, that refers to the mouth of the Riachuelo River. In the 1880s, my ancestors were among the first Italian immigrants from Genoa who arrived at the port of Buenos Aires and claimed La Boca," he boasted proudly. "We brought the color and passion!"

"And what's so special about *La Boca*?"

"Everything! *La Boca* is the birthplace of the TANGO! The Genovese were fishermen, so naturally, a red light district soon popped up on the port. The fishermen needed music and dance to wine and dine the damsels – so as the story goes, Spanish Flamenco mated with the Cuban Habanera, and the Tango was born.

"The *Caminito* (walkway) near the port is the most colorful place in Buenos Aires. The fishermen built simple wooden or corrugated zinc houses, still standing, and painted them with the bright, leftover paint from their boats. There you will find the best tango cafes, markets, and restaurants. You must eat at *El Obrero* (The Worker)."

Jotting down notes as fast as I could, I asked Santi, "Is it affordable? I'm traveling on a budget?"

"Affordable, darling? You will be a queen in my city if you have US dollars – with the current exchange rate, you'll be able to buy the restaurant."

"Hurray, I can't wait! Is there anything else I should see?"

"Everything! The city became a haven for commerce with the rest of the wave of Spanish, French, German, and Jewish immigrants. Although we are a majority of Italians, they call Buenos Aires the Paris of South America because of the Parisian architecture. We even have the widest avenue in the world and the most diverse, beautiful city anywhere. You'll see!"

"Sounds great, but I prefer the off-beat, bohemian quarters. What about the gauchos?"

"Ah, the 'Argentine cowboys' – nomadic horsemen that live, work and wander in the grasslands of Argentina. They are rugged men, outsiders, and even historical outlaws. I can tell you're drawn to cowboys."

It was true. Since our family trip to Tombstone, Arizona, when I was about eleven, I have been fascinated with the 'Wild West.' My brother, Spike, and I re-enacted the shootout at OK Corral countless times. Wyatt Earp and Doc Holliday were our heroes! We collected cowboy memorabilia, and my brother even vowed to return to make that frontier outpost his home one day.

"Well, I have some Argentinean friends from Ibiza, and they told me to get in touch when I arrive. They live in Río de la Plata and have friends with an *estancia* (ranch) nearby. Perhaps I'll run into some gauchos while I'm there?"

"Ha, my dear one, at best, you'll find some tourist show with guys dressed up as gauchos, putting on a show with *boleadoras*. That's a type of throwing weapon made of weights on the ends of interconnected cords, used to capture animals by entangling their legs."

"Heaven forbid, I don't want to witness some poor animal knocked down by a whirling weapon. I'll scratch that off my list immediately. But I would like to find some antique silver buckles with the silver chains on either side." I'd keep one for myself and turn a good profit on the rest.

"Try the flea markets or the San Telmo Antique Fair. You'll probably get a good deal since those belts are not in demand. People prefer gold here; not much prestige with silver." I noticed Santi was sporting a solid gold Rolex Submariner.

"Santi, your English is amazing and very American. Did you ever live in the States?"

"No," replied Santi, "I attended the International School in Buenos Aires, and absolutely everything was in English. Most of the teachers were from the States."

"Ah, that explains your American slang - sounds much better with your sing-song Spanish/Italian accent," I commented. Yes, Santi was charming and attractive, but I wondered how I would shake him loose after our flight landed. I know how sticky charmers can be.

"You mentioned Ibiza several times - tell me more about that Spanish island. There's a buzz about that small island becoming the new 'sound capital.' Many Argentines have migrated to Spain because of the opportunities opened through the breakneck speed of rapidly spreading tourism. Also, any socialist or communist-minded compatriots are fleeing from the upcoming change of events in our government. Isabel Perón is hanging onto the presidency by her teeth, but I see a military coup d'état on its way. There will be an explosion any day now!"

"Yikes, it sounds worse than Chile. Let's see if the pilot makes a warning announcement to Americans when we touchdown. I'd hate to forfeit authentic tango instruction, all the affordable food, and antique silver buckles just for some political whim."

"Haven't you heard about all the young leftist sympathizers disappearing in Buenos Aires? The rightwing Argentine Anticommunist Alliance (AAA) is on the move."

"Well, I hope they can hang on for a week or so." I had not been following my mother's advice about buying a Herald Tribune weekly to avoid countries in war or revolution. They say ignorance is bliss . . . . I wonder!

Looking sheepish, Santi cooed, "By the way, my girlfriend is picking me up at the airport, and she has a temper like a lion. She's dangerously jealous. I hope you don't mind if we say *adios* on the plane."

I nearly roared with laughter. I was worried about how I'd shake this Romeo, but now he'd become a trembling mouse. How can you look so macho and become so terrorized by a woman? It's clear that Santi was a natural-born flirt, so I guess he'd pressed his luck on too many occasions. I couldn't wait to see his shrew - she must be a real knock-out for him to toe the line.

"Oh, that's fine, Santi. I won't let on that I know you. I certainly don't want to ruffle the feathers of your girlfriend. *Un millón de gracias* (Thanks a million) for all your helpful tips about where and what to do in your city of passion and color!"

* * *

The plane landed without incident, and there was no anti-American warning announcement, so I lugged my oversized handbag into the airport up to the information desk. On my way to check out a cheap and central pension, I stopped by the money change office to investigate the dollar rate for the Argentine peso. My eyes lit up, and my stomach rumbled. Santi was right; I'd be living like royalty! Of course, the black market, which was hard to avoid, would be pursuing my US dollar.

"Wahoo!" The 4-star Sheraton Hotel was only four bucks a night. I had been spending up to two dollars for a crummy room with, at best, a stained hand basin. Now I'd be basking in luxury.

I grabbed a taxi, and the driver immediately offered me a better exchange rate and sped off to my destination. The Sheraton Buenos Aires was located at the Plaza San Martin, near the infamous port and the ideal starting point to everywhere. I checked in, flung my bag into my flawless room, and headed out to find the best restaurant.

It must have been about 75 degrees, and I was nearly back to sea level. My energy level shot through the roof, and I discovered I was skipping wildly down the street singing, "Oh, When the Saints Go Marching In." I scanned the streets for homeless children I might befriend, but none were in sight. The only kids I saw were being pushed in Rolls-Royce strollers or dressed to the hilt in kids' designer clothes, walking hand-in-hand with their well-groomed, sleek parents.

I felt an unexpected culture shock. I could have been in Paris, Milan, or Madrid – there was no clue that I was still in South America. Good thing I had taken Mandy and Mark's advice to dress European – if not, I might have been arrested in my Andean folklore outfit.

Within about twenty minutes, I felt at home and relatively anonymous. Like a chameleon, I blended into my Argentinean surroundings and only lacked some gold jewelry. I was still wearing my boots and would give them a quick polish. My flared jeans and crisp white blouse were spot on. Perhaps I'd invest in a silk blouse with the inviting exchange rate.

Yes, I looked a hundred percent Argentine, but if I opened my mouth with my vague American-accented Spanish, I'd be tagged as a Yankee gringo. In that case, with the anti-American sentiment, I would tell a bleached lie and say I was Canadian – that is, if anyone asked.

Due to the current political climate, I decided it was safer to remain low-key. I'd call my friend from Ibiza, Ana, and see if she could meet me at my hotel. But, first, food - glorious food! It was nearly 7 pm, time for the restaurants to revive. The chic closed eateries had a sign on the door, *Abierto para la cena a las 22:00* (Open for dinner at 10 pm.) I did see a few would open at 9:30 pm, but my blood sugar was plummeting rapidly.

I made an about-face and headed back towards the seedy neighborhood with street food. The bohemian quarter, near the port, would indeed have some street vendors hawking food for tourists. Hallelujah, I spotted some food stalls with several scraggly customers.

Some fair-haired backpackers were ahead of me, and I prayed they wouldn't wipe out the *empanada* inventory. Finally, my turn! *"Que le gustraia señorita?"* (What would you like, Miss?) I knew I was an excellent imposter since the vendor addressed me in Spanish.

Not to break the mood, I pointed to a pastry-filled surprise and what looked like blood sausage. I was served the delicacy in a newspaper and hoped I wouldn't be poisoned by yesterday's news. I found a wall to lean on and gulped down the last morsel. A refreshment stand was nearby; fortunately, they had *Yerba Mate* (Yerba Mah-tay).

Yerba Mate is more than a drink. It is the ancient Andean superfood discovered by the Spanish colonizers in the 1500s. Made from the leaves and twigs of the yerba mate plant, it resembles a holly-like shrub that is steeped in hot water. It has the strength of coffee, the health benefits of tea, and the joy of chocolate. I'd only sip one to avoid being wired all night and quenched my thirst with a tall glass of pineapple cider.

Oh yes, Argentina's national dessert is the addictive *dulce de leche*! My mother feared my string bean frame would reflect her culinary skills, so she tried to fatten me up on that delicacy back when we lived in San Souci Forest. By merely boiling a can of condensed milk (bain-marie) for several hours, the sweetened milk transformed into a creamy caramel that even surpassed devil's food chocolate cake. It was her secret calorie bomb, unknown to the American public.

In a digestive stupor high on sugar, I crawled back to my hotel and hoped I wouldn't have a sugar crash that would only stimulate my appetite. I needed protein fast and fell asleep munching stale peanuts.

I awoke with peanut crumbs covering my pillow and a zest to conquer the second-largest city in South America. I called Ana from my convenient room phone, and she said she'd take the next train to Buenos Aires. "I have twin beds in my Sheraton suite," I added, "Just in case you need a place to sleep."

"No problem, my boyfriend, Bautista, lives a stone's throw from the port. Let's meet at your hotel at about 5 pm."

"Awesome, Ana. I'll be waiting for you in my hotel lobby." Perfect timing, I thought. I'd have a chance to hit the flea markets to look for antique gaucho belt buckles and explore La Boca, the colorful zone Santi raved about.

Ana was a force to be reckoned with. She was nearly my height - slim but curvaceous. Her huge, dark eyes betrayed her every thought and offset her warm, strawberry-blond hair and bronzed olive complexion. Her biggest weapons were her beauty and no-nonsense verbal retaliations.

Ana had lived in London for nearly five years and snagged a likable entrepreneur while perfecting her English. She was not shy about voicing her need for financial security, thus had her clever, rich 'partner' swing a deal with NYC Arlene, owner of *La Tierra* 'in' bar in Ibiza.

Intimidating but fun and adventurous, Ana became the reigning queen of Ibiza nightlife in the old port of Ibiza City. As the new proprietor of *La Tierra* (The Earth) bar, we hit it off instantly. Our taste in men was drastically different, but our sense of fun was identical.

The last time I saw Ana, she was headed to Argentina for Christmas, and I was off to the US for my first trip back in three years.

"Don't forget to call me if you ever get to Argentina," were Ana's last words. Even though her family lived in *Mar de Plata*, she didn't think twice about the five-hour train journey to Buenos Aires. She could tango with expertise and would certainly know the best dance cafes in La Boca of the San Telmo neighborhood.

I remembered what my Spanish friend, Alejandro, told me in Ibiza, "Don't be tempted if an announcement is made for volunteers to come up on the dance floor to learn flamenco. Only gypsies or Spaniards born in Andalucia (Southern Spain) can pull off that dance. A tourist trying to do the flamenco will look as awkward as a cow on ice." I would try and remember that advice if the opportunity arose with a tango demonstration.

The flea market was a treasure chest full of odds and ends, and I lucked out by finding two stunning gaucho buckles, with three silver chains on either side, to be buttoned onto wide leather gaucho belts. I could always get the leather belts made to order in Ibiza by one of the many Argentine artisans that had migrated to the island. I hauled my treasures back to the hotel, including a mauve silk blouse I would inaugurate this evening. I showered, decked out, and was in the lobby at the agreed hour of 5 pm.

* * *

Within minutes, Ana and Bautista pushed their way through the revolving door as if they owned the place. All eyes shifted over to them – Ana was dressed to stop traffic. She wore a backless, flaming red micro-mini dress with matching spiked heels. Bautista sported a white linen suit, emphasizing his deeper-than-deep tan. I smiled at their audacity and wished I had packed my turquoise sequined catsuit.

As Bautista and I were introduced, a wry smile crept across our faces as we realized we were carbon copies. I was a female version of Bautista - how very amusing. Bautista's wavy brown shoulder-length hair framed a face that could have been my twin. Ana laughed out loud, "I've been waiting for the opportunity to get you two together." By the way, Bautista is my boy friend, not my boyfriend – so you can have him if you want." She chuckled again, proud of her attempted matchmaking skills. "Let's go before our car is towed away."

Bautista opened the car door and flung his arm out in a Don Juan gesture. I hopped into the back seat, and we took off with the radio blaring. "A friend of ours has recently opened a restaurant and tango bar on the outskirts of Buenos Aires, so we thought we'd try it out," revealed Ana enthusiastically.

"Out-of-sight," I was all for it but explained, "I'm not exactly dressed for clubbing."

"You are absolutely perfect, Tyke," assured Ana. "You see, Bautista and I have been tango partners since high school. We want to show off, so we've dressed to the hilt. It's still too early, so we'll stop for some wine and appetizers."

"OK, but I'm inviting you this evening," I insisted. After all, Ana had spent the afternoon on a train, and Bautista kindly drove us around. My dollars would go a long way!

It was twilight when we headed down a rural road for about ten minutes, and Bautista announced, *"Debe estar cerca."* (It must be close.) Ana pointed to the bright lights just around the corner and shouted, "Stop, stop, pull in here!"

We had come face to face with three men dressed in military uniforms, toting machine guns. They were standing in front of an electric-wired fence protecting a military base. I wondered if we rolled into the twilight zone. In a flash, Ana's head swung back to me, and she ordered, "You are the sister of Bautista. You are deaf, and you cannot speak." I nodded. My lightning-fast mind realized we were in deep trouble, and if my identity as an American was discovered, we might soon be behind bars.

"Sal del auto!" (Get out of the car!), shouted one of the menacing-looking military men. I saw Ana and Bautista pale and get out of the car. I followed suit. We stood there while they opened the trunk, rummaged around, and then ripped the back seat out of the car. Another guy shouted, *"Busque en el frente, armas o explosives."* (Search the front for weapons or explosives.) I could see steam coming out of Ana's ears.

"Qué diablos crees que estás haciendo?" (What in the hell do you think you're doing?), shouted Ana. I took a deep breath and inwardly screamed for help, "Holy Spirit of God, we need a miracle! HELP!" A curious thing happened - a colossal condor started circling overhead, issuing a series of hisses and snorts. We all looked overhead while Ana taunted the men, *"No sabes quienes somos?"* (Don't you know who we are?) I wondered who we were.

Suddenly, what looked like a pale pigeon, landed squarely on my head. Did my windblown hair look like a nest? I had read that condors preyed mainly on dead carcasses and hunted small birds and animals. Was the condor going to swoop down and swallow the pigeon? I instinctively wanted to scream, but I was supposed to be deaf and dumb.

The tough military men screamed, "Brujas, brujas . . . . .salgan de aqui!" (Witches, witches . . . . .get out of here!) The men ran back into the military base, locked the gate, and ran into the cement block building. We looked at each other, I shook the bird out of my hair, and Ana said, "Throw the seat into the back of the car and let's get out of here."

Bautista reversed the car at fifty miles an hour, and we sped back the way we came. Ana burst into laughter and said, "Argentineans are really superstitious. Those guys are going to have nightmares, and rightly so!" The radio was blaring again, and we went happily on our merry way. I tried to piece together our impossible getaway and how it happened. There was no logical reason.

"*Mufa*," muttered Anna, as tears of laughter rolled down her cheeks. I guess her joyful emotion was also a release of tension. "*Mufa*?" I queried.

"Yes, *mufa* is a local expression for someone who brings bad luck. The hissing condor, the nesting dove, plus my red hair were the perfect combo that set those macho men into a tailspin. My country considers redheads bad luck, so I use L'Oreal Excellence 8 Reddish Blonde hair color. It gives an extra kick to my threatening demeanor."

Ana, a bombshell with a black belt in Jiu-Jitsu, was mega-daunting. It was fortunate that she chose me as a friend - heaven forbid having Ana as an enemy. Of course, I had been told more than once that I had a 'don't mess with me' aura. Plus, my brother had sergeant-drilled me in self-defense while growing up in San Souci Forest. As a matter of fact, I had not encountered one single negative incident throughout my travels in the Northern Hemisphere, nor a hitch, here in South America.

La Milonga Tango Club was only five minutes away but set back off the dusty road. It was still early, so there were no cars, but they were now rolling in rapidly. Due to its location, only the local 'in crowd' hung out in this gem of a club. As we entered, we were pelted with approval, and I reveled in the glory that reflected off my companions. Ana and Bautista were well known on the tango circuit, and come to find out; they had been the Junior Champions of Buenos Aires.

I was impressed to see a full orchestra setting up. There was a double bass, a bandoneon (a relative of the accordion), a violin, flute, piano, and a glittery vocalist. The place was huge – perhaps the size of a small roller skating rink. I was content to be an observer and looked forward to an entertaining evening. After the tango competition, dinner would be served. No one would think of dancing on a full stomach.

At least a dozen couples stopped at our strategically placed table, and Ana introduced me to all her friends. Argentines are 'cheeky,' giving a greeting kiss on only one cheek. However, they don't make a kissing sound but only graze cheeks. I thought Bautista was being a bit fresh until I discovered these strangers were all offering me an 'air' kiss. There were not many singles in the room, and I was glad, for once, not to be the protagonist.

A bit insecure about attempting the tango, I felt in my element with impromptu dancing. Without having to work out a meticulous routine with a partner, it would be difficult to detect a faux pas. Tango is a precision dance; as we all know, 'it takes two to tango.' The marvelous music started up, and I felt itchy to dance.

About eight couples slinked onto the dance floor and swung into their seductive routines. The dancers and their outfits were galactic, with every hue of the rainbow represented on that dance floor, ricocheting bursts of color off the polished surface. Ana and Bautista stood out like stars swirling across the Milky Way.

They were a cut above the rest, and the dance was all about seduction. Therefore, executing the fancy footwork and simultaneously transmitting a cool allure involved synthesizing body, mind, soul, and spirit! I wondered how it was possible that all those intricate kicks and swirls didn't entangle the dancers lightening fast legs - leaving them gasping on the floor, locked together in a pretzel position.

One by one, couples were eliminated until Ana and Bautista remained alone on the floor amidst a sea of wild applause. They bowed graciously from the waist, extending their arms, swirling their wrists, acknowledging appreciation to one another and then the audience. They were dramatically showered with flowers. Ana then joined me at the table, and with a bewitching twinkle in her eye, I wondered what was next.

Bautista remained on the dance floor, and when the applause subsided, he announced that he had just opened a tango school in

La Boca. He then looked me squarely in the eyes and motioned for me to join him. I could feel my ears turning red under my heavy mop of wavy, waist-long hair. I looked for an escape route, but there was none. OK, I'd be a good sport. After all, I didn't know anyone.

It seemed that Bautista wanted to use me as an example to show how *anyone* could learn the tango with the right instructor. He led me through the basic steps of walking backward, forwards, and sideways, slowly dragging one foot inward. I had a vision of myself kicking the guy in the shin, accidentally crippling him. Luckily, no kicks were involved.

Slow, slow, quick, quick, slow, quick, quick, slow – I caught the rhythm and flowed with it. Only Bautista's discreet hand pressure enabled me to follow his lead. Miraculously, I hadn't tripped on my feet or his. Imitating the previous dancers, I tilted my shoulders and head back slightly and looked in the opposite direction for a dramatic effect.

Now a twirl into a pivot and a dip backward over Bautista's left knee, while he appeared to be in an elegant lunge position, with his right leg extended backward. A deep dip brought our noses only inches away, which sparked an explosion of applause.

I made it through the experiment unscathed and headed back to my table when Bautista caught my hand and twirled me back onto center stage to execute a proper bow. I was miffed I wasn't wearing something super sassy.

We had a lovely dinner of grilled strips of sirloin with chimichurri (olive oil, vinegar, chili flakes, oregano, crushed garlic, and cilantro), accompanied by palm hearts and avocado. Fruit salad followed, and naturally, *dulce de leche*. I was warned never to eat watermelon combined with red wine since that was '*mufa*,' bad luck. I obeyed.

It was nearly midnight when Ana and Bautista dropped me off at the Sheraton. "We'll be back at noon tomorrow to show you around La Boca!"

"Great," I replied enthusiastically, "I can't wait to discover every inch of that bohemian quarter!"

Takes Two to Tango

* * *

Looking forward to my chic room and inviting hot tub, I ended up waterlogged and longed for a soothing sleep in La La Land. However, my mind kept flickering back to our early evening episode at the military base. I had heard how hundreds, if not thousands, of young adults were disappearing daily. They were thought to be withering away in hidden prison camps tucked away in the countryside.

Ok, Ana's reddish hair might have had something to do with our escape. However, I felt it was clearly a move of the Holy Spirit. My mind drifted back to Cusco and the powerful teaching that James had given us at his Bible study. Jesus told his disciples they would be better off if he went away, then he would send the Holy Spirit. And the Holy Spirit would remind them of everything he had told them and lead them into all truth. Jesus then told his disciples to wait for the Holy Spirit, who would give them power from on high so that they could be His witnesses to the ends of the earth.

After all, I had prayed a prayer of desperation. The full impact of the condor circling overhead, and a dove nesting in my hair, could have only been a God-incidence. The foreboding omen certainly sent the gunmen fleeing for safety, allowing our getaway. How humbling to contemplate that God Almighty had devised an escape route for us.

Why were we so favored? Am I supposed to be witnessing to the ends of the earth? How on earth will I do that? I had heard God would take our mess and make a message out of it. I hoped so. I wondered if the birds were only an illusion. However, the bird poop on the collar of my new silk blouse was all too real. Drifting off into a deep delta slow-wave sleep, I awoke in the same position seven hours later.

Feeling invigorated, I bounced up, ready to devour the complimentary buffet breakfast. I scoffed down something of everything in sight and snuck a few bananas into my bag for later. It was the perfect time to explore the city center since I'd be heading back to *La Boca* with Ana and Bautista at noon.

I jogged to the famous opera house, Teatro Colón, belting out James Brown's paradigmatic tune, "I Got You." "Wow! I feel good, da-da-da-da-da-da-da . . . . .!" Yep, it felt good to be back down to sea level where I could hop, skip, jump, plus sing, at the same time.

Boom! There it stood majestically - the Colón Opera House was as imposing as I had imagined. The horseshoe-shaped halls were perfect for echoes, and the three floors of boxes were made of soft materials such as fabric, wood, and carpet. The brochure in my hotel room said that many of the great orchestra conductors who performed there said it was the world's best lyrical opera house.

Luckily, the door was open, and there was no uniformed employee or entrance fee. It was early, and I was clearly the only one there. Whoa, it looked as sumptuous as La Scala in Milan. I would try out the acoustics with an aria from my signature song, "Summertime." Okay, "Porgy and Bess" wasn't serious opera, but when I sang *fortissimo* (loudly) with vibrato, I could escalate to the highest notes.

I scanned the orchestra area and the three floors of boxes to ensure I was alone - then tip-toed up the steps to the stage. Feeling like a desperate diva - I dramatically tossed my hair over my shoulders and sang as if my life depended on it.

Singing *acapella* (without instrumental backup or a microphone) would be a challenge. I took a deep breath, opened and relaxed my throat, raised my soft palate and released my breath in a steady stream, and bellowed, "S-U-M-M-E-R-T-I-M-E and the livin' . . . .!"

Enthralled by the way my voice reverberated around the opera house, becoming richer and fuller as it echoed back to me, I wrapped up my performance by placing my right hand over my heart and bowed from the waist. Returning to an upright position - I blew gracious kisses to the *'audience'* with both hands simultaneously. My melodramatic finale fed my pumped ego, and I basked in the burst of happy hormones released by my forceful song's vibration.

While contemplating another bow, to my horror, I heard unabashed applause coming from a dark corner near the closed entrance. A single masculine voice shouted, "Encore!"

My emotions were mixed – I was either being discovered, or else I was the victim of sarcasm and would soon be carted off to the clink. Ultimately, I was trespassing. In Louisiana, trespassing is considered a misdemeanor, so the penalties are not as severe as a felony - unless the homeowner can prove they are in imminent danger. In that case, shoot and kill is acceptable.

My imagination was running wild until a lone gentleman, armed with a broom, moved into the light and exclaimed, "*Mi sueño de toda la vida es cantar en ese scenario.*" (The dream of my life is to sing on this stage.) "*He trabajado aquí durante veinte años, escuché a los mejores tenores del mundo.*" (I have worked here for the past twenty years and listened to the best tenors in the world.)

I invited the dear man onto the stage and promised to lock the doors and I'd cover for him while he sang. I'd take the blame if we were discovered. I saw he had trouble with the steps and gave him a helping hand. "Just hang onto my arm," I encouraged him. He announced proudly that he would be singing the famous aria, "*La*

Donna é Mobile," from Giuseppe Verdi's opera, "*Rigoletto*." That preferred aria of many tenors translates into "Woman is Fickle." It was a well-known melody, and I didn't take it personally.

While the petite version of Pavarotti practiced some vocal scales, I dashed to the entrance and double-locked the door. It seems the opera house didn't officially open for another half hour. Without knowing the opening hours, I merely pushed the door, abracadabra, and walked in.

During my many visits to Italy, I discovered that all Italian men could sing, some better than others. The Italian language was invented for singing, especially in operas. The long consonants are so crucial because it helps the singer with breath support, projection, and expression. At least that's what my Roman friend, Flavio, a connoisseur of opera, explained to me in detail while demonstrating.

The lyrics of "La Donna é Mobile" rushed forth like a category five force hurricane from the moon-shaped mouth of the talented janitor. I would never have fathomed that such volume and projection could be emitted from that pint-sized Pavarotti. Awestruck, I felt goosebumps rippling from my scalp down to the soles of my feet, and I tried to hold back tears of emotion. I lost the battle and wept. The aria was full of mirth; however, knowing that this man of humble means was having his dreams become a reality tugged at my heartstrings. We ended up weeping together in a soulful embrace for the sheer beauty of the moment.

A shiny brass name badge revealed the operatic virtuoso was *Señor* Mario Rossi. As he worked his way down the steps sideways, step by step, I took his arm to steady him. "What happened to your leg, Sr. Rossi?"

"*No es mi pierna, necesito un reemplazo de cadera.*" (It's not my leg, I need a hip replacement), revealed the man. At that moment, I felt a nudge from the Holy Spirit. In the silence of my heart, I cried out, "Holy Spirit, it's all yours!" I was a beginner – I wasn't qualified to pray for a creative miracle! An inner voice reassured me, "You are right. No one is qualified, especially you. My power will be perfected in your weakness."

Hmmm, that must have been a message from God Almighty because my over-inflated ego wouldn't have allowed me to say that to myself. What a relief, I sighed inwardly. I meekly probed in my best Spanglish, "Sr. Rossi, do you have a small amount of faith, even the size of a mustard seed?"

It sounded like he replied, "I have a lot of faith, and my wife has an altar in our bedroom with fresh flowers for the Virgin Maria."

On a roll, I asked gently, "Do you mind if I pray for your healing?"

Sr. Rosi's eyes widened; he smiled and replied, "*Quién sabe, tal vez eras una ángel gringo – sí, adelante.*" (Who knows, maybe you're a gringo angel – yes, go ahead.)

Placing my hand about a foot from the singer's right hip, I commanded, "*En el nombre de Jesucristo, ser curado!*" (In the name of Jesus Christ, be healed!)

I didn't hang around for the results since it was the opening hour of the opera house, but in faith, I thanked God for healing that humble tenor with the huge voice. I had become convinced that God might heal through me since I felt so inadequate. I remembered Michael and Lidia's encouraging words back in Quito, "It's not about your ability – but your availability."

However, I was finding it difficult to stay focused on being available. I was so easily side-tracked. I wasn't sure if I was in step with the Holy Spirit or dancing to the beat of my own drum. Unknowingly, I was being swept up into the outpouring of the Holy Spirit that was rippling across the South American continent. It was picking up speed, building momentum, and I wondered where the tsunami would hit. Could I be eccentric, plus have fun, and still qualify as a PR agent for *Yeshua*?

After all, *Yeshua* (Jesus) went to parties and even transformed water into wine. King David danced wildly before the Lord and sang his way through the Psalms. I asked the Holy Spirit to wave a red flag in front of me when I was headed down a dead-end street and to shout loudly when He needed me for a healing or some other heartfelt task.

Aware that the Holy Spirit was gentle as a dove, never demanding or pushy, I realized, ultimately, it was up to me to be receptive. Yes, I would focus on being open-minded. I felt like a spiritual shift had occurred – I wanted my life to have eternal significance.

Meanwhile, I would look for a Yerba Mate stand to have a mid-morning pickup before making my way to the Plaza de Mayo. Yerba Mate was more than a tasty lift - it was an art form. Served in a hollowed-out gourd and sipped through a metal straw, it was a social event that brought friends together or enabled you to make new friends.

I found the ideal Yerba Mate hut just around the corner and sat down at a long table. I asked the girl seated next to me, passing the gourd filled with Mate, if she knew Jesus. I figured the direct approach was the best. I had seen street evangelists in action; they spoke so down-to-earth and naturally about the supernatural.

"Of course, I know Jesus," the girl said, pointing across the table. A guy stood up, extended his hand, and with a warm smile, said, "Well, who are you? You look Argentine, but you have an American accent." I corrected him, "Actually, it's a Canadian accent," I said sheepishly. Heaven forbid - my street evangelism was floundering.

"I'm Marie France," I offered, "And your name is Jesus?"

"Absolutely, Jesus Romero at your service. You must be a university student here perfecting your Spanish."

"Uh – no, I'm just visiting your amazing city."

"Well, today is my day off, and I can show you around," offered the gorgeous guy.

"Actually, I have Argentinean friends who I'm connecting with later, and they're taking me to La Boca,"

"And how did you know my name and that I was here?" The guy started to look skeptical.

"Ah, I only asked this nice girl next to me if she knew Jesus, but I meant another Jesus."

"Well, Jesus is a prevalent name in South America. Do you know his last name?"

"Um – yes, it's Jesus Christ," I whispered.

With a burst of laughter, the guy admitted, "You gringos sure have a strange sense of humor!" I decided to laugh along with him rather than pursue my original plan.

I paid up and scooted off as soon as possible, trying to figure out a new tactic for spreading the 'good news' of Jesus. Perhaps the

Lord's plan for me was exclusively in the healing department. I'd wait for a confirmation. Meanwhile, I'd have to fine-tune my approach.

As I walked over to the Plaza de Mayo, I had less zip in my step and not much wind left in my sail. However, I refocused on the operatic event of the morning and thanked the Creator of the universe that he *did* have a plan for my life. I just had to discover it.

* * *

Plaza de Mayo, the principal square of Buenos Aires, was set in a park of nearly five acres. Its name commemorated the May Revolution in 1810, which started the process toward the country's independence from Spain in 1816. There remains a bitter-sweet relationship between the two countries, but the facility for Argentines to migrate to Spain has improved relations.

The famous *Casa Rosada* (Pink House) could be seen from a distance. Like the US White House, it houses the president's executive office. It's referred to as the Royal Palace, but the President's official residence has been relocated for safety.

I could visualize Eva (Evita) Peron standing glamorously on the balcony with crowds roaring their approval. Not only Argentines loved her. The world adored her. Evita was responsible for the passage of the women's suffrage law and formed the Peronista Feminist Party in 1949. She also introduced compulsory religious education into all Argentinean schools. However, the right-wing was now gaining power and popularity - the city was a time bomb waiting to explode.

It looked like a political demonstration was happening, so I shot some prayers in that direction and kept moving. After viewing the massive Metropolitan Cathedral and hum-drum City Hall, I returned to my hotel. Visiting umpteen magnificent churches, cathedrals, and museums in South America, I was experiencing cultural fatigue and longed for a day in the country.

There seemed to be more emphasis on the church buildings and the golden altars, with statues embracing baby Jesus, than on having a relationship with the living King of kings and Lord of lords. 'Church building' in Spanish is *iglesia* - derived from the Latin word – *ecclesia*. The definition of *ecclesia*, 'an assembly of people,' morphed from 'a gathering of people who worshiped Christ' into the actual 'structure' where the people worshiped. The building seemed to have taken pre-eminence over the reason it was built.

Perhaps it's my rebellious streak, but nature had become my comfort zone for worshiping. Personally, I felt a closer connection to our Creator within His own setting, where you could hear the wind blowing and birds singing. You could look towards heaven and see the sky rather than acclaimed frescos in stages of restoration.

As I strolled back to the hotel, I absorbed the contrasts of the brash but elegant, rough, and refined city of *Buenos Aires* (Good Airs). The eclectic architecture was an intriguing mix of neoclassical, art-nouveau, and art-deco styles. Nevertheless, I looked forward to discovering more of La Boca, with the brightly colored shanty town structures up and down the port's *Caminito* (little street). Locals of Buenos Aires are called *porteños* (people of the port) because so many of them historically arrived from Europe by boat.

With half an hour to freshen up – I showered, then dampened, gelled, and scrunched my wavy hair, separating the locks with my mega afro comb. Slipping into my embroidered jeans and tie-dye t-shirt, I draped my antique beaded scarf around my long Modigliani neck. I was tempted to wear my gaucho silver belt buckle but refrained. I grabbed my hand-woven Peruvian puma bag and exited bohemian-chic.

Waiting in the lobby, I kept my eye out for Bautista's vintage Mercedes, so I could hop in without them having to park. My friends arrived nearly on time, and, like clockwork, I rushed out and hurled myself into the back seat.

"What a divine scarf," exclaimed Ana. "Did you find it on Portobello Road in Kensington?"

"Definitely," I admitted.

"I almost wore one of the beaded dresses I bought from you in Ibiza," commented Ana.

"Yeah, what a bonanza find. I still have a few silk chiffon floral ones from the Roaring Twenties. As soon as I return to Europe, I have the fashion shows in Florence and Milan, then a trip to India, and I'll be in Ibiza end of May at the latest. Since I'll be flying to my island from London, I'll scour Portobello's early-hour buyers' market for more treasures."

"*Fantastico*, just remember to show me everything first," Ana begged.

"Of course, you're my best publicity," I assured Ana.

Bautista laughed and said, "Hey, chicas, donde vamos?" (Hey, girls, where are we going?)

"La Boca," confirmed Ana. "You know the best places since it's your neck of the woods."

Bautista was tall, slim, and attractive - but above all, he had style. He also had manners and knew the art of dealing with boisterous women. He understood English but was shy at communicating in a language he hadn't yet conquered. Fortunately, I spoke Spanish unabashedly, even if I omitted most prepositions and didn't often conjugate in the proper tense. As long as I could communicate, that was plenty enough for me.

I gathered from Ana that Bautista grew up in the San Telmo port area. The fourth generation of Italian immigrants who fished or worked on the wharf - he was breaking the mold by becoming an entrepreneur. Bautista had finally opened his own dance studio. He had danced his way around the clubs of *La Boca* since his early teens and was everyone's friend. He also played several instruments, including the accordion.

"*Hemos llegado,*" (We've arrived) announced Bautista. I felt instantly relaxed. I could see that Bautista was nobility in his neighborhood. All the locals greeted him. The men extended their hands, and the ladies gave him affectionate air kisses. We walked along three picturesque city blocks along the edge of the river inlet. They were dotted with street market vendors shaded by large white umbrellas on elevated sidewalks.

Yes, Bautista had an intrinsic elegance that disguised his modest upbringing. He was dressed casually in black designer jeans with a black linen shirt worn open over a snug black t-shirt. Black was the official tango uniform for male dancers, and Bautista emanated seductive class. As we walked down the length of the celebrated *Caminito* (little street), made famous by the electric-colored houses and the tango restaurant clubs, I felt like I was on a movie set with two megastars. All male eyes darted towards Ana as she swished along in her alluring white mini dress that coordinated with the sparkle of her perfect smile.

My friends were dressed to perform, so some fun PR was in store. Ana was a loyal friend and a lady who didn't waste her time on frivolity without accomplishing a goal. She was always balancing future repercussions with her uncanny foresight. Some described her as calculating, but I labeled her clever, talented, pragmatic, and warm.

As we made our way through the artisanal stalls, we were unexpectedly showered with applause by a group of musicians setting up in the middle of the street. "Hola amigos, vuelves en diez minutes y échamos una mano." (Hey, come back in ten minutes and lend us a hand.) Bautista nodded and said, *"Por supuesto!"* (Of course!)

The entire neighborhood's livelihood was rocked in the tango cradle that turned the streets into an improvised dance floor. Tourists abandoned the city center and flocked to the emblematic port and hundred yards of *El Caminito*. After all, the tango was the national symbol of Argentina.

Ana turned to me and confided, "Bautista has been attracting crowds on the *street* since he was a toddler. He was born to dance – and so was I. We first met here and often returned to liven things up, especially on the weekends. This is what I have missed the most since I moved to Europe. Hey, what about a 'Tango Night' at La Tierra . . . . . or even Pacha?"

"I'm all for it," I agreed.

Ana lowered her head and whispered, "When we start to dance, and there's a good crowd gathered, maybe you could volunteer as a tango novice. Good to drum up some business for Bautista. His studio is next to the 'in' restaurant, The Obrero, and he offers intensive courses for tourists who are only in town for a few days."

I couldn't help but laugh, "Absolutely, I'd be honored to help. I only hope I can remember the footwork from the other evening."

"Come on, Tyke, you're one of the best dancers I know, plus you could sell a bikini to an Eskimo." I winked at Ana when I fully grasped that my upcoming job would be as an innocent bystander, as well as hawker, pitch person. Why not? It would give me a sense of purpose and a way of coercing my friends into a day at a gaucho ranch in the countryside.

The musicians started playing, so we wandered back slowly, pretending not to know one another. I mingled with the tourists. Spontaneously, Bautista tapped Ana on the shoulder, and she looked surprised when he invited her to dance. Within minutes she had become an extension of Bautista's every move. The crowds lapped it up, and a small child passed the hat after the grand finale. Great tactic, I thought.

Then Bautista nonchalantly invited someone from the crowd to join him for a dance. A plump lady with well-worn tennis shoes, obviously American, waved her hand eagerly. I raised my hand half-mast, and Bautista beckoned, "Don't be shy young lady. I'll show you what to do step by step." At the end of our dance, I shouted, "You are an awesome teacher! Can I take some more intensive lessons privately - I'm only here for a few days."

"Yes," answered Bautista with his melodious accent, "My studio is only a block away."

"What if I get a group together? Will you make a good price?" I pleaded.

"Depends, not more than eight people so that I can spend one-on-one time with each of you."

"Who wants to sign up with me for an intensive class tomorrow?" I asked. Of the forty people gathered around us, about fifteen hands shot up. Ana gave me a small notebook and pen, and I scribbled down the names of each hopeful person, folded the paper, and tossed it into the hat. Okay, I'll shake up the names, and let's have a volunteer pick out the eight winners."

One by one, each winner impulsively screeched with emotion - then Bautista led us to his studio about a block away. "The session will be three hours at $10 an hour," announced Bautista. "Class will begin at 10 am tomorrow, don't be late!"

"Wow, that would cost double in the States!" I provoked mass hysteria, and more people were desperate to sign up. I looked to Bautista, and he agreed to give another session in the afternoon, starting at 4 pm. I signed up the remaining seven tourists, now waving their hands wildly.

Bautista was bubbling over with amusement. "Tyke, I'd like to invite you to a first-class meal at the best restaurant in town," exclaimed Bautista. His eyes darted over to Ana, "*Crees que tu amiga consideraría convertirse en mi agente?*" (Do you think your friend would consider becoming my agent?)

"*De ninguna manera, ella hace lo suya,*" (No way, she's a free-wheeler,) replied Ana with a laugh.

We arrived at a lackluster muddy red entrance that looked like it led to a sleazy bar. Bautista gallantly held open the door to what looked like counter-chic chaos. The walls were covered from top to bottom with signed photographs of the internationally famous.

Prize fighters, soccer stars, musicians, movie stars, bullfighters, politicians, directors . . . . .absolutely anybody who was anyone!

However, *El Obrero* (The Worker) opened in 1910, catering to the thousands of Italian laborers arriving in Argentina. The menu was nearly identical, but the tables now bragged white linen tablecloths, although shabby and stained. Whatever the case, I felt privileged to be in that dismal, smoky workers' café.

"So what's the magic formula?" I asked Ana. "The secret is the superior quality beef. Served on chipped plates with bent forks, it outclasses even the prime cuts served at the up-market downtown steakhouses that are triple the price."

Bautista introduced me to Guillermo Vita, whose father-in-law bought the establishment in 1954. "It's still the same building from 1910, and we still have the same tables and chairs," he bragged. "The waiters here, and I'm one of them, greet every arrival as a new member of the family." With that, he pressed his cheek to mine and welcomed me as if I were a celebrity.

Then Bautista ordered sirloin for three with fried potatoes and his favorite red house wine. "Our cattle are the best in the world – no hormones or antibiotics." My steak was grilled crisp on the outside and juicy inside. "Delicious," I murmured. I had more of a seafood palate, but what the heck? Steak is synonymous with Argentina.

Our meal opened the door for my suggestion to visit the countryside and watch the *gauchos* (cowboys) at work, driving the cattle.

"The real gauchos work on the fertile *pampas* (plains), and you don't want to see a nearby tourist show. I'll take you to visit my good friend who trains polo ponies. It's only about sixty miles from here, and you'll see the best landscapes. Bautista, darling, can I borrow your car to show our helpful friend how polo ponies are trained?"

"Sure, Ana, Monday is okay, but I'll need the car back by 7 pm."

"Thanks, Bautista, love of my life; I'll bring you a surprise."

Ana obviously had perfected the art of how to charmingly whittle whatever she wanted out of her illustrious, talented friends. But she was incredibly generous with her time and favors, so it was all fair play.

I looked forward to our foray into the countryside to visit Ana's polo-playing playboy. However, remaining true to my tango commitment, I was at Bautista's studio at 10 am sharp the following morning for my perk of three hours' worth of free lessons.

Bautista used me as his star pupil and teaching partner. I even felt confident enough to add a few strategic kicks into my tango repertoire, and I accomplished and polished my 'dip' to a T.

* * *

Ah, I needed a breath of fresh air in the countryside! I was longing to hear birds singing and soak up some wide-open spaces. I spent my formative years in the country outside New Orleans, and we always had several horses. Nevertheless, I would humor Ana by going with her to visit her *guapo* polo pal. My brother, Spike, used to entertain my gang of friends and me with his Wild Bill Hickok stunts. At full gallop, he would swing one leg over the saddle and hit the ground with both feet, then swing over to the other side and repeat without missing a beat. Rodeos attracted the horsey He-Men in Louisiana, Texas, and Arizona. Polo was much too civilized – a cross between golf and hockey.

Ana was a daring, accurate driver, and we arrived at her friend Nacho's ranch in no time. She explained to me that her friend was a man of almost mythic proportions. As charming as he was notorious, he lived fast and large, a legend of the *glitterati*. He was a champion polo player who hobnobbed from one glamorous occasion to the next, drawing on his Argentine mystique and impeccable manners to ingratiate himself with the global elite.

I figured the guy must be past his prime if he's teaching polo ponies instead of riding them. But, I would be polite and enthusiastic as always. Having attended the prestigious Hurlingham Club in Fulham, London, I had watched some nobles whacking the ball around like an adult version of lawn croquet. One thing I noticed about Ana was that she drew a menagerie of men friends from every walk of life, but they all had one thing in common, they were all drop-dead attractive. I was curious to meet Nacho.

The impressive entrance to the property announced boldly - *Alba* (Sunrise) Polo Club. I jumped out of the car to ring the buzzer, and voila, the wrought iron electric gate slid open, and we rolled into the vast landscaped estate, flying. It took about ten minutes to arrive at the stately, two-story white stucco hacienda with typical red clay roof tiles. A stable, large enough to house at least a few dozen horses, was adjacent to the house.

I was wearing my slim-cut, high-waisted blue jeans, with my boots pulled up over my jeans. Accentuating my classy ranch look, I wore my mauve silk blouse with a scarf knotted loosely around my neck. To top off my casual country 'look,' I wore my Panama hand-woven hat from Ecuador. The fedora brim with an indented crown was slightly off-center from being packed so often, sending an 'I'm too cool to care' message. Ana wore designer jeans with a white, backless halter that augmented her deep, flawless tan.

While Ana pulled up to the hacienda and parked, The Marlboro Man walked up to us casually and opened Ana's door - then he leaped over the hood to open my door.

"Hola Señorita Annie Oakley! Are you planning on riding some polo ponies with me today?" The Marlboro Man then flagrantly gave me the once-over and said, "Long strong legs, symmetrical body, and an impressive mane. Ana, is this the foreign filly you brought me to break in?"

We all laughed at my expense, and I knew this Italian-looking Argentine would be a fun guy. Nacho was perhaps forty, the tipping point for a man. In my book, men looked like boys until their temples grayed and a pleasant sun-squint furrow developed between their eyes. Okay, Nacho was polo aristocracy, but he looked rugged, nothing like the polo polite gents in London. His black wavy hair was fashionably long, and his huge hazel eyes smiled mischief.

"Come on, Nacho," teased Ana, "Be on good behavior with my girlfriend from Ibiza. I promised her a day in the country and said you'd be more amusing than some sweaty gauchos. She's been helping Bautista out with his new tango school."

"Alright, girls, let's go over to the stable, and I'll show you my prized ponies." The stable was impeccably spic-n-span, and the horses were well-groomed and awaiting a caress from their master.

"You'll notice I prefer mares – they're built better and have softer tempers, strangely enough. You can have your thoroughbreds. I prefer *Criollos* (Mustangs) – the native horse of the Pampas. They have a reputation for long-distance endurance linked to low basal metabolism."

"Are they native to South America?" I asked.

"Actually, they evolved from horses imported from Spain and have been allowed to run wild in Argentina for three hundred years - that's why the breed is known for its hardiness and stamina. They are the most durable horses in the world and my best friends. They are my passion, hobby, and livelihood," replied Nacho, matter-of-factly.

"And what about all your lady friends?" laughed Ana.

"They're too erratic and expensive! I find solace in my darling Criollos – they live to please me. I can depend on them through thick and thin."

"So, what's the art of teaching these athletes?"

"A relationship built on one hundred percent trust. I treat my horses with tender, loving care, and they respond with top performances. In high caliber professional tournaments, I take eight horses for each game - a different horse for each *chukker* (seven and a half minute session)."

"Nothing to compare to a good rodeo horse," I quipped.

"Maybe, but I know several rodeo heroes who have switched to polo because it takes the same skills, but the pay is triple!"

"Hey, will you give us a demonstration?" I begged.

"Okay, I have to work out a few mares anyway."

"Come over here and meet my yearlings – my future superstars. I'm building trust with them now and will begin their training in a year or two, depending on how they mature. Training a polo pony is slow, but the rewards are immense. Bonding is vital, and the training takes six months to two years. My ponies reach full potential and are the most valuable between six to eight years."

"So long?" I blurted out in disbelief.

Nacho nodded, "The ideal polo pony has a combination of speed, endurance, intelligence, and a love of the game. The pony must have strong leg bones to be able to carry riders at full speed and stop or turn at a second's notice. I have to put some ointment on Melinda's fetlock (ankle). I'd hate for her to be ineligible for polo due to a weakness in that crucial joint."

"I'm sure the ointment will help but have you tried prayer?" The moment the words spilled out of my mouth, I knew it was too late to retract them or try to re-scramble them into another meaning. Nacho stopped, looked up at me seriously and said, "No, but why not - I'm up for anything that will strengthen this filly's fetlock. She's my favorite – smart as a whip, sensitive, and talented."

The ball was in my court. I could feel my face flush when I placed my hand near the pony's hoof and prayed under my breath. Nacho, looking intensely into my eyes said, "Thank you, my friend. I always have my horses blessed on the feast day of St. Francis of Assisi, the patron saint of animals. I am convinced I have a guardian angel who also looks after my ponies."

"I can vouch for that," said Ana with a wry smile. "As I see it, being a polo player is about balancing aggressiveness with self-confidence. However, it is vital to have a sense of passion, discipline, and commitment to your horse's welfare."

"You see, that's why I adore Ana - she reads me like no other lady. She has an innate degree in psychology," Nacho laughed.

"It's just that I understand the philosophy of ego-addictions. From my point of view, the synergistic combination of horses, adrenaline, teamwork, and competition are the key factors that make polo addictive. Nacho is a more than willing victim," confirmed Ana with a grin.

"Okay, now a short demonstration with one of my mature mares." Nacho saddled up the horse, who seemed pleased to have been chosen, and then he walked it out to the practice field. After the usual warm-up exercises, Nacho explained he would do some spins and sliding stops with back steps.

"Horses know exactly how you are feeling and mirror it back to you. Often the reflection is unexpected. Horses are excellent teachers of self-awareness. If your horse is agitated, there's a good chance you are also," he explained.

I could see that Nacho was in his element – his first-class horsemanship trumped his egocentric attitude. I had a growing respect for his perfect balance, flexibility, strength, and control. After breaking into spontaneous applause, I remembered Polo etiquette fell more in line with a golf match than a football game. I curbed my emotions and yelled softly, "bravo, bravo!"

Ana and I declined a polo lesson and opted for swimming in the Olympic pool. "Okay, girls, work up an appetite, and I'll get my cook to start a wood-burning fire for an outdoor *parrillada* (barbecue). Towels are in the pool house."

"*El almuerzo esta listo*" (Lunch is ready,) shouted Diego, the stable hand/cook. We were served grilled tenderloin and, tasty but tough, *entraña* (skirt steak) with *chimichurri* sauce. Grilled potatoes and a large shared salad of palm hearts and cherry tomatoes rounded out the meal. For dessert, we were served homemade *dulce de leche* ice cream. Yow, I'd have to do some more laps to liberate the calories, or better yet, I'd take a brisk walk around the manicured estate. That way, I'd allow Nacho and Ana to indulge in a *tête-a-tête* and catch up on any personal news.

As I walked over to the lake to try and spot the black swans Ana raved about, it dawned on me that perhaps the young up-and-coming men's fashion designer, Ralph Lauren, knew something that I didn't. The emblem he chose for his stylish men's clothing line portrays a polo player on a galloping horse! In his right hand, the rider holds a mallet in an attempt to strike a ball. Some even predict Lauren will soon be a global leader in design marketing and distribution of premium lifestyle products. The upstart designed his first Polo collection in the late 60s – a mere five years ago.

I could imagine that Ralf Lauren must have visited Argentina before having his emblem brainstorm. Could it be that your modern-day American male's fantasy is playing Polo? As strange as it seemed, Lauren's marketing strategy was working.

Making my way back to the hacienda, I spotted Diego at the stable and passed by to bid him and the ponies farewell. He was exercising the yearlings in the fenced-in pasture and waved for me to come over. *"Mira, Mira, ella camina sin cojear."* (Look, look, she's walking without a limp.) *"El ungüento funcionó!"* (The ointment worked!) *"Nacho será loco de content!"* (Nacho will be over the moon!)

Diego went sprinting back to the house to find Nacho and break the good news that his favorite yearling, Melinda, was not lame anymore but galloping around with the other ponies.

I looked up, thanked our heavenly healer, and then traipsed behind Diego at a slower pace. I could hear laughter coming from the pool and found Nacho and Ana sprawled out on a sun bed, taking in the last rays. Diego waved his arms around flamboyantly, explaining to Nacho that his favorite yearling was as good as new.

By now, it was late afternoon, and Ana announced that we'd have to be getting back to the City since she promised Bautista she'd have his car back by 7 pm. I sighed while reflecting on the glorious, fairytale day.

As Nacho walked us to the car, I expressed my deep gratitude for his awesome hospitality. It was rare for a man to be so handsome and talented yet kind and well-mannered. His wealth and good fortune had not spoiled him.

As we approached the car, Nacho cupped my hand with his strong, calloused grip, placed it palm down over his heart, and held it in place for what seemed an eternity. He then looked directly into my eyes and whispered, "Thank you for becoming a part of my life – I will never forget this day. An angel has sent you here. Melinda thanks you also."

They say, 'eyes are a window to the soul,' and I experienced a close-up view of a tender, gracious soul. What could have been considered melodramatic, I received with the sincerity that it was meant.

Nacho swept Ana off the ground and gently placed her in the driver's seat. "Expect to see me sometime soon in Ibiza - I have a European tournament coming up in May." Nacho then grazed his lips across Ana's forehead and said, "*Hasta pronto, querida,*" (See you soon, darling.) He then remained in the same spot until we were out of sight.

I was stunned as I sat there meditating on the jumble of elements that birthed the definition of *a perfect day in the country*. We rode back to the City in silence. As Ana pulled up in front of my hotel, she looked at me with moist eyes and said, "He stole my heart when I was eighteen, and I've never quite recovered." It was the only time I'd ever seen the vulnerable side of Ana. She quickly recovered her smile and said with exuberance, "See you tomorrow!"

Having often heard the expression 'Latin Lover,' I had now experienced the true definition. That intrinsic quality is not something that can be learned or copied. I discovered that what I witnessed was not a plot or a gimmick - it was raw, transparent, momentary emotion that was unabashedly transmitted with all sincerity. It was mindboggling and illogical but true. I was on my way to understanding a unique breed beyond analysis and was all the better for it.

I had slept as never before and awoke electrified - ready to head back to the bohemian quarter for a final sift through the market stalls. I also surprised Bautista by joining his morning tango class as a paying client. Wanting to invite him and Ana out to lunch before heading off to Rio the following day, I was fully aware that their input enabled me to experience Buenos Aires in an unequaled and unforgettable way.

By now, I felt like an intermediate tango student and was flattered that Bautista again chose me as his partner. I strutted my stuff and inserted a few more intricate kicks without fumbling. No, nothing worse than being a hypocrite – no false humility for me. I realized humility was overrated since it was like underwear, essential but indecent if it showed.

Ana met us at El Obrero for our farewell lunch, and Sr. Guillermo placed us at the best table. All eyes darted our way since we looked pretty theatrical, and everyone there was on the lookout for the rich and famous. Bautista was dashing with his black tango ensemble - his shirt casually unbuttoned to the waist. Ana wore another knock-out micro mini and, wearing my Panama fedora, someone asked me for my autograph. I scribbled Carly Simon, not to disappoint her fan.

There was a buzz that Maradona, the teen 'wonder boy' of soccer, was in the corner with his trainer and a few other players. Signed soccer jerseys were strung across the ceiling on a cord, thus honoring the legend of nimble-footed international soccer elite.

I had mixed feelings about leaving Buenos Aires. It was a city that plucked at my heartstrings. It was a city where I could live – cosmopolitan enough that it felt European, yet it incorporated an exciting blend of Hispanic and indigenous traditions.

Back on the colorful street, we embraced with sincere hugs – *"No adiós,* but merely, *hasta luego."* (No goodbyes, but merely, see you later). I'd see Ana back in Ibiza within four months, and perhaps Bautista would emigrate there one day. I thanked them both for their warm caress of friendship and hospitality and blew them kisses as I walked away. I would be heading for my ultimate destination in South America - Rio de Janeiro!

11. RIO DE JANEIRO, BRAZIL

The flight from Buenos Aires to Rio was only three hours, so that would put me into the city at about noon, with plenty of time to find my way to the iconic Copacabana Beach. I settled back into my seat, looking forward to catching up with journal entries and reviewing highlighted paragraphs in my Smith Wigglesworth book. What good fortune, I had the window seat for great views, and a Portuguese couple plopped down in the other two seats. I couldn't understand a word they were saying. Just as well, I opened my journal and was glad to have some uninterrupted hours.

With about twenty minutes left before arriving at the Galeao Airport, I started to get that familiar drum roll and then the swarm of butterflies, signifying a new adventure was in store. I was on the home stretch - Rio had been my destination since my South American trip was first birthed in the subway of New York.

When Ruggero, my friend from Rome, leaped over the center partition of the escalator at Times Square and 42nd Street, offering me bargain-priced tickets to anywhere - Rio de Janeiro popped into my mind. Since the stops were unlimited, I decided on eight capitals of South America. Why not? However, Ruggero warned me that his brother, a TWA agent, said not to change or re-route the ticket. The only downside was I had to pay cash, but all that for 200 dollars was an absolute steal. I guess TWA had to drum up business for the post-holiday slump.

I wore my hair in a high ponytail to look less suspicious and my clean jeans and white shirt to appear anonymous. I breezed through customs/immigration with flying colors and headed to the hotel info desk. Without making reservations, I always found an adequate hostel with an airport agent. Of all the airports I'd landed in over the past three years, I never had a language problem. Someone always spoke some version of English, if only to fleece the American tourists. However, I hit a roadblock in Rio. Spoken Portuguese was not remotely similar to Spanish, and no one spoke Spanglish.

The exchange rate with the Brazilian Real was outrageous. Every dive listed in the info catalog was too expensive. I chose a dismal-looking hostel that was not remotely near anything of interest. Oh well, everything would work out; it always did, la-la-la. By now, I had a heavy, bulging bag and roll-on hand luggage that fit into the plane's overhead compartment.

I found my way to the bus, even if it was a rip-off. Only twelve miles to the mid-city terminal, and there I would have to get a taxi. From then on, the bus system and metro would suffice. I waited an eternity for a cab, and when we finally arrived near the center, utter pandemonium broke loose. The traffic-frazzled city was thick with dust and pollution. I had a flashback of my luxury Sheraton in Buenos Aires and wished I was there.

Shaking off my negative attitude and embracing Rio with a smile was the only way to survive. I was armed with three names of friends of friends, along with their phone numbers. My rule of thumb was to call my contacts from a hotel, not a bus station. It seemed less desperate and a lot classier. The taxi pulled up to a grim, brown cement-block hostel. I paid the exorbitant fare and lugged my belongings into the makeshift reception. At least I was given a ground-floor room with a bathroom down the hall.

I opened the door, and to my dismay, there was a big fat roach, belly up, in the middle of the floor. I'm not sure what was worse - the roach or the fluorescent green color of the shabby room. Curiously enough, the bed was ridiculously high. Okay, I had extra long legs to hop onto the spring-less mattress - but what about small people? They'd need a step ladder. I sat down, perched upon my bed, and a single tear rolled down my left cheek. I dried it with the back of my hand and decided, no matter what, I would have the time of my life!

Hoisting my belongings onto the bed, I pulled out my bikini and crammed it into my shoulder bag. The receptionist pointed me to the bus that went to Copacabana. As grim as my hostel was, it was only two blocks from the beach road. I hopped onto bus 432, and after a fifteen-minute ride along the seafront, I spotted the mythical Copacabana Hotel and pressed the buzzer to get off. I walked briskly towards the hotel with confidence.

When I emerged from the revolving door, I was blasted with refreshing air conditioning and the heavenly scent of coffee and donuts. I resisted the urge to pounce on the courtesy donuts and guzzle some coffee and casually continued to the lounge, where I sat down to get my bearings. I cooly spied out the layout. I spotted the pool and the ladies' room, where I could change into my bikini. I'd wear my long white blouse unbuttoned, over my swimsuit, as if it were a beachwear accessory.

I was getting ready to make my move when a dashing young waiter asked me what I wanted to drink. "Uh, a coke, please." Ugh, he caught me off guard - oh well, I was thirsty. The coke was served in a frosty glass with a slice of lemon. At least the efficient waiter spoke English so that I could pick his brain. He returned with pretzels and peanuts – perfect.

"This is my first trip to Rio. Could you suggest the best beach?"

"Yes, madam, the Copacabana beach in front of you. It is two and a half miles long, and the promenade is the most famous worldwide. The currents are mild so that you can swim safely."

"Thanks for that tip - I really appreciate it," I replied. "By the way, do you have a public phone here, not to go back to my room?" For my conscience, it *would* be easier than a bus ride back to my room at Hostel Horrible.

"Yes, the phones are in the alcove to the right of reception." He then whispered, "Try Ipanema Beach. It's less than two miles south of here, and the atmosphere is younger and livelier."

"Thanks, so kind of you to share that info!" I wondered if that meant I needed to tip the nice guy. The coke was nearly the price of my room. At least I'd finish up all the nuts and pretzels. I had the bright idea to call my contacts from the hotel phone, so when they asked me where I was, I could honestly reply *Copacabana Hotel*. It had a better ring to it than Hostel Javier.

"Hello, may I speak with Mrs. Astrid Meyer?" I asked politely.

"Um momento, por favor" (One moment please).

"Olá, esta é a Sra. Meyer, com quem estou falando?" (Hello, this is Mrs. Meyer, with whom am I speaking?).

"Do you speak English? I am a friend of your daughter, Petra. I just arrived in Rio."

"What wonderful news - I would love to meet you and hear all about my dear Petra."

"I was with her several months ago in Paris, and she asked me to call you if I made it to Rio," I explained.

"What a fortunate stroke of serendipity! Can you come over this afternoon so I can meet you? I plan to go to the mountains tomorrow to escape this awful heat. I have a huge favor to ask you."

"Sure, I can come over. What time and where are you? Petra didn't give me your address."

"Tell me where you are, and I'll tell you the shortest way to get to my condo."

"I'm at the Copacabana Hotel right now," I said honestly.

"Perfect, you're not far away - I'm on the beachfront of Ipanema. It's only a short taxi ride from where you are. Better yet, come over in half an hour for some late lunch. My building is Ocean View - twelfth floor, apartment four. I'll advise the doorman, and he'll let you in."

"Ah, well . . . . . err . . . okay, I guess I can change my plans. I'll be there in half an hour," I stuttered. What did I have to lose? I just hoped the huge favor was something I could handle.

At least I'd walk around the hotel pool and check it out for another day since I knew the Atlantic would be freezing. And yes, I'd take a short stroll along the emblematic, undulating black-and-white mosaic promenade synonymous with Rio. It was all quite surreal, but it felt right! Randomly, a tune popped into my mind, and I started humming, "The Girl from Ipanema goes walking . . ."

Before leaving the hotel, I freshened up in the ladies' room and was glad I had chosen a mother-friendly outfit to travel in. I was good at mesmerizing mothers. I looked respectable and would be a charming bearer of good news for Petra's mom.

When I first met Petra in Paris at Alan Kowaski's impressive townhouse, I wondered what such an understated, wholesome-looking girl was doing there. Usually, Alan was into flashy, glitzy ladies – at least in Ibiza. Petra was tall and slim with shoulder-length auburn hair that was thick and wavy. She didn't conceal her freckles with foundation but appeared to be a well-scrubbed, studious German student.

Surprisingly enough, Petra turned out to be Brazilian. She explained that her parents emigrated from Germany to Brazil after World War II. Her mother wanted her to perfect her French in Paris and absorb some European culture and refinement. How she ended up with Alan, I'll never know. He was into promoting rock stars and was presently organizing and booking top pop groups for tours around France. Well, they say opposites attract.

Petra was quite hesitant about striking out to discover Paris, so I became her friend and guide. She insisted I stay in one of their guest rooms whenever I was in Paris, so our friendship grew. I introduced her to the street fashion boutiques in the Saint-Germain des Prés area – then the haute couture designs in Rue du Faubourg Saint-Honoré. There, I had my over-the-knee kid leather custom boots made during my first visit to the 'City of Light' and excitement.

Petra was happy to discover the famous *Les Puces de Saint-Ouen* (Flea Market of Saint-Ouen) and all the art deco shops where I hawked the treasures I found in the London pre-dawn buyers' markets. We went to the latest American 'original voice' films at Odeon and often ate out in the nearby Vietnamese Restaurants. I felt pretty protective of Petra – she had been thrown into the deep end of a fast and furious lifestyle without knowing it.

* * *

A few taxis were waiting outside the Copacabana Hotel, so I decided to treat myself since I felt luxurious and didn't want to risk being late for my rendezvous with Petra's mom. The hotel doorman opened the taxi door wearing a huge smile and a bright red uniform – then he slammed the door with a frown. Perhaps he expected a tip?

"Ipanema Beach – Ocean View Apartments," I told the taxi driver – feeling rich and important. In less than ten minutes, I arrived at my destination and saw the building's concierge was outside waiting for me. "Miss Tyke?" I nodded, and he opened the door. Presto! As I rocketed to the 12th floor, I looked forward to the panoramic expanse of the Ipanema beachfront.

What a posh elevator and delicious thick carpet. I rang the doorbell and an unexpectedly petite lady, looking indigenous, said, "*Boa tarde*" (Good afternoon). I figured that Petra took after her father's side of the family. Then, a tall, slim lady of about fifty came into view and confirmed she was Petra's mom.

"Hello, I'm Astrid, Petra's mother." It was apparent - Petra was a dead-ringer clone. I formally extended my hand, but she hugged me. Not very German, but I responded warmly.

"Welcome to Rio de Janeiro! I am thrilled that an angel sent you here just in the nick of time."

"Time for what?" I asked politely.

"Come in and sit down – what would you like to drink?"

POW, what a spectacular view! "I'll just have some water, please."

"How about some iced tea? Maria just made some freshly brewed Darjeeling."

"Oh great, yes, that would be perfect," I smiled.

"Now tell me, how is my precious Petra?"

"She was doing great when I last saw her two months ago."

"You see, I'm so worried that she's married a man who is after her inheritance."

Gulp, "Well, Alan seems to be in love with her," I exaggerated. I thought - so that's it. I hoped Petra's mother wasn't right, but it did seem to ring true. I wondered if the huge favor she would ask me was to poison Alan or, perhaps, push him off the third floor of his mansion? I started to feel very protective over Petra and furious with that scoundrel, Alan.

"Can't Petra put a block on her bank account?" I asked.

"Yes, she can, but she won't. She's of age, and the accounts are in her name. I think she feels if she blocks her accounts, she'll lose her husband."

Bright deduction, I thought to myself. I suspected Alan was up to something. Alan was such a flirt and really paid no attention to Petra. All I could think to say was, "Maybe we should pray for Petra and the situation."

"Oh, I do," confessed Astrid, and then she started to sniffle. "I just have to give it to the Lord because there is nothing I can think to do."

"Maybe we should pray that Alan's pop-star tours are successful. Or that he would acquire a conscience?" I offered with a heavy heart.

"Sorry, Tyke, this is your first day in Rio, and I don't want to put a damper on it. The favor I wanted to ask you is if you would kindly stay in my condo while I'm gone for two weeks to the mountains. Maria, my housekeeper, is afraid to sleep here alone. I know you must be very comfortable in your hotel, but this would mean a lot to me. I would be able to leave with peace of mind. I cannot bear to think about being here for Carnival. It's so hot, and there is so much noise and traffic. The city doubles in population, starting in a few days."

"Don't you worry! Of course, I'll keep your housekeeper company while you're gone," I muttered, fighting off a euphoric urge to scream and leap for joy.

"I cannot thank you enough! Lunch is ready – do you mind if we sit inside since the terrace is steaming," explained Astrid.

"Absolutely not. The view from here is just as good," I said comfortingly.

"Maria is a good cook, and she'll do all the shopping - just let her know when you want to eat lunch or dinner here. She will be so happy when I tell her you can stay."

"I don't speak Portuguese, but I've managed with sign language throughout Europe, the Middle East, and the Far East. I'm a good communicator; I'll be just fine." I could hardly keep my cool. I hoped I wouldn't throw up from the excitement of it all. I breathed in deeply, 1-2-3-4, and out again 1-2-3-4.

"When would you like me to come over tomorrow?" I asked.

"I'm leaving at 9 am, so any time after that, the sooner, the better," replied Astrid.

"Would you like another filet mignon or more potatoes or egg *farofa*? There's a lot left."

"No thanks, Astrid, I've had plenty - it was delicious"!

"Would you prefer passion fruit or *brigadeiro* (condensed milk, cocoa powder, butter, and chocolate sprinkles)?

"I love passion fruit and haven't had any since Bali."

They say, 'for a dream to come true, you must wake up first.' This setup far exceeded anything I could have imagined. If I was dreaming, I didn't want to wake up.

"Please, stay as long as you like, Tyke, but you'll have to excuse me – I must run to the drug store and then start packing. I can't wait to spend time with you when I return!"

"Thanks for a lovely lunch, Astrid - I have a list of things to see and do, so I'll be off. Have a cool time in the mountains, and we'll catch up in two weeks," I reassured her.

With an air kiss on both cheeks, I was off humming, *"The girl from Ipanema . . . . . .!"*

Back down on the lawn, I felt I had to do some *jetés,* or a few cartwheels, to release the euphoria that had been bubbling up. I needed a plan of action - a list would put some order into my jumbled, scattered thoughts. Okay, I had to grin and bear one night in my Hostel Horrible, and I'd be in paradise the following day.

My top priority was to see The Protector of Rio - the enormous statue of Christ the Redeemer, with His arms outstretched to all humanity. Next on my list was to purchase a ticket to *the* Carnival night extravaganza. It would be held in a tent as large as the Barnum & Bailey three-ring circus. There were also special sky-high priced VIP tickets for boxes that overlooked the dancing masses. Those prestige boxes were where the movie stars, sports elite, and vulgarly rich hung out. On second thought, I'd better get the ticket first since the statue wouldn't be going anywhere.

It was nearly 6 pm, so I returned to my roachy room. I wanted to advise the receptionist that I'd leave early the following morning. It had been a long day, starting in Buenos Aires, and I wanted to get settled into my hostel before dark since the neighborhood appeared dubious. I was warned not to wander around at night since the crime rate was off the charts. Anyway, I wanted to have an early start the following day.

Astounded that I slept so well - I jumped down from my bed, gathered my belongings, and headed for the checkout. I decided to taxi to Ipanema, leave my stuff at Astrid's condo, and then take the bus to the ticket office before noon. It was only three days until Carnival, and I couldn't afford to miss the primary reason I came to Rio. I inherited *Mardi Gras* genes from my New Orleans ancestors, and I was drawn to Rio like a queen bee to honey.

I did challenge myself at times, wondering if I was more interested in dropping the phrase, "Oh yes, Carnival in Rio was divine," or if I really desired to get hot and sweaty and dance the samba 'til I dropped. I hoped it was the latter, but I wasn't sure.

"Yikes," I gasped as the bus stopped. I couldn't believe what I saw – at least a hundred people were in line at the ticket office. I looked around for a slick ticket scalper. There was none. I was ready to pay double to ease the agony of waiting, but against my instincts, I stood at the end of the line. Three hours later, I drifted away, drenched in sweat, clenching a soggy red ticket. That ticket was my entrance to utopia - the makeshift dance floor within the titanic tent that would transform my life. For better or worse, it would become future nostalgia.

I must admit, I was proud of my long-suffering patience and consoled myself in the refreshing condo pool back at Astrid's place.

Maria, the housekeeper, had prepared a mouth-watering lunch, and I thanked my lucky stars for so much good fortune until my conscience started to nag me.

"If you were willing to pay double for one entrance ticket, why didn't you buy a few extra tickets for some of the *favelados* (slum dwellers) waiting in line with you?" Yes, why didn't I think of that? I was disappointed that I had missed an opportunity to pass on some of the blessings I had received. I would do better next time.

Maria had a meltdown when I tried to wash the dishes after lunch. She wouldn't even allow me to pour myself water. Looking insulted, she grabbed my bottled water and filled my glass. Maria seemed so grateful that she could wait on me hand and foot. It was so unjust but very comforting. I would look for a unique gift for her.

* * *

Astrid had told me I was welcome to use her phone for local calls, so I decided to call the other two contacts I'd been given. My jet-set German friend from Ibiza, Eva, had recommended I phone a guy named Axel. He sounded like a Formula 1 driver, but she said he was actually into banking and had lived in Brazil for the past decade.

"Hello, may I speak with Axel?" I asked boldly.

"Speaking, and who are you?" he retaliated.

"My name is Tyke, and I'm friends with Eva and David from Ibiza."

"How are they, and where are you?" Axel asked.

"I'm at Ipanema Beach, staying with a friend's mother. I arrived yesterday from Buenos Aires and will be here for a few weeks. Eva said to be sure and call you to let you know that she and David are looking forward to meeting up with you in London this Spring."

Axel's tone changed, sounding like a long, lost friend. "Oh, how fantastic - you're here just in time for Carnival."

"Yes, I planned it that way," I laughed.

"Well, my girlfriend and I will be going to the event of the year next Friday if you'd like to join us."

"Do you mean the Carnival samba-dancing event in the huge tent?" I asked.

"Yes, I have a few extra passes for the VIP boxes that overlook the samba competition, and we'll be snacking on caviar and sipping champagne. It *is* the event of the year!"

"Wow, how amazing! You've twisted my arm! Thanks a million."

"Give me your phone number, and I'll let you know when Sonia, my lady, wants to arrive. We're not far away, so we can swing by and pick you up Friday evening. Remember to dress up – anything goes."

"Awesome! I look forward to meeting you two and dancing 'til dawn."

There was a lesson to be learned. It is best to phone *all* contacts first before standing in the scorching sun for three hours to buy an obsolete ticket. Ah, but I could now offer the ticket to Maria and still buy her a gift. So, not all was lost - my blunder had a silver lining.

I had only forty-eight hours to polish up my samba before D-day. I realized that Copacabana Beach was the accessible epicenter for learning carnival samba. That dance had become the heart of

Rio - with its pulsating rhythm and African influences that rippled and joggled every existing muscle of the anatomy. I think Brazilian men from the favelas were born with 'six-packs' - even children had muscles. All the guys on the public buses doubled up their t-shirts to expose their impressive midriffs.

Copacabana Beach was a mere hop, skip, and a jump from Ipanema, so I was there in a flash. I found a small group of shirtless and bikini-clad dancers and mimed their moves with expertise. I was familiar with the basic samba, but they perfected it in quadruple time.

It was all about the 2/4 - 4/4 rhythm in a major key, with a happy, upbeat tempo! The marginalized from the poorest neighborhoods became the super-stars during Carnival. They had been creating their flashy ensembles the entire year – sinking most of their savings into three days of non-stop dancing.

The samba schools, also originating in the shantytown district, had become the soul of Brazil – bringing the people together, regardless of their economic position or class. Either dance or soccer was the slum dwellers' ticket out of misery. Afro-Brazilian Pelé is regarded as perhaps the greatest soccer/football player in the game's history.

Struggling in the sand to capture the 4/4 beat, I shifted my weight from one leg to the other – throwing my hips from side to side. I was determined to nail that lightning-fast rhythm. Breathless after about twenty minutes, I left a hefty tip in the hat and moved on. I would practice back in the cool condo.

Of utmost importance was my outfit. I couldn't compete with the samba queens, but I'd do my best to dazzle. With my humidityfrizzed hair, deep dark tan, and XL lips – I could have easily passed for a *Pardo* (a mix of African, European, and Indian ancestry). My lengthy hair concealed my lack of backside oomph, but I'd try to shake a tail feather as fast as I could.

I passed several carnival shops selling glittering bits and pieces, but nothing to compare with the meticulous homemade creations of the samba schoolgirls. I settled on some sequined short-shorts and a matching midriff top. I then purchased a rhinestone tiara that I could adorn with plumage - full stop. I didn't want to overdo it. The Brazilian dancers wore skimpy, colorful thongs and bikini tops, so in comparison, I would be dressed conservatively.

There was so much excitement on the streets, with neighborhood parties breaking loose and people dancing everywhere. I walked the beachfront for two days, absorbing the party atmosphere and studying the local dancers - awaiting Friday evening to roll around.

Axel called Friday noon to let me know he and his girlfriend would pick me up at 10 pm for the 'event of the year.' It seemed a bit late, but he said it was better not to arrive too early and hang around until things warmed up. I hoped my ensemble would not be too boring. I told Axel that I'd be waiting downstairs at the designated hour. Tossing a shawl around my shoulders, I covered up a bit while waiting.

A BMW pulled into the circular entrance of the condo at 10 pm sharp. A normal-looking guy of about forty was at the wheel, and a blond lady was in the passenger seat. I waved, and he lowered his window, "Yes, can I help you," asked Axel.

"Yes, I'm waiting for a guy called Axel. My name is Tyke."

"Oh, what a surprise, we didn't expect you to look so authentic," muttered Axel. "The door is open; please jump in," he stuttered. The lady was pretty in a very mundane way. She fit the bill of a Sloane Ranger - the typical upper-class Brit in London who lived near Sloane Square. They were girls who looked like they'd been trapped in a time warp – wearing tweeds, pearls, and twin sets.

"So amazing of you two to invite me to join you for this incredible happening," I said with a smile.

Turning around with eyes as large as saucers, Sonia glared at me and said, "What an amazing wig you are wearing! How did you pump your lips up, or are they wax? You look like a bona fide ghetto girl. You will blend in perfectly with the masses!"

"Thanks," I replied. I was so pleased with myself for achieving the 'look' I so desperately wanted to capture. I started to feel really self-confident with my choice of attire and couldn't wait to dance up a storm. Axel and Sonia must have felt spellbound, bringing someone so precisely adorned for the occasion.

Axel pulled up to the tent entrance and handed me my ticket, explaining that he and Sonia would park the car and meet me in the VIP box. I was elated that I didn't have to make an entrance with that outmoded couple – they'd put a damper on my entry. Perhaps they were nice people but so old-fashioned.

Eva, our mutual friend, was a dead ringer for Catherine Deneuve. She had been married briefly to a Spanish duke and still carried the title of *duchess* in her passport. We were like chalk and cheese - she wore classical designer, and I sported the latest trend or vampy beaded dresses from the twenties. Perhaps we were each other's alter egos, but we meshed well together and had fun. I think Eva liked to shock her pretentious friends with my unconventional quirks. That was the charm of Ibiza.

As I gracefully climbed the stairs to the 'luxury loge,' a flurry of paparazzi jumped out and started snapping their cameras wildly. I was embarrassed by the commotion, but nevertheless, I wallowed in the attention. I wondered if they had mistaken me for Carly Simon - strange since I wasn't wearing my fedora hat.

Once on the platform, searching for my seat number, I heard a continued ruckus going on and turned around to see what was happening. Raquel Welch was trailing me. She wore a long white sequined gown with a plunging neckline and a crown. Of course, she was the reigning queen of curves in the USA. I was willing to share the limelight and was relieved that I wasn't the only one wearing sequins. I welcomed her with an air kiss.

"Hello Raquel, welcome to Rio," I exclaimed.

"Thanks, forgive me, I've forgotten your name," she replied.

"Tyke, from New Orleans," I said with enthusiasm. Raquel smiled and turned away. I hope she didn't feel envious of my youth and lanky legs. She was at least a decade older. Oh well, I was here to have the time of my life! An array of drums beat, tambourines rattled, and whistles blew from below. With such pulsating rhythm, I couldn't sit still - however, I waited politely for Axel and Sonia to arrive. I would then confess that since I didn't drink champagne and the caviar was too salty, I would go downstairs and dance with the crowds.

Phew, Axel and Sonia finally arrived, and when I sheepishly explained that I was heading downstairs to dance, Sonia appeared relieved. Oh well, different strokes for different folks. I hoped I didn't intimidate Sonia - I certainly wasn't after her boring banker fiancé.

As I descended the steep steps, I heard Axel calling, "Hey Tyke, check back with us in a few hours." Good idea, I thought – I knew I'd be thirsty by then, and maybe they'd have a few edible *hors d'oeuvres*.

Working my way into the innermost sanctuary of the dance floor, I heard the drums reverberating through every fiber of my being. I not only heard and felt the rhythm – I became the rhythm. The double-time samba was infectious. I felt like I had an outboard motor connected to my hips.

Being surrounded and immersed in the reckless samba sound made me question my ancestral roots. I felt I was transported to another dimension - was I in a dance trance? I was on automatic pilot and wondered if I would continue my frenetic pace until dawn. Whoa! The music stopped – what happened? Had the world come to an end?

No, the female individual samba competition was going to begin. Everyone vacated the dance floor, and sixteen girls, each representing the best of her samba school, lined up in the order of her performance. There was a considerable amount at stake here - the winner would not only receive adulation plus a monetary reward - she would receive a one-way ticket out of hell. She'd have an opportunity to shake the dust off her spiked heels and prance out of the slums.

There was live international news coverage, and the winner would be swept into the spotlight of the public eye and regurgitated onto the stages of the world's top clubs. I heard Las Vegas scouts were waiting to bag their prey.

Feeling dehydrated and famished after my dance-a-thon, I returned to the VIP box to regain forces and secure a bird's eye view of the upcoming competition. My body glistened from samba sweat, and I noticed a few reproachful glances that I interpreted as sour grapes. The rest of the ladies in the luxury loge were overripe and past their prime. There was even an audible complaint, "I didn't know they allowed riff-raff into our elite box."

However, I remembered it would be edifying if I were generous with encouragement. It would be verbal sunshine and cost me nothing - warming hearts and enriching lives. These older people in my box needed some affirmation. I didn't intend to show off my youth and vitality. It just happened. I would spread some encouragement to each of my inmates.

The competition lasted about an hour since each contestant had four minutes to impress the judges. I agreed on the winner – she displayed more shakes per second than a malted milkshake. The crowds roared with approval, and then the drums and whistles advised the masses that it was time for everyone to start dancing again. I had a calorie rush from all the appetizers and found it impossible to sit still.

Explaining that I was ready to soak up more samba with the masses below, Alex reminded me to touch base with them by 3 am. "Remember Tyke, this celebration initiates Carnival - there will be four more days of parades and dancing in the streets, so pace yourself."

Growing up in New Orleans, I was all too familiar with Carnival chaos. There was usually a week of mayhem before *Mardi Gras* (Fat Tuesday). The following day, Wednesday, commenced lean lent and sobriety. At least that was the idea amongst pious Catholics if they actually existed - I never met one. However, they refrained from eating meat on Fridays as penance, and instead, they ate shrimp, oysters, crabs, or fish. I never understood the logic of that punishment.

Anyway, I still had two hours to dance myself silly until my time was up, and I'd have to return to the 'box' of bitter-sweet party poopers and reconnect with my hosts. Feeling wired, I figured I could find a party in my Ipanema neighborhood, but first, I'd check on Maria. I wanted to ensure she wasn't wide awake waiting for me. After all, I told Astrid I would keep Maria company.

Axel and Sonia dropped me off at my Ocean View condo without any fanfare or follow-up invite, so I imagined they were dog-tired and ready to conk out. I waved goodbye and blew kisses from the door as they sped off into the night.

The words, *pace yourself*, were ringing in my ears, and I decided to give in and go to bed. Maria wasn't home yet – she was probably still rocking out at the Carnival gala. Good for her! Yep, Axel was right. The Carnival festivities raged on. Dancing and singing rippled like wildfire through the stands lining the jam-packed streets. Each samba group, with up to six thousand dancers, presented a symbolic theme with a specially written samba song, costumes, and giant floats.

Rio had been my target and the goal of my trip, but now I was beginning to experience 'fun fatigue' . . . . .if that was possible. I was coming to the end of my rope, or rather, my tether. I sensed a spiritual force drawing me back to my source. I felt as if God Almighty, in His mercy, had me graciously attached to a retractable leash. It allowed me to wander around at free will, just so far, then when I was nearing the end - my Master would gently reel me back in again. What an incredible comfort.

Forty percent of the Brazilians in Rio lived in the *favelas* – they worked hard and scrimped and saved to celebrate for several days without restraint. That was not my story – I began to feel quite decadent since I had lived a 'my way' lifestyle for so many years. It was all about balance – being in this world without becoming worldly. Trying to keep an eternal perspective without getting caught up in a fleeting 'feel good' syndrome - learning to enjoy beauty and artistry without becoming addicted to it.

I was starting to understand the highlighted verse in my Gideon Bible, "*Delight yourself in the Lord and he will give you the desires of your heart. . . .*" (Psalm 37:4). I now realized that those desires in my heart were placed there by The Almighty. Primarily the desire to be loved and to give love.

I had been wired to give back – something I couldn't take credit for. It had been only several weeks since I had left La Paz. My focus was on street children, and I planned to help orphaned and deprived kids here in Rio. But where are they? I heard the police were often rough with them, especially during Carnival. They were a nuisance during the high season in Rio. There were possibly a million visitors for Carnival - helping to sustain a considerable chunk of the city's income. I guess the police shuffled them out of sight.

* * *

Next on my list of must-see 'wonders' while in Rio was Christ the Redeemer (*Cristo Redentor*). Like Jesus Christ, the statue is believed to protect the urban environment, similar to a roof over your head. *Cristo Redentor*, as important as any shelter, with arms outstretched ninety-three feet wide - is thought to protect the soul while welcoming the world to Rio.

The Redeemer stands ninety-eight feet high and commands the most magnificent 360º view of Sugarloaf Mountain, Guyana Bay, Copacabana, and Ipanema Beaches. The massive statue is situated on top of Corcovado Mountain, on a peak of 2,300 feet. Only about six miles from the center of Rio, it is accessible by bus, train, and taxi. The key is to wait for a cloudless day so the views would be optimal.

I figured I really should call my third contact, Nico. I didn't want Petra to think I was ungrateful since she raved about how entertaining he was and very sportive - plus good-looking. As she went to school with Nico, I knew he'd be several years younger, thus too juvenile for me. However, I called him.

"Hello, may I please speak with Nico?"

"Who is speaking, please?"

"My name is Tyke - I'm a friend of Petra Meyer from Paris."

"Oh, how is dear Petra? She's like a daughter," said the mother of Nico, I presumed.

"She was fine when I last saw her in November," I replied.

"My son Nico isn't here right now. I'll have him call you."

"I'm staying at Petra's mother's place in Ipanema." The lady's voice converted into an embrace, and she said abruptly, "Wait, Nico just walked in."

"Hello, Nico here."

"Hi, I'm Tyke, a friend of Petra. I'm staying at her mom's condo in Ipanema!

"Whoa, say no more! I'm off to the country for the weekend but will be back on Monday. I'll take you to Corcovado, and we can have lunch in the clouds."

"Sounds great!" Good thing I called - I'd hold off on visiting Christ the Redeemer.

"I'll pick you up about 11 am," replied Nico, with an air of confidence.

"Good, I'll see you then," I answered coolly. Just as well, I thought, since there'd be a ton of tourists visiting the monument on the weekend. Especially with the crowds left over from Carnival, plus I still had a bit of adrenaline hangover.

Maria had been in the kitchen for at least an hour - cutting, chopping, and cooking. Wafts of wonderful food scents were elevating my appetite. I had probably lost at least three pounds dancing non-stop the past four days.

"*Almoço está pronto*" (Lunch is ready), announced Maria. I was starting to get the hang of the Portuguese accent. The vocabulary was a distant cousin to Spanish, but the accent was way out in left field.

"*Ya voy*" (I'm coming), I replied in Spanish. "What a spread!"

"*Feijoada*," beamed Maria.

"I recognized the succulent national dish. Black bean stew cooked with different cuts of salted and smoked pork, plus tomatoes, cabbage, and carrots. Rice, parsley, and peeled orange slices were served separately in earthen pots, plus a large mixed salad.

Salivating, I lifted my orange juice glass in honor of Maria's culinary performance and cheered, "Brava!" Then I dug into the familiar dish similar to New Orleans' number one soul food – red beans and rice. I felt the calorie rush and my face blushed as I scooped up my second large helping. I thanked Maria profusely and tried to help clear the table, but I was sternly stopped in my tracks.

Before getting bogged down in a digestive stupor, I decided to head up to the historical center. Bus 2017 would transport me nine miles up along Copacabana Beach and deposit me smack dab on the main square, a short stroll to Old Town Rio.

It was customary for an entire family to take a bus in their swimwear. I must admit, bus travel was slow but highly entertaining. Most bus people were likely to be undressed - on their way to a beach destination. I admired their lack of self-consciousness and blasé attitude about what they had or were missing. I felt well dressed in my cut-off jeans and off-the-shoulder smock top. Hoisting my blanket of hair up into a high ponytail, I stayed cool and showed off my huge hoop earrings.

It was good to walk off some calories from my mega-lunch and take in the sights of downtown Rio. I read on the bronze marker that the Portuguese royal family arrived in 1808 and built what is now called The Imperial Palace. That mansion would have blended into the New Orleans French Quarter, filled with Spanish architecture.

I discovered a charming pedestrian street lined with colonial mansions that must have housed the aristocrats and then rambled past the Tiradentes Palace – headquarters of the Brazilian National Congress until 1960. The Lapa Arches (an aqueduct that dominated the scenery) was a major tourist stop, and I felt like I was being swallowed up by the clicking masses. I guess it would take another week before the out-of-town Carnival crowds evaporated.

Another bronze marker explained that in 1888 slavery was abolished in all forms, and things slowly changed. Due to a lack of affordable housing, they didn't foresee that the favelas (slums) would spring up – giving birth to the samba.

My hair was almost kinky with the tropical climate, and I was constantly followed in the souvenir shops. Yes, I could have easily been mistaken for a local slum dweller. My deep tan and oversized lips confirmed what the shopkeepers were thinking. They always spoke to me in Portuguese – *O que você está procurando?*(What are you looking for?). My response, "Nothing," did not amuse them.

There were still no street children in sight. Perhaps I'd find some on the beach if they were banned from the Old City. I was ready to head back down to Ipanema to explore the eclectic shops and people-gaze from a quaint café. Ipanema had become my comfort zone. Back on the same bus headed south, I was once again slack-jawed by the jumble of illicitly dressed passengers that enabled swimwear to become obscene. Thongs on the locals worked, but gringos stuffed into Brazilian bikinis were a significant offense to the senses. I focused on the ocean.

Humming, "The girl from Ipanema . . . . ," I pressed the buzzer to get off at Copacabana, so I could gingerly zigzag down the wavy mosaic walkway and enjoy people goggling. Small groups of locals were still rocking out with radios blasting samba tunes as they burrowed their feet into the sand with a 4/4 beat. You could see sparks flying. On several occasions, I applauded and gave thumbs-up appreciation while popping some bills into their upturned hats.

Life was good in Rio. With luxurious, free accommodation on the iconic beach of Ipanema, I decided to scratch my flight to Caracas, Venezuela, and take advantage of an extra week in paradise. The fashion shows in Milan and Paris didn't start until mid-March, so I had time to zip back via New York City to London with time to spare.

* * *

I was on the lookout for Nico's cream-colored Mercedes. He said he'd pick me up at 'my' condo at 11 am. I hoped he hadn't forgotten. He came whizzing up the entrance waving, only ten minutes late. Screeching to a stop, he jumped out of his prestige car, addressing me in perfect English, "You must be Tyke!" He then proceeded to give me an air kiss on both cheeks. "Any friend of

Petra is a friend of mine." He opened my door and ushered me in with a whistle, "You sure have long legs – shall I adjust the seat for you?"

"No need," I replied, "this is perfect." I wore my cut-off jeans that seemed to have shrunk in the wash. My bright yellow midriff top accentuated my dark tan. I wore my hair free and wild and would hike it up if I got hot.

Nico looked North European with his sandy blond hair and huge green eyes. Perhaps, post-war, his ancestors also emigrated from Germany. He was about five-feet-ten and built like a gymnast – compact and muscular. I guess you could describe him as cute. He was too young for me, but he seemed to be an attentive and helpful guide for the day.

"I am so glad Petra gave you my name and number – I miss her so much. She had been my girlfriend since we were fourteen. Her mother sent her to Paris to a swanky finishing school, and she fell in love with a gold digger."

Not sure how to tactfully reply to Nico's tricky but accurate assessment, I supposed he heard all the details from Petra's heartbroken mother. "Well, maybe Petra will see the light, get fed up, and return to Rio," I replied comfortingly.

"I'm counting on it," whispered Nico, "But today is the perfect day to check out Corcovado Moutain and Christ the Redeemer," Nico added, "I can show you the best way to get there. Rock climbing to the statue is my first choice. The K2 route is only five hundred feet long, and every pitch offers interesting and varied climbing, from friction to knob face, to lieback - all with a breathtaking view."

Nico was so excited about taking me rock climbing - I hated to disappoint him, "Sorry Nico, but I don't have my rock climbing shoes with me." It was true. I hated disappointing him further by admitting I'd never been rock climbing. However, I climbed the mountains in the foothills of the Himalayas in Nepal. But I decided to keep that tidbit of info from him. I didn't want to entice Nico into thinking I was sportive - he was way out of my league.

"Too bad," replied Nico, "Petra and I used to go rock climbing almost every week, so I thought you'd enjoy it." I couldn't help but reflect on Petra's fear of shopping alone in Paris, so that data was hard to digest.

"We loved to go rock climbing on Sugar Loaf Mountain. It is one of the monolithic granite and quartz mountains that rise straight from the water's edge as you enter Guanabara Bay. I'll point it out to you when we get up to Christ the Redeemer. Hey, I know what you'd like, we'll go to the botanical gardens first, and then it's just a twenty-minute drive to Corcovado Mountain.

"Perfect, sounds like a dream," I replied with tempered enthusiasm. We arrived at the botanical garden in no time. The grand entrance to the gardens – nearly a mile long, was lined with a hundred and fifty Royal Palms. It was regal beyond description. Nico parked the car, paid our entrance fee, and we jumped into a souped-up golf cart.

Boy Wonder then zoomed around the magnificent park at breakneck speed. I wondered if we would get arrested or fined. He sped around at least thirty of the fifty acres, naming each exotic plant or tree and from where they were imported. Arriving back at the starting point, I had to catch my breath. My hair was matted, and I had whiplash of the neck, but I diplomatically raved about how much I enjoyed the whirlwind tour.

The next stop, Corcovado Mountain, situated in the beautiful Tijuca National Park, was one of the largest urban parks in the world. Nico explained that the hike started from Parque Lage and would take approximately one hour and a half up the mountain to arrive at the massive statue.

"Oh," I exclaimed, "I'm wearing my city boots. It would be easier with my worn-in hiking boots or tennis shoes."

"The out-and-back trail is about five miles and takes four hours to complete, but the route we're taking is a piece of cake. On the other hand, I could drive up to the parking lot in Paineiras. There they supply official vans to transport visitors up to the top."

"I would adore a nature walk, but to tell you the truth, I'm getting hungry – and I don't want to risk a hypoglycemic attack," I exaggerated.

"Well, I have a dark chocolate bar, just in case," smiled Nico.

"I'll try to hold out until we get to the restaurant. Perhaps if we drive to the parking lot and then van up, that would be the surefire way of arriving on time for lunch," I pleaded.

"Done! I just hate for you to miss the magnificent hiking trail experience. Next trip, bring your rock climbing shoes and hiking boots," insisted Nico.

"Absolutely," I exclaimed.

We made it to the parking lot in about fifteen minutes. Mid-way up the mountain, Niko left his car, and we were jammed into an official transport van that deposited us not far from the base of the statue. I saw glimpses of the iconic *Redeemer* at the top of a stairway to heaven.

"Oh, it looks like we still have a long climb," I commented.

"Only two hundred and twenty steps," confirmed Niko.

"Great, I need to pump some oxygen into my leg muscles," I said, proud of my anatomical knowledge.

"Yep, climbing stairs is a neat way to amp your core muscle power. It sculpts and tones your body. It also works the major muscles in your lower body – glutes, hamstrings, abs, quadriceps, and calves," explained Nico casually.

"Are you a personal trainer or physical education teacher?" I asked.

"No," laughed Nico, "I'm a maritime lawyer."

"You are by far the youngest and most athletic lawyer I've ever met," I said with sincere amazement.

"With your long legs, you'll be able to climb two steps at a time. By the way, do people here speak to you in Portuguese? You look exceedingly more *carioca* than I do," winked Nico.

"Oh yeah?" I queried. "What's *carioca*?"

"It is a demonym used to refer to anything related to the City of Rio de Janeiro. You could be a poster girl for Brazil."

I laughed, "When I was in Buenos Aires, I was Italian. Now that I'm in Brazil, I've become Brazilian. If I'm in New York, I'm Jewish. However, when I'm in Paris or North Africa, I'm Arab. You see, I'm a chameleon - it takes a lot of practice."

We were nearly halfway up the steps when I glimpsed a welcoming sign, Corcovado Restaurant. Hallelujah, my glutes, hamstrings, abs, quadriceps, and calves could have a rest and a refueling. Nico politely opened the door, and I ran in. We were ushered onto the patio and seated under a large green umbrella with stunning, clear views. The waiter greeted Nico by name, and their ensuing conversation gave me time to excuse myself.

Before devouring lunch, it was the ideal time to do a few ballet exercises using the protective railing on the patio to hoist up one leg, then the other. Stretching was strategic – it helped elongate my tendons and enabled more flexibility. After a few lunges, I returned to my chair, hungry enough to eat a horse – or at least a pony.

Nico suggested we have thin slices of filet mignon with a unique melted cheese, roasted potatoes, and a mixed salad with everything under the sun. I agreed while trying to stifle my salivating glands from producing an untimely drool and spoke loudly to muffle my stomach's rumbling.

Feeling filled up and satisfied, we continued our trek up the rest of the steps that led to the base of the colossal statue of Christ. It was all about the incredible views because it was hard to focus on the statue at such close range. Nico informed me that 'Cristo Redentor' stood ninety-eight feet high with an arm span of ninety-three feet.

He added, "Christ the Redeemer was built using reinforced concrete and had an outer shell of six million soapstone tiles. It's believed that the workers who fabricated the tiles often wrote notes on the back, meaning this landmark is full of hidden messages. Construction of the statue took nine years and was finished in 1931, making it the tallest art deco statue in the world. It will probably be voted one of the New Seven Wonders of the World."

"What I find extraordinary, Nico, is that I haven't seen any street children in Rio. Not in the old town, the beaches, or here - a top tourist destination. I heard there were thousands of orphans and abandoned kids living on the streets in Rio. Where are they?" I asked.

"Well, I see them regularly at the soup kitchen in our parish," replied Nico.

"Do you have parishes here, rather than counties – like in Louisiana?"

"No, I'm speaking about my church parish," answered Nico. "The police are quite brutal with the children during grand events such as Carnival. Many of the kids are expert pickpockets and also grab bags - then outrun their victims. The city can't afford to lose tourists due to their fear of robbers."

"So, where are they hiding?" I asked.

"They're in the *favelas* (slums) sleeping rough. I'm trying to organize housing facilities for the kids and schooling, but it's hard with the current government," admitted Nico. "However, other churches have joined the bandwagon and are also opening soup kitchens."

I was shocked that Nico was involved with a church and the street children. He had even become an activist. Petra had clearly lost the plot in Paris. She was swept off her feet by Alan's false 'knight in shining armor' chivalry, plus all the jet-set hype and rock stars surrounding his lifestyle. I didn't like to interfere in my friends' relationships, but I would have to tell her to block her bank accounts and return to Rio before it was too late. Come what may, my conscience wouldn't allow me to remain silent.

"Do you have a personal relationship with Jesus?" I questioned Nico before considering that I might be trespassing on his privacy.

Nico laughed, "Typical American, no filter system in your communication. I like it. Actually, it was at Pittsburgh's Duquesne University where I received my law degree and joined the CCR."

"CCR, what's that?" I asked.

"Catholic Charismatic Renewal," replied Nico with a kind smile. "The movement was birthed at Duquesne University in 1967, eight years ago. A history professor and a graduate student were baptized in the Holy Spirit in a charismatic prayer group of Episcopalians. Then, through personal contacts, the experience of the Holy Spirit soon spread to the University of Notre Dame, and then to the University of Michigan - the rest is history."

"So you started the CCR here in Rio?" I asked.

"Not really, the Holy Spirit did. I shared *my* experience with my parish priest here in Rio. He admitted that he had intellectual knowledge about Jesus, but the truth dropped down to his heart after he had an experiential revelation of the Holy Spirit. The third part of the trinity, the Holy Spirit, has been brushed under the carpet for centuries."

I nodded my head in agreement, "I know what you mean."

Nico continued, "Due to control issues, the church hierarchy hasn't wanted believers to know about the power available to them through the indwelling of the Holy Spirit. The power to follow Jesus' teachings and the empowerment needed to spread the gospel with signs, wonders, and miracles. There was also fear of the supernatural, and still is.

"Jesus said to his disciples before ascending to heaven, 'But verily I tell you, it is for your good that I am going away, the Holy Spirit will not come to you; but if I go, I will send Him to you.' (John 16:7)

"Christ then said, 'But the comforter, the Holy Spirit, whom the Father will send in my name, will teach you all things and will remind you of everything I have told you.' (John 14:26)

"You see, it is the Holy Spirit here on planet earth, dwelling within the hearts of believers, carrying on the ministry of Jesus until His return for us. We are the hands, the feet, the mouth, and the heart of Jesus. Believers are being mobilized all over the continent as the Holy Spirit sweeps through each country. We are experiencing favor in South America, and the supernatural is becoming natural."

I stood there dumbfounded. I did not expect this young, cute, sportive lawyer to expound on such a taboo topic with such authority and confidence. He would be a world changer – actually, he already was. The world of many of the street children was being radically changed.

"Nico," I asked, "Are you going to be the Smith Wigglesworth of this generation?"

"I doubt it," replied Nico. "God also needs workers from the business world, especially honest lawyers," he laughed. "My grandfather and father are both legal eagles and are changing the image of lawyers here in Rio. I feel called to follow in their footsteps. Since I share an office with them, I don't have specific hours and can manage my time to accommodate supervising the soup kitchens and appealing to government officials.

"I am also introducing other church parishes to the Charismatic Renewal movement. Brazil is the country with the largest quantity of Catholics worldwide. But the teaching within the church has most often been 'turn or burn' rather than teaching about the grace and love of God.

"You see, Jesus came to bring truth and grace. 'But when he, the Spirit of truth comes, he will guide you into all truth.'(John 16:13) The church needs to understand that 'God's love has been poured out into our hearts through the Holy Spirit.'(Romans 5:5) It is only through truth and grace that people will be drawn to Jesus – not fear. It is not our performance that makes us worthy or acceptable to God. It is His grace.

"For it is by grace you have been saved, through faith – and this is not from yourselves, it is the gift of God – not by works, so that no one can boast. For we are God's handiwork, created in Christ Jesus to do good works, which God prepared in advance for us to do." (Eph.2:8-10)

Nico continued, "It's God's Word that keeps me humble. I don't take credit for my actions since He prepared this work for me in advance. My job is to stay in step with the Holy Spirit and discern where He's leading me. A major problem has been that Mass had been spoken only in Latin until 1965, and believers were not encouraged to read the Bible – so they were at the mercy of their local priest or their grandmother's superstitions."

"Whoa, Nico, hold on – you're going too fast. I can't absorb everything. Have you memorized the Bible? How do you pull those verses out of your sleeve like a magician?"

Nico paused with a smile, "Sorry, once I get going, I can't stop. It's in my DNA. I've been programmed as a lawyer to state my case clearly. Hey, let's get on with the tour. Would you like to climb up to the head of the statue and walk out onto the arms of Jesus? It is so awesome; you won't regret it! Or perhaps you don't have your arm-walking shoes with you," he grinned.

* * *

I accepted Nico's challenge and was looking forward to it. I had been well watered and fed and was feeling electric! "I hope there won't be a long line to hang around in with all the people up here," I nagged.

"Nope, only us," replied Nico.

"How's that? Are you a VIP up here?" I questioned.

"The statue is the first open-air sanctuary in the world and is administered by the Catholic Church. Therefore, you need authorization from the Bishop. Also, you can only climb up to the head when there is a maintenance inspection and the scaffold has been installed – plus, we need permission from the Guardian of the Sanctuary and the availability of an employee to accompany us."

I was relieved and disappointed at the same time. "Too bad, I was looking forward to the bird's eye view of Rio from up there."

"Hey, I wouldn't have asked you if it wasn't already arranged. I took a visiting priest up last week because he looked fit."

"How fit do you have to be? I hope I pass the test?" I thought to myself if I could crawl down the four-foot high passageway, two hundred feet into the belly of the Great Pyramid of Giza – I could easily climb the scaffolding upright.

"You'll be alright, Tyke. I saw how you skipped up the steps from the restaurant. Also, you're thin enough for the narrow squeeze points, and you appear to have the strength and resistance to do it. If not, I'll carry you," said Nico laughing.

I could feel the familiar drum roll as I psyched myself up for the ascent. Of my plethora of oddities, fear of heights was not one of them. I was thankful to have discovered that when I had to cross the swinging bridge suspended over that fathomless gorge in the Himalayas. Even though many of the weathered, wooden planks were missing, iron cables were anchored at either end to hang onto in case a plank broke.

Nico went to speak with one of the maintenance men, motioning for me to come over. "Mateo will be our guide," explained Nico. Mateo offered a strong, calloused handshake, and I complied with a firm grip and a smile. So far, so good.

When we entered the statue, I was given a hard helmet, just in case, and a harness that consisted of a waist belt and two leg loops. I stepped into the leg loops and buckled the strap snugly around my waist. Mateo attached a rope to my harness and motioned us toward the rickety stairs. Ladders were set at inclines, switching back and forth every twelve steps.

Looking up, there was enough light to see the endless switchback of steps. It would have been daunting; however, a single trusty handrail ran up the right side of the makeshift staircase. Mateo hooked my rope to his harness, and another maintenance man remained at the bottom - perhaps to catch me?

We started climbing slowly, and I became euphoric when I discovered it was easy. At least the first six sets of twelve steps each were easy, and then I started to sense my leg muscles rebelling. I was embarrassed to request a five-minute rest break and regretted not packing a banana – for more power. I took a swig of water and shot some desperate prayers up to my Creator, then announced, "Ready!"

Only six more sets of twelve steps each, and we would arrive at a door that exited out onto the shoulder of Jesus. Phew! I made it, legs trembling, but I succeeded! When I crawled onto Christ's rounded, broad shoulder and looked around, I realized it was worth the pain to gain such a sublime view of my surrealistic surroundings. I greatly respect the maintenance men who kept Christ the Redeemer in tip-top shape.

Nico was right behind me and encouragingly said, "Hey, aren't you going for a walk?" I explained that the view was more than sufficient from my seated position. The massive right arm was about forty feet long and perhaps eight feet wide. It was wide enough for a stroll, and I *was* in a harness; however, I felt glued to the smooth, reassuring shoulder.

"Okay, move over to the left so I can step over you," Nico responded. He then casually walked the length of Christ's arm and sat down on His hand. He was roped up and haltered also, but it gave me the heebie-jeebies. Nico then pointed out all the most exciting views and began to sing.

After about ten minutes, which seemed endless, I worked my way backward into Christ's neck, feeling exhilarated. Nico joined me in the narrow channel, and Mateo asked if we wanted a superior view from the crown of the head.

"Of course," replied Nico. I shrugged my shoulders, and Nico pushed me upwards. There was a narrow opening that I had to lift myself up into, and Nico and Mateo followed. In a crouched position, Mateo pushed a circular plate upward and swiveled it back into our small chamber. "Stand up and take a look, Tyke. You may not be coming this way again soon," whispered Nico.

By now, we were in the clouds, but I could see the entire Atlantic coastline and the whole expanse of Guanabara Bay. I needed a release and a response to the beauty surrounding me. I whistled, not a polite girlie whistle, but a full-fledged truck driver's eardrum perforating whistle.

"Hey, calm down, Tyke. We don't want a rescue team coming up here for us," Nico warned.

I was riding a wave of ecstasy until a single thought broke into my intoxicated exhilaration. The thought was sobering - how were we going to get down? Walking down twelve sets of staircases backward would be doubly difficult. I wished I could fly.

Nico broke into my spiraling thought pattern, "Tyke, would you like to descend in the halter – it's the quickest and coolest way to get back down. If not, it might be slow-going, backing down those wobbly steps."

I heard myself reply, "Great, sounds awesome!" What was I thinking? I'd never been rock climbing or descending – I didn't know what to do. "Do I need lessons?" I asked Nico. My courage was crumbling.

"No, you're in a seat-halter - you merely remain seated, and Mateo will slowly lower you down. It's how all the workers descend or arrive at the spot they need to repair. There is ongoing restoration taking place – mostly damage from lightning."

"Oh okay, if you say so, Nico," but why don't you go first, and I can watch your technique."

"Yeah, why not, if it will make you feel more confident," said Nico.

Nico was right - it looked straightforward. He descended without a hiccup and remained there looking up at me. However, Nico was the size of a giant ant, which meant that I was totally dependent on

Mateo – I hoped he could do it again. I started to pray a desperate prayer of "HELP!" I reminded myself to relax and enjoy the ride down. I practiced my deep breathing exercises while Mateo checked my halter, the ropes, and the carabiners. He then tightened the strap of my helmet, which made me a bit suspicious.

I heard myself screaming "GERONIMO" and prayed I wouldn't end up like Custer. Something extraordinary happened – I felt a total sense of oneness with the Creator of the Universe as if I was wrapped in a down-filled quilt of peace, seated on the wings of an angel. I wondered if I was delirious or if I had fainted. I felt a strange peace envelop me.

When my feet touched the ground, Nico was there to steady me. Applause broke out like fireworks, and we were the heroes of the moment. Nico kissed my forehead and said, "See, easy-peasy. I knew you could do it, even without your statue-descending shoes."

With that comment, I burst into laughter and continued laughing, almost hysterically, until we reached the van that would deliver us back down to the parking lot and Nico's car. I needed another tension release and kept giggling at intervals until we arrived at the condo. It was almost dusk, and I asked Nico if he wanted to join me for one of Maria's gourmet meals.

"I'd love to, but I have a meeting back in the office with an important client – give my regards to Maria," responded Nico. He then cut his car's engine, looked me squarely in the eyes, and said, "Let the Holy Spirit become your algorithm, and remain sensitive to His leading. It's good that you are proactive, but remember, you don't have to perform. I can sense that you are a people-pleaser – but the Bible clearly states, *"Woe to you when everyone speaks well of you....*" (Luke 6:26). Keep your eyes firmly focused on Jesus, and be ready to swim upstream against the current.

"God has a special mission for you – you're a good communicator. Stay grounded in His Word, and remain dependant on Him."

"How will I discover His unique mission for me?" I asked. "To tell you the truth, I wanted to conquer South America and put some more 'been there, done that' notches in my expanding travel belt. Plus, I wanted to discover the unique beauty of this Continent and the patchwork of colorful cultures – but most of all, I just wanted to have fun.

"However, I've been hijacked by the Holy Spirit at every turn. I want to share the miracles I've experienced and the raw faith of the indigenous believers I've encountered. Still, I know from experience that people might seem indifferent or feel intimidated. I think you have to live it to understand it."

"Perhaps the Lord wants you to write it down and share it in a book one day. It's less invasive than trying to squeeze your experiences into a timely conversation," offered Nico. "And remember, God has planned what He has designed for you to do in advance, so don't run ahead of the Holy Spirit. Wait, pray, and be sensitive to His leading. He will place the desire in your heart when the time is ripe."

When I first met Nico, I wondered what pearls of wisdom I could share with the young guy and hoped for an opportunity to speak about Jesus. I discovered that age has little to do with wisdom. He had become a living example to me of how it is possible to remain in the world without becoming worldly. His head and heart were clearly in the heavenly realms, but his feet were planted firmly on the ground.

Nico was mature beyond his years. Not only was he spiritual - he was kind, versatile, pragmatic, and magnetic. I would pray for his ministry to the street children and that Petra would soon wake up and return to Rio. I think Nico will be waiting for her, with outstretched, forgiving arms – like 'Cristo Redentor.'

Digging into my handbag, I pulled out a business card from my mother's art gallery, *Adventures in Art*. Handing the card to Nico, I explained that I was on the move without a fixed address, but he could always contact me via my mom. Or better yet, if he ever visited New Orleans, my mother would have a place for him to stay.

Nico got out of the car and politely opened my door, giving me an affectionate air kiss and reminding me, "Worry is a misuse of your imagination, so don't waste your time on it. And above all, don't forget, it's *not* about religion. It's about a relationship - with The King."

I thanked Nico for the unforgettable day and his phenomenal patience with me and my untimely quirks. I stood at the entrance to the condo and waved farewell until his car was out of sight. I had met a young man who knew me better than I knew myself. He had spent the day with me, catering to my every whim, without expecting any obvious external reward. I would not forget him. And I will never forget the street children hiding in the slums. I would stay in touch with Nico and sponsor a few of his kids.

Astrid had returned from the mountains refreshed, and I filled her in on my sensational sensory overload in her absence. I promised to have a serious talk with her daughter, Petra, and gave her my mother's calling card. I was thankful for my tireless, adventurous mother, Peggy. She constantly mopped up after me and, with open arms, received the motley lot of strangers I sent her way. However, she would be more than pleased to entertain Astrid or Nico.

I would have loved to stay longer in Rio, but I was on a tight schedule. I needed to stop in London before flying to Florence to commence the Spring Fashion Shows. Since I would skip my stop in Caracas, my pre-scheduled TWA flight would deliver me to Miami nine hours later. Okay, Ruggero had warned me not to change my ticket, and I wouldn't - I would only eliminate one stop. I felt optimistic. However, I prayed for mercy.

The Miami airport was swarming, but with my trusty U.S. passport, a sweaty agent prodded me into the less lengthy line at the chaotic customs control. I had been primed by a savvy traveler never to make direct eye contact with an immigration officer - that would automatically relay a message of guilt. Of course, I dressed like a nerd and wore my hair in a braided bun. I made it through customs without even a luggage check, which would have only perplexed the agent. No red light flashed, and no armed police officer whisked me away, so I deemed myself safe—only one more challenge.

I had to check into my final TWA flight to New York within several hours. Luckily the ticket agent was weary-eyed and didn't notice the omitted flight. Phew, I had a seat near the front. I never quite grasped the logic or courtesy measure of having chain smokers seated in the last ten rows. I'd get smoked, as usual, reeking of stale cigarette fumes and have to fumigate my clothing and double-wash my hair as soon as I got to my friend's house in London.

12. LONDON

From New York's Kennedy Airport, I had a direct night flight to Heathrow – so I'd try to capture three middle seats to spread out and snooze. It was still off-season, so I hoped to avoid a crunch. I requested an aisle seat, so I could bolt to some convenient sleep seats as soon as the 'fasten seat belts' sign stopped flashing. Like musical chairs – three of us dashed for the vacant spots, but my legs were longer, and I won. I immediately laid down to mark my territory and even ate dinner in a reclined position.

I awoke refreshed, breezed through immigration and customs, and headed to retrieve my baggage. When I tipped a porter for helping me, his tender reply, "Thanks, Luv," felt reassuring. London was my comfort zone - it felt like an oversized, kind village. Milk was still delivered to doorsteps, and people dared to leave their soiled clothes in suitcases outside their front doors for Jeeves - the gurus of dry-cleaning.

When I accidentally stepped on someone's foot while waiting for the bus, *they* pleaded, "Sorry." I mean, how polite is that? Although I hadn't had a permanent address for more than three years, traveling non-stop, I had a permanent closet at my friend's place in Fulham Broadway. I quite enjoyed couch surfing.

The airport bus deposited me at Earl's Court, and I taxied to Sloane Square. From there, the 22 bus took only twenty minutes to

Tink's place, allowing me a picturesque ride up King's Road. London in the mid-70s was by far the most exotic city in Europe! It was a multicultural, diverse, and tolerant city. There were few dress codes or social norms, so I felt at home.

As I jumped onto the double-decker city bus, the cockney driver shouted, "Up the apples, Luv."

"What apples," I replied.

"Apples and pears – STAIRS," he ordered, pointing upwards. Ah yes, cockney rhyming slang - the typical coded East End London lingo. I staggered upward with my luggage.

I sat scrunched up next to a plump Indian lady draped in a sari reeking of curry. Across the aisle was a young woman covered in a hijab. To her right was a teen with bright pink hair, chains, and a nose ring. In front of me was a granny with a high lace collar and grey hair tucked neatly into a bun, and her seatmate wore long tangled dreadlocks. As diverse as the passengers were, they had one thing in common – they all smoked. Upstairs was the smoking section . . . uff.

I knew London like the back of my hand. For the past three years, it had been my point of entry and exit . . . . . from everywhere. With daily flights to and from most of the seventy ex-colonies of Great Britain, there was always a bargain to be had. I could also count on some modeling jobs or photo shoots to tide me over until the next seasonal fashion shows or jewelry sales.

Six months previously, I conveniently lost my passport and applied for a new one. Traveling was now effortless without an accordion of fold-out extension pages filled with stamps from Indonesia, India, Nepal, Afghanistan, Tunisia, Algiers, Morocco, and the likes.

Now there was no trace of my hippie-trail activity or suspicion of smuggling. Anyway, my upcoming flights would be tame. I'd fly into Florence to meet up with Roberto Cavallini for the fashion week and then to Paris.

I think London was the official capital of style – the home of street fashion. I was mesmerized by the mind-bending inventiveness of designs sported by the trendy pedestrians strolling the streets.

Punk-ware was starting to take off. Punk epitomized a D.I.Y. attitude as a reaction against the consumerism of the 70s Post Modernism and reflection on the socio-eco reality. Vivienne Westwood was the reigning queen of the flash fashion movement. I saluted her shop at 430 King's Road as we passed World's End, heading up to Fulham Broadway. Only five minutes until I reached my destination – Mirabelle Road.

* * *

I rang the doorbell several times, hoping someone would stir. Tink opened the door and squealed, "Tyke, you're back! I'll help you with your bags." Tink was the spitting image of Janis Joplin. However, her voice and personality resembled Little Bo Peep.

Tink's enigmatic presence was baffling, but once you got to know her, you realized she was intrinsically a humanitarian, by nature bohemian, and by choice a vegetarian. She was, above all, a true ailurophile. She loved felines, and her huge grey Persian cat, with emerald eyes, ruled her home and her heart.

My closet was conveniently in the living room near *my* couch. On occasion, Tink's roommate was away, and I was permitted to hang out in Ros' room. I first met Ros in Rome at a quaint upholstery shop in Trastevere. They also did alterations.

The shop, located in the picturesque old quarter, was near my friend's walk-up apartment. I glimpsed a sewing machine and dashed into the shop when my green suede hot pants exploded, and Ros allowed me to hide behind the door in my knickers. She replaced the zip in five minutes flat. How kind was that?

When I next crossed paths with Ros, it was in London at my Roman friend's apartment in Lowndes Square, not far from Harrods. Gio, who drove me across the Sahara, was remodeling an Italian bank and taking English lessons from bi-lingual Ros. She was wearing an exquisite chenille jacket that caught my eye, and she confessed her roommate had designed it.

Then Ros declared, "Hey, you're the girl with the green hot pants and broken zipper!" Ros was from Wales but lived in Rome for several years, perfecting her Italian. It was more than a coincidence that we met up again. She invited me back to her flat, so I could buy some antique chenille stuff to sell in Ibiza.

And that is how I met amazing Tink. She was a true artist who designed and pieced together her creations from antique fabrics. Each piece was a 'one-off.' She would scour the buyers' markets at daybreak, and I would tag along. Tink encouraged me to follow at a reasonable distance, with my coat inside out, so that her prices wouldn't escalate. I was looking for art deco jewelry that I could resell in Paris and make a good profit.

Our friendship and partnership flourished. I introduced Tink to my cross-section of eclectic friends from Ibiza currently residing in London. I'd even invited them over for an advance chance to buy

Tink's creations. Everyone fell head over heels for her unique fashion. Tink couldn't sew fast enough to meet the demand. "How about hiring a few extra sewing ladies?" I suggested. "Impossible," she explained, "Each garment is pieced together with my innate, artistic eye."

Tink was not born for a high-octane lifestyle. As long as she could keep up her sizeable two-story house, protected by frozen rent, she was content to eke out enough to go on holiday and to the nearby pub. Her hospitable nature enabled a string of musicians and travelers to drop by whenever for a meal or a pint - never a dull, drab, or dreary moment at Tink's tavern.

What took a slight adjustment was to remember to stockpile fifty pence coins to feed the electricity meter - if I wanted the luxury of a hot bath. On more than one occasion, I had to hop out of a bubble bath and drip to the meter with frosty house temps of 46 degrees F. I discovered most Brits were partially amphibian and didn't succumb to the needs of pampered ex-colonists. I now fully understood why the Brits had stiff upper lips.

If I had an interview for a fashion shoot, I'd jump onto the bus and head to Peter Jones department store on Sloane Square. There they had heated facilities. Veering away from euphemisms, the English deemed a bathroom had a bath. If not, it was called a toilet, lavatory, or loo. It often took a while for my make-up and fingers to thaw out, but that only added to the adventure of it all.

I couldn't wait to tell Tink all about my South American adventures. However, I hoped she'd ask, not to feel that I was force-feeding her.

* * *

"By the way, Tyke, anything exciting happen in South America?" Tink asked casually. Trying to appear laid-back without imploding, I responded, "Yeah, I witnessed some out-a-site miracles."

"Cool," responded Tink without asking for details.

Previously I had explained to Tink about my extraordinary life-changing encounter with *Yeshua* (Jesus). She casually responded that she had gone to church with her parents as a child and still prayed once in a while.

I quickly discovered the most counter-productive thing I could do was to announce, "Guess what? I've become a Christian." That encouraged my peers to think I had joined some cult or flipped my lid. However, saying I had become a follower of Yeshua was accepted and applauded.

Most everyone I knew had a guru, a master, or a 'guide.' Zen masters were particularly the trend due to their non-violent approach to everything. Most Zen Buddhists believe that achieving enlightenment by seeing one's original nature is achieved without the intervention of the intellect. Zen is big on intuitive understanding and not so keen on philosophizing.

The Beatles had become disenchanted with Maharishi Mahesh Yogi's Hindu teachings, although TM (Transcendental Meditation) remains popular. Repeating unique Sanskrit words or mantras to achieve a state of inner peacefulness is on the rise.

Okay, different strokes for different folks, but none of the other religions, belief systems, or teachings included the concept of **grace**. Only Jesus brought the perfect balance of truth and *grace* (undeserved favor). Grace is the love-saturated rescue plan that took Jesus to the cross. *"God so loved the world that he gave his one and only Son, that whoever believes in him shall not perish but have eternal life."* (John 3:16). What?

Nothing, but nothing comes close to that promise. To Buddhists, eternal life is a gray area. They don't believe in a self or a soul. Everything in the manifest world is impermanent. When a person dies, they are continually reincarnated until they gain "enlightenment." After entering a state called "nirvana," it is unclear if it is an eternal state. The work of perfecting one's self enough to be reincarnated into a higher state sounds like a futile attempt at self-salvation.

According to a collection of revered Hindu texts, all beings are souls and thus spiritual in nature. Even though the body is temporal and eventually dies, the soul is eternal. After death, the soul is reincarnated, taking birth in another physical body or form.

Of course, once again, the attempt to relive your life in order to be reincarnated into a *better* body depends on your karma from a previous life. Trying to work your way into a better life seems quite pointless. I guess Hindu women have the incentive to perfect their karma so they have a shot at coming back as men.

The Muslims believe that God will judge each individual by their deeds and that heaven awaits those who have lived holy and hell for those who have not. Now that is a very logical belief system. It makes sense, but it is totally void of grace. What a burden to have to earn your own right standing. Can you ever be good enough to reach the mark?

So why was there an allergic reaction to calling myself a Christian? Every reason – Christians, through the ages, have not been great PR agents for Christ. Mahatma Gandhi said, "I like your Christ, but not your Christians. Your Christians are so unlike your Christ."

How true. I guess that's why Nico told me to keep my eyes focused on Jesus. Christians are fallible and so confusing. I warned people that I was a work in progress and explained that it's not my performance that will get me into heaven, but only God's *grace* (undeserved favor). Perhaps it sounds too easy – maybe people like to struggle and toil.

During my trip through South America, my hypothetical Bible knowledge moved from the theory stage into reality. I experienced firsthand miracles like those performed by Jesus and His disciples. Jesus commanded his followers to spread the gospel with signs, wonders, and miracles – thus giving power to His Words. It is evident that Jesus *is* the same yesterday, today, and forever.

Enthusiastic about sharing this good news, I had been warned to stay in step with the Spirit. So, I would wait until I received a nudge from the Holy Spirit. Meanwhile, I was in my favorite city, so I decided to enjoy it!

* * *

Tramp Nightclub was the talk of the town. A friend living in London, who I'd met in Ibiza, told me I could enter the chic club using his business card. I wanted to try out his card and the dapper club's dance floor. I talked Tink into coming along. Not to arrive too early, we waited until 9 pm and then caught the bus to Piccadilly Circus – which deserved its jolly name. Clowns were hanging around the circus, better described as an assortment of second-class street entertainers. From there, it was a short stroll to the trendy Tramp club.

The double-decker buses were slower but far more scenic than the sooty Underground, leaving me looking like a chimney sweep. We were dressed to kill, but no one blinked an eye. I wore my body-hugging flared jumpsuit with my flashiest gaucho belt and green platform boots with lightning bolts. Tink wore an antique lace gown and a shawl.

When we arrived, it was 10 pm, the perfect time for an eye-opening entrance into a classy club. I whipped out my friend's business card while the doorman's eyes darted back and forth, then up to down. We looked like the odd couple, but he motioned us in. It seemed like time stood still for several moments. Everyone stopped to check us out, hoping for a celebrity, and trying to figure out who we were.

Fortunately, I knew a few guys who were regulars at the Potter's Pub on King's Road, where the Rolling Stones hung out. They motioned for us to join them, so we slinked over to their table with increasing confidence. Very posh indeed, with carved wooden panels covering the walls and old masters' paintings that spelled *class*. Stylish sofas lined the walls – so every seat had a clear view of the inviting but decadent dance floor.

However, the crucial element was the music! I hoped they had a hip D.J. with a rockin' repertoire of the hottest dance tunes. The place looked a bit too refined to relate to the right rhythm for footloose fancy-free dance, but as they say, you can't read a club by its décor.

The first tune was "Rock and Roll All Night" by Kiss, followed by "Sweet Emotion" by Aerosmith. Whoa! YES! I grabbed the rhythm and dove in. Dancing, like singing, activates the sensory and motor circuits of the brain – creating comfort, relaxation, fun, and power. Once I started dancing, wild horses couldn't drag me away. Tink had warned me that the public transport stopped at midnight, but I assured her that my treat was a taxi back to her place if we passed the limit.

When Tink tapped me on the shoulder, it was 3 am. "Maybe we should head home, or else they'll lock us in," she warned me.

"Wow, I can't believe we've been dancing non-stop for nearly five hours. I feel like I could fly. At least the calorie burn will help me to remain size 8 for the upcoming fashion weeks," I replied.

"Okay, Wonder Woman, but I can't fly, so we'd best get to Piccadilly Circus for a taxi," laughed Tink. Our make-up had slid off our faces hours ago, and we glistened with over-exertion sweat. I hoped Tramp's liability insurance would cover the dent I danced into their highly polished wooden floor. I was surprised to discover I was one of the last left rockin' out.

No taxis outside of Tramp, so we trudged over to Piccadilly, laughing the whole way. We were experiencing an endorphin high, and I just hoped we didn't overdose. "YEA, there are still three taxis!" I reported happily. The first taxi rolled down the window and asked us where we were going.

"Fulham Broadway," exclaimed Tink. "Sorry, Luv," replied the cabby, "I'm only going east – I'm on my way home at this hour." The following two cab drivers responded likewise. I wondered if our alien appearance put them off.

Tink responded philosophically, "Why don't we walk? It's only three miles."

"At this hour, don't you think that would be risky?" I gulped.

"I doubt it. Even assassins will be asleep by now," reasoned Tink. So we headed west to Green Park, then to Hyde Park, past Harrods, and up the entire length of Fulham Road. During our trek, we only saw a handful of cars and two taxis that I tried to wave down - to no avail. While singing with intervals of hysteria and storytelling, we arrived at Tink's place in less than an hour and a half. I carried my boots that last half hour and hoped I hadn't trampled through dog poop or diphtheria.

In New Orleans, you gambled your life by walking several blocks at night. It was known as 'the city that never sleeps.' Even supermarkets were open 24-7, and madmen patrolled the streets at all hours. Front page news in London covered stories such as, "Woman gets her 'bum' pinched while on the Underground," and other such heinous crimes. I couldn't imagine returning to New Orleans to live, but it was a nice place to visit if you carried a gun.

Only a week until I'd fly to Florence for the Petite Dona fashion shows. Thanks to new arrivals such as Roberto Cavallini, Florence became a mecca for the international style set. The Tuscan capital was Roberto's hometown, and he drew a broad audience of admirers and buyers. I needed to knock off a pound or two to slip into his slinky models. I borrowed Tink's beat-up bike and pedaled into oblivion, up to Hampstead and then down to Richmond. Then ten miles east to Canary Wharf and Greenwich, back up to Wembley Stadium.

* * *

Pedaling up King's Road, heading back to Tink's place, I stopped at the Chelsea Antique Market for the last scan of their collection of 20s flapper dresses and beaded silk chiffon gowns. My re-sale strategy was to wear the dresses a few times, break them in, and then resell them for at least double the price. My clients snapped them up, especially Mama Lula in Rome. She'd then quadruple the price for her movie star clientele, and everyone was happy.

I then checked out the ABC Cinema to see what was on. "Shampoo," the frivolous film about a playboy hairdresser in Beverly Hills, starring Warren Beatty, Julie Christie, and Goldie Hawn, seemed like the perfect way to wind down from my upsurge of activity. I wanted to invite Tink out for the evening. She was a homebody, and I had to pry her out of her homegrown comfort zone. She reluctantly accepted my invitation as if politely doing me a favor.

We started at The Casserole, where we'd be guaranteed to run into Ibiza people and rock musicians. Yep, I knew or recognized about a third of the regulars. The Jesus rock group, "*Sheep,*" looked like they were grazing in the corner. 'The Lonesome Stone' rock opera musical brought the Jesus people to the U.K. in 1973, and they dared to rent the Rainbow Theater, the top rock venue, for two solid months. They were sold out to 2,700 people, but I managed to snap up a ticket.

The *Sheep* were influenced by Jefferson Airplane and had a Californian style fused to a full-on declaration of the Gospel truth. The Jesus People Movement had germinated and was taking London by storm. It had become cool to be a follower of Jesus in the alternative atmosphere of gurus, other religions, no religions, and the new age setting. I had always been a rebel. Born south of the Mason-Dixon line in the US, I was a legitimate confederate and a rebel by birthright.

During my university days, I hung out with the bearded guys from the bohemian left and was ostracized. Then, my lack of interest in drugs, hallucinogenics, and horoscopes made me suspicious during my encounter with the hippie movement. Now, being a follower of Jesus, I was accepted but kept at a distance – until people realized I wasn't a goody-two-shoes or a blatant party pooper.

The curious thing was, I got just as goofy and disorientated as everyone else - without drink or drugs. I knew it was impossible to convince someone of something that only the Holy Spirit could reveal. *"Not by might nor by power, but by my Spirit, says the Lord Almighty."* Zech 4:6)

* * *

Alitalia offered the best deal for a one-way flight to Florence - so I bought the ticket on the spot and had just two more days to wrap up my time in London. I wanted to scour the markets and Portobello Road once again for enticing tidbits I could hawk in Florence and Paris.

"Tyke, telephone," shouted Tink from the other side of her messy mansion.

"Hi Angie, what's up?" It had been ages since I'd seen or heard from her.

"I just thought I'd check with Tink to see if you were in town. Did you know that you're on the front page of today's Evening Standard?"

"You're joking! It must be a look-alike," I shot back. Suddenly my heart started to race when I realized that the front page of any newspaper, especially the Evening Standard, only carried bad news - because that's what sells. There were lots of female terrorist members of the Irish Republican Army. I wondered if I looked like a member of the IRA.

"What are the headlines with the photo?" I questioned Mandy.

"Go to your nearest newsstand and buy a copy," she laughed. "You'll be surprised – I was! I didn't realize you were so interested in politics and had such profound views."

It was late afternoon, so I dashed out to the newsstand, where I could also buy some Milky Ways to reverse my sugar plunge provoked by the shock of Mandy's untimely message.

Nearing the newsstand, I felt butterflies doing the samba in my stomach. I picked up a paper and was taken aback by the bold title of bad news. Then, my photo was directly below the horrid headlines, smack dab in the center of the paper. Yep, it was me, alright. I wondered what I was accused of saying.

I am Innocent

"American model, living in London, has her say on whether President Nixon should stand down - more on page 11." I decided 'model' sounded better for an interview than wheeler-dealer. After all, I had just done some photo shoots for my friend Marisa, who had an exotic collection of antique Chinese kimonos cut up and reshaped into enticing evening wear.

London Photo Shoot

I burst out laughing with relief when I realized that the funny-looking photographer who stopped me as I exited American Express actually worked for a newspaper. I thought it was only a 'pick up' line when he asked about the President.

American Express had become the global post office for traveling Americans. A place they could receive their mail and buy traveler's checks – or photographers could find US citizens to interview. Phew, I bought several copies to mail one to my mom in New Orleans. She'd be delighted that I made front-page news without starting a war.

I convinced Tink to meet me in Ibiza in May and to lug as much stuff as she could carry so that I could connect her with clients. After the fashion weeks were finished, I'd jet over to India to pick out the best silver snake belts from the nomads of Thar Desert, then up to Kathmandu to visit my adopted boy Mahesh.

13. FLORENCE AND PARIS

My flight took off at noon, so I'd be in Florence in time for a late lunch – perfect! I decided to wear my suede Cavallini outfit to prove to Roberto how much I cherished his present from the previous shows six months ago. After spending my youth trying to straighten my kinky curls, I finally embraced the lioness look and went so far as to wind up clumps of hair and bobby-pin them into tight knots. This trick enabled me to attain an even wilder look by simply brushing out the corkscrew curls into an unruly, tangled mane.

With nimble artistry, I wound up about fifty pin curls and stuffed them up under my fedora hat for a neat, chic look that would enable me to whiz through customs. All was going well until the guy at customs ordered me, *"Togliti il cappello"* (Take your hat off). My automatic response was, "No." I didn't want to be humiliated by having my fifty clumps of pin-curled hair spring out of my hat in a Rasta fashion.

It was a showdown - he again ordered me to take my hat off. I swiveled my head left to right and back again to signify NO. I could see Roberto and Johanna from a distance waving. The customs guy blew a whistle, and several security guards toting weapons surrounded me. I guess they thought I had dope hidden under my hat.

"Okay, okay," I relented and lifted my hat off. I stood behind a post to stuff my hair back up under the hat and confidently carried on.

The men looked baffled and somewhat embarrassed and motioned me through customs without even checking my designer leather bags.

"*Ciao Bella*" (Hi beautiful), announced Roberto, as he gave me an unabashed hug. "*Qual era el problema lá dietro?*" (What was the problem back there?) asked Roberto and Johanna.

"Oh, nothing, the usual. They wanted autographs," I fibbed.

"Of course, you look like a star in that creation of mine." Roberto's specialty was animal prints on supple suede that fit like a second skin. I stopped at the ladies' room, yanked the bobby pins out of my hair, ran my fingers through my yard-long tresses, and exited a wild woman.

I brought curls to a new level. My hair resembled a wayward Afro reacting to a tropical storm. "*Bellissima*" (Very beautiful), raved Roberto. Of course, his prize pet was a Mountain Gorilla named *Dolcezza* (Sweetie), revealing his unusual taste in beauty. I guess I was Roberto's gimmick model who brought his animal prints to life. He also allowed me to wear his cape ensembles since I could mimic the toreros by twirling the capes around as if taunting a snorting bull.

Yep, it was good to be back in Florence. The Florentines were gregarious, friendly, and generous. Mark Twain described Florence as the "city of dreams." It was the birthplace of Renaissance art and architecture, with breathtaking views at every turn - nothing short of spectacular. We pulled up to Roberto's restored palace, knowing the following week would be hard work - but it was rewarding to be a pioneer in his expanding emporium.

Johanna and I leaped out of the Range Rover and entered his domain through the massive arched entrance while Roberto parked around the corner. We had become friends, and I stayed with Johanna while in Munich, and she visited me in Ibiza. Actually, she was a lot of fun, despite her clockwork, boot camp timetable. I liked her predictability - 10 pm in bed, and 6 am, she arose with the roosters. The downside was that we were sharing a room. I had packed a flashlight to read after 'lights out' and roam into the kitchen for a midnight snack.

Roberto gave us a preview of the garments he had chosen for each of us. His favorite prints were leopard, zebra, snake, and giraffe – often fusing the fabrics, patterns, and textures into one sublime ensemble. Birds and feathers were thrown into his collage of God's creation sensation. He explained that he preferred me in his giraffe prints since my neck was slender and long, so I stood up straight and tried neck stretching calisthenics.

As his fame drew buyers from afar, Roberto's catwalk extravaganzas became the talk of the town. He used shock therapy to showcase his creations and was not only an artist but a natural-born promoter. His people skills paralleled his innovation in fashion, and the resounding result was a roadmap to success. He had quadrupled his seamstress staff in only three years but refused to outsource his fashion. His hands-on attention propelled his success, and he personally chose each and every button.

We would push on to Paris with only one day off, so I used my time wisely and made the rounds of my previous contact shops. I was intuitive about what would sell, but I was nearly fleeced by the local merchants, selling my gems for a song. I hoisted the prices to include my flight and a bit more, so I could knock off something for a discount. I had forgotten that bartering was a way of life and officially the national sport in Italy.

The week in Florence was more than successful and a tried and true warm-up for strutting down the catwalks in the world's fashion capital. Paris not only embraced its mystique as the land of love and romance, but it also embraced the fashion buyers streaming in that would boost its economy.

* * *

We were Paris bound as usual in Roberto's four-door V8 Range Rover. His spacious vehicle was packed to its gills with his latest designs, plus all the delicious delicacies from his natal region of Tuscany. I once again shared the back seat with porky – a huge hind leg of dry-cured pork, better known as Prosciutto de Parma. Cases of reserve red wine, Barbera d'Alba, were under my feet, and an assortment of the best potent cheese was at my fingertips. I was prepared for the twelve-hour journey to the City of Lights – the undisputed capital of fashion and center of café culture.

The Tuscan landscape, filled with vineyards, olive groves, and ancient hamlets, softened the impact of Lamborghinis and Ferraris that whizzed around us without mercy. Sure and steady, Roberto merged smoothly into the chaotic Parisian rush hour like slicing butter. He maneuvered his four-by-four monster as if it were a sleek Maserati.

Italian drivers were amusingly frenetic. However, Parisians behind the wheel were hopelessly homicidal. Roberto had nerves of steel, and his single-mindedness enabled him to remain in a cushioned bubble, excluding any signs of stress or trouble. He worked around the clock while remaining unruffled as he orchestrated every detail of his large-scale, expanding venture.

Roberto dropped us off at our revamped Palace Hotel in the center of the medieval old city – Île Saint Louis – the heart of Paris. He reminded us, "Be ready tomorrow at 7 am. I'll pick you up and head to the *Prêt à Porter* (Ready to Wear) fashion fair to set up the stand." Roberto was meticulous about arranging his display of new designs and the irresistible 'entertainment' corner where he would invite his clients to the delicacies of his Tuscany region.

Hospitality is a dominant gene in Italian temperament. It flows naturally like fine wine and is inviting, never contrived or insincere. Roberto's relaxed, easy-going personality propelled his networking with finesse. He was naturally charming and drew people to himself like a powerful magnet.

It was another week of unparalleled excitement and success. We broke protocol and had a ball on the runway as I encouraged the other models to step out of their trance and dance. We started a new trend, and other models tried to copy us but fell short of the mark without the break-free designs to back up the euphoria.

On the last day of the Paris shows, I decided to give our runway spectacular a grand final with some extra pizazz. Punctuating Roberto's flamboyant designs with a few jetés leading into a non-stop pirouette, I heard an ear-piercing crack as the stiletto heel of my left shoe flew over the bewildered spectators. Plunging into a nose dive onto the carpeted runway, I tucked my head under and rolled into a somersault, ending up in a somewhat graceful split.

The attentive crowd was on their feet – some gasping and others looking horrified. However, the mood instantly transformed into cheers and wild applause. The other models calmly danced around me as if my faux pax was planned. When I came to my senses, I stood up and called for Roberto. He approached me, shouting, *"Brava, Brava, Bellissima."* He then lifted my hand, and we bowed in unison.

You can run but you can't hide.

Modeling was amusing and initially my goal – but it had now become a mere stepping stone in financing my global adventures. I discovered that 'trade' was an intrinsic part of my personality; therefore, wheeling and dealing came naturally. On payday, I would head back to London, where I could find the best deal on flights to everywhere. After stocking up on treasures in India and Nepal, I would return to Ibiza in time to sell my silver snake belts and bask in the sun while reconnecting with my worldwide collection of friends.

14. INDIA AND NEPAL

The rock-bottom cheapest fare I could find to India was with Aeroflot Airlines. London, with a stop-over in Moscow, then New Delhi – perfect! The plane was filled with locals from New Delhi returning from visits with relatives in London. The handful of Russians was obviously not used to flying since they hung onto every word of the air hostess and looked around to locate the exit rows. Most curious of all, they appeared to have been held captive from another era. Their clothing and hairstyles were World War II vintage, and their expressions were bleak - as if they had just discovered Santa Claus was a lie.

I had enough time during my layover in Moscow to hop on a bus and head to the city's center. Wanting to check out the famous GUM department store facing Red Square, I was surprised to discover it was a miniature city - formed by three street-like arcades intersecting at right angles. A fountain was featured in the center of the building, and the entire complex was encapsulated by a glass dome that let in natural sunlight.

For such a gleeful setting, the people looked just as grey and cold as the weather. They either avoided eye contact with me or glanced over with hardened disdain. I guess they were brainwashed that Americans and Europeans were capitalist heathens to be shunned at all costs. It seems they were a bit slow at catching on that Communism wasn't working. It was almost sixty years since the Russian Revolution of 1917.

Were the people so naive to believe that their classless system, in which private property was non-existent, excluded their elite leaders who led luxurious lifestyles? It seems their commanders were re-labeled and re-cycled versions of the Tsar. I hoped my frivolous existence might pry them out of their lackadaisical inertia. Couldn't they see that Marxism and Leninism boasted an ideology that had hit an iceberg and sank like the Titanic?

Perhaps my bright green platform boots with the red and yellow lightning bolts were a bit over-the-top, but they were comfortable for travel. I then skipped over to the walled Kremlin, the medieval fortress founded by the Rurikids ruling dynasty.

St. Basil's Cathedral looked like Walt Disney designed it. Still, I read that the mysterious multicolored patterns on its domes were meant to give a visual representation of Heavenly Jerusalem. That didn't sound very Orthodox to me, but why not? It was cheerful. On that note, I dashed back to catch my return bus to Sheremetyevo International Airport.

I was just in time to board and glad to see we had a jet, so that meant only about seven hours non-stop to New Delhi. I scrunched up comfortably in my window seat and was pleased to have time to write in my journal and reflect on life. However, after an hour and a half, the plane started to descend. What? A voice droned over the speaker system, "We will soon be landing at the Baghdad International Airport in twenty minutes."

Waving my hand wildly, I caught the attention of the elderly stewardess and asked if the plane was having engine problems. She looked bewildered and said, "No, this is our usual route to New Delhi."

"What," I shrieked. "My ticket says non-stop to Delhi."

"Oh, that's because there wasn't enough room on the ticket to add that part." I shrugged and tried to breathe deeply for five minutes. I recalled the wise proverb, "You get what you pay for." I'd chalk it up as an exotic, unscheduled stop and tried to feel privileged.

There was a cultural shift on the next leg of my trip. A fourth of the passengers exited, and a swarm of Saddam Hussein clones piled in. Baghdadi Arabic controlled the airwaves, and the piercing, guttural sounds were a mix of someone clearing their throat while gulping entire potatoes. I was good at imitating accents but decided not to.

Pleased that a plump Indian lady sat down beside me, I nodded and placed my hands together prayerfully, and offered, "Namaste." She politely returned the greeting, which was our amusingly clever but short interaction for the next six hours.

I spent the last hour of the journey psyching myself up for my shambolic arrival in New Delhi. I had a sense of pure relaxation, riddled with a foreboding sensation. I prayed that one of my usual "boys" would be at the airport to prevent a dozen kids from hanging on me while I struggled to the taxi stand.

Traveling light was essential so that I could sprint ahead of the crowds. With my long legs and lightning bolt boots, I jumped into a taxi before the "*baksheesh*" kids could catch me. "Narula Hotel - the short route," I panted. If not specified, it was considered fair play for the cabby to take his pale passengers on a wild goose chase. This was my fifth trip to New Delhi in three years, so I knew the ropes.

* * *

The street children in South America were solemn and cautious, while the kids in the streets of India tended to be boisterous and annoying. However, the fact remained that they were all undernourished, and even worse, they were vastly under-loved.

My heart was melting for those children, and I knew I could try to save a few if I couldn't save them all. They desperately needed to know their worth and how profoundly their creator loved them. I felt a transformation taking place that was beyond my control - my heart was being wrenched open for those pesky little vagabonds. My worldview was being dismantled.

After settling into my raw room with the bare necessities, I went to the reception desk to ask about Arjun – my friend, guide, and protector. When limping through New Delhi in survival mode, eighteen-year-old Arjun cushioned my culture shock and converted my stay into a victorious encounter.

Mr. Patel was there to greet me warmly and break the good news about Arjun's upcoming marriage. "Will Arjun continue working here at the hotel after he is married?" I asked.

"Yes, mum, my nephew would never give up such a prestigious job as bellhop *Boy Friday*."

"Will he be coming back tonight?" I inquired.

"He now fills in for me during the night shift," bragged Mr. Patel, "so he'll be coming in at 10 pm sharp."

"Great!" I exclaimed and then ran out to find some fuel. Curiously enough, curries in London were superior to those I'd eaten in India - however, the vegetarian dishes in Delhi were delectable. I fought off fatigue after my calorie rush, but the anticipation of seeing Arjun kept me revved up.

I couldn't wait to see his expression when I surprised him with a Seiko, battery-powered, quartz wristwatch. Quartz watches were the latest innovation in timeware, and I knew it would give him the prestige and incentive to keep climbing his corporate ladder with confidence.

At 10 pm punctual, Arjun arrived to relieve Mr. Patel and tucked his thermos of hot coffee under the counter, along with a hardy *samosa* snack. He would be sitting there alert until 8 am the following morning. I stood up and walked around the counter into Arjun's full view. His eyes brightened, and a huge smile danced across his expressive face. He greeted me with a warm *namaste* and bowed deeply from the waist rather than the usual nod.

"Good evening, Arjun - congratulations on your upcoming marriage! I brought you a small gift." Arjun fumbled while opening the small package, and then his eyes widened as he extracted the watch and slipped it onto his slim wrist. I knew not to appear too intimate since that would be considered a cultural blunder.

"A real quartz watch! I've read about this clever invention but never thought I would own one. Thank you, mum, you are like family to me. You are too kind." I think Arjun blushed, but his complexion was too dark to detect it. He had a synthesizing mindset that could absorb a lot of information. You could see him reflecting on it, and then he would organize it, regurgitating what would be useful and discarding the rest.

"I am so proud of your promotion to the reception desk," I said sincerely. You've been not only my trusty guide but also my bodyguard - transforming the pandemonium of the train station into a play station. I am sorry you won't have time for me when I'm here. I will miss you!"

"No, mum, I am still here for you – always. I only need four hours of sleep, mum. I will soon have my own auto rickshaw." I was merely six years older than Arjun but felt like a maternal older sister.

"I'm leaving tomorrow for Rajasthan at noon and will return to Delhi again in several days, and then I'll head up to Nepal for a week. Does my trip to the train station fit into your schedule?" I asked pleadingly.

"Oh yes, mum, of course, mum. I will take you to the right train track at the right time. Don't you worry, mum." He then endearingly wobbled his head from left to right to left again. His body language meant either 'yes' or perhaps 'thank you.' It could also signal his understanding of something – head wobble nuance was an art I finally conquered.

My long day, starting in London, caught up with me after my foray through Moscow and a two-hour layover in Baghdad. Ready to conk out, I confirmed my morning departure with Arjun and headed up to my no-frills room for a deep sleep draped in my curry-perfumed hair.

* * *

Arjun was waiting in his auto rickshaw when I exited the hotel at 11 am. With the polished expertise of a Formula I driver, he dodged holy cows, potholes, bicycles, and lunatics without blinking an eye or losing concentration. He insisted on escorting me through the swarming masses of humanity at the train station, heading towards the ticket office with brazen authority – he extended his right arm stiffly, like a snow plow.

Ticket in hand, we wove our way around the roped-off section advertising free vasectomies. The sign boasted, "Bring a friend and get a free Coca-Cola." We made our way to track number 22 – Jaipur. Arjun instructed me where to hop on, and then he remained there waving until the train was out of sight. I had slipped him an envelope to show him my appreciation, but he refused to take it. I'd look for a wedding gift in Jaipur.

My mega modeling earnings were converted into traveler's checks and tucked snugly away in my body pouch. I anticipated buying up all of the hand-woven, snake-like, silver tribal belts that Mr. Anand could find. It would take about four and a half hours to arrive in Jaipur, the capital of Rajasthan, so I treated myself to a first-class ticket. Traveling in style, I relished the time I had to reflect on where I was going - both physically and spiritually.

The Holy Spirit had stuck close to me as I traveled all around South America, but lately, I felt an uncomfortable separation. I wondered how to get the Holy Spirit working again. I'd try turning it off and back on again, and if that didn't work, I'd call the manufacturer. I knew that only with the help of the Holy Spirit would I have the power to make the changes I needed to make in my life. I was confident He was always present, ubiquitous, and omnipresent. It was me who had side-stepped away.

I pulled out my pocket-sized Gideon Bible and read over the verses I had highlighted until I felt centered again. That always worked. I was finding it challenging to balance *my* ambition with God's mission. Until they meshed, I knew I'd feel scattered. What I needed was a faith lift. *"Now faith is confidence in what we hope for and assurance about what we do not see."* (Hebrews 11:1). It seems that faith begins where reason and logic end.

Sven, the Viking I'd met in Colombia, told me that 'faith is daring to believe God's promises.' Yes, that was the answer – that's what the indigenous believers did. They believed the Words of Jesus were true and acted on them. The source of their miracles was simply faith – never diluted with doubt.

* * *

As the train pulled into the Jaipur station, my emotions began to ramp up in anticipation of returning to the Pink City, with all its tribal charm and gypsy influence. I would head to my standby hotel, *Khatu Haveli* (Old House). I knew what to expect there, and it was only a stone's throw from the Bapu Bazaar. I had stopped wasting time bargaining over rickshaw and taxi prices, which amounted to mere pennies. That sensible and generous decision eliminated the time and stress involved when I needed to move around swiftly.

The wise words of Maya Angelou reverberated around my conscience, *"Do the best you can until you know better - then when you know better, do better."* On my first trip to India, it seemed vital to battle for each rupee – but considering the dire straits of most rickshaw coolies, I started to tip my drivers.

Divit, the hotel bell boy and my usual transport, greeted me with a broad smile, a charming head wobble, and an endearing

Namaste. I adored the adventure of discovering new frontiers, but there was something cozy and comforting about returning to the familiar. I found that discovery somewhat disturbing but would dissect the innuendos another day.

Checking into the hotel, I requested my usual interior room. Although it was a bit dark, the soothing solitude outweighed the need for glaring light. After all, I'd be out from dawn to dusk - I needed a refuge from the ceaseless noise and activity of the boisterous city. As usual, I had the receptionist book me a ticket to see the Cobra Gypsy Dancers at the Oberoi Hotel.

Skipping over to Bapu Bazaar, I was on the lookout for Mr. Anand. I'd politely ask him to bring his collection of desert treasures to his market stand, thus skipping the ritual of a long, drawn-out meal at his home. Instead, I'd barter for the belts on the floor of his shop while his brother kept an eye out for clients. In Europe, ethnic jewelry was still on a roll and particularly in demand for the sun-bronzed bellies of the clubbers and fun-seekers of Ibiza.

Meanwhile, I'd shop for an authentic multi-colored Kalbelia circular skirt. With bits of shell and mirror sewn on, plus embroidery woven into their emblematic patterns, my interpretation of the snake dance would take on a new dimension. Those skirts weighed a ton, but I'd wear one back to London since it would be too bulky to pack.

I booked a rendezvous with Mr. Anand the following morning and was not disappointed. Silver was shunned in India, and rustic, handmade jewelry even more so. I had a monopoly on the nomads' treasures. Exhibiting a nonchalant attitude, I snapped up the exquisite antique silver snake belts one by one. We sealed the deal with a handshake, and I reminded Mr. Anand that I'd be back within six months for more.

The Kalbelia dancers had become synonymous with Jaipur. Their tribes from the Thar Desert had spent centuries eking out a living by extracting cobra venom to sell as potions or medicine. However, since the agile ladies' exotic cobra dance was taking the night circuit by storm – many of the Kalbelia families had traded their tents and camels for colorfully painted horse-drawn caravans and moved to the edge of town.

To honor the multi-talented dancers, I would wear my rainbow-colored circular skirt and anticipate an opportunity to swirl together with the stars. I arrived at the Oberoi early and was ushered to a front-line VIP table. The handsome head-waiter treated me like royalty as I greeted him, *Namaste*, then slipped him a well-earned gratuity.

While the musicians were warming up, Sabina, the lead dancer, spotted me and knew by now I was on their side and would pose no threat. She lifted her hand to quiet the musicians and announced, "I see we have one of our former dance students here tonight, so maybe she'll demonstrate what she learned from us." I laughed inwardly - Sabina was an excellent saleslady, as well as an artist. Although I'd never attended, I heard their school was booming with tourists and long-haul hippies.

Of course, she was taking a gamble on me, but I took up the challenge and decided to dance myself into oblivion. I wouldn't let her down. Since Kalbelia dance schools were becoming the rage, I'd do my best as her PR agent. After all, she was the first in town.

As the music started, the ladies, one by one, outmaneuvered each other with an extraordinary exhibit of their specialty. I was relieved to have time to study their moves - it had been six months since I was last in Jaipur. I prayed an S.O.S. prayer and leaped up onto the stage. I swung into my signature moves, which included gyrating, shimmying, and pirouettes. Like dancing flamenco, I naturally coordinated my arms, wrists, and finger movements.

Feeling the music as I entered into a rhythmic oscillation, I became the dance – it took over. I whirled endlessly, gyrating like a belly dancer and shimmying as if I had motors embedded in my shoulders. Did I dare to attempt a backbend while shimmying and try to grasp the upright ring with my accommodating overbite? Why not!

I tucked my head further back, grazing my forehead on the floor, and grasped the ring between my teeth. Hallelujah, I got it! As I shimmied my way back to an upright position, I was drenched with applause. I placed my hand over my heart and bowed from the waist, as Bautista had taught me after our tango demo back in Buenos Aires.

After soaking in the glory of the moment, I graciously swept my outstretched arm in front of the dance troupe, plus musicians - inviting a standing ovation. Sabina took my hand and looked into my eyes, so I grabbed her cue and announced, "I owe my skills to this amazing lady and her dance school." I wondered if I was part gypsy.

* * *

It was an intense, productive, and fun few days in Jaipur, but I was already looking forward to being in Nepal. I missed Mahesh and couldn't wait to hold him in my arms. I drew a bit of attention as I boarded the train wearing my three yards of colorful Kalbelia skirt and matching top - since it was too hefty to carry. My silver belts were heavy enough, but at least I wore as many as possible.

It was necessary to have the silver belts certified and sealed in New Delhi, proving they were acceptable antiques to be exported. Who knows how old the belts really were? But, that way, I'd have no problem exiting India or entering the UK with my treasure. Meanwhile, the Delhi bureaucrats were content to send me to three separate offices, charging some insignificant amount at each dismal place without even inspecting the belts.

Mr. Patel kindly allowed me to store my luggage at the Narula Hotel until I returned the following week from Nepal. Booking a direct morning flight with Air India would give me an optimal view of Mt. Everest. I consider Kathmandu my all-time favorite place in the world. Flying into the plush green valley of Kathmandu, encircled by the globe's highest mountain range, was nothing short of magical. It was my mystical, harmonious valley – my utopian Shangri-La.

I stepped out of the aircraft into the intoxicating crisp mountain air, shaking off the heat and humidity of India and thanking God for creating such an eye-dilating wonder. I then headed directly to my safe spartan hotel, the Panoramic. However, this time I had a panoramic view of Mt. Everest rather than the economy back-alley room. I threw my big bag into the corner, dashed out to rent a banged-up bike, and then sped into the center of town. I needed to get under Kathmandu's skin to feel at home.

Cycling around *stupas* (huge white mounds housing Tibetan holy relics), on through a bazaar of Buddha shops selling prayer flags and other temple essentials, I peddled up hippie road - dubbed Freak Street. Still the epicenter of the hippie trail, it seemed to have been stuck in suspended animation since the late '60s.

My first stop was the Ying Yang restaurant - one of the remaining all-time anchors for professional hippies and locals. It was there I first met Mahesh, my adopted boy. More or less the same crowd was there to 'turn on, tune in, and drop out.' I had a few triple and quadruple embraces with friends I'd made over the past three years. The hug philosophy was - the more people involved in the caress, the more vibes were felt. Okay, if you say so.

To be fair, most of the crowd that hung out at Ying Yang were productive professional hippies – mostly artists, authors, and musicians. They were adaptive, intuitive, and compassionate. Their self-reflective, analytical traits made them incredibly understanding of other people. Therefore they were willing helpers for Vidhya, the Nepalese restaurant owner. Inspired by his father, who opened the first orphanage in Kathmandu, Vidhya went out of his way to cater to the practical needs of street children.

On his weekly 'fast day,' when the restaurant was closed, Vidhya produced a banquet for the orphaned and abandoned kids – whether Indian, Nepalese, or Tibetan. The kids lined up outside, waiting for Vidhya to open the doors. They would then file in barefoot and sit politely at the tables. The counterculture regulars from the restaurant were all there to help serve and clean up after the youngsters. I decided to chip in and join the workforce.

I wore the large, silver, antique Portuguese cross I bought in Goa. It often became the focus of attention. "Hey, Tyke, have you become a Jesus freak?" asked an artist friend. "Yea, it's awesome!" I replied. Funnily enough, Jesus freaks fit into the 'cool' spectrum of spiritualities – whereas Christians were treated with suspicion since they echoed the establishment. It was more about a personal relationship with "The King" rather than a religious exercise.

Anxious to see Mahesh, I asked Vidhya if he knew where I could find him.

"Probably out on the playing field next to the orphanage," he replied.

"I'll work my way over there since I'd like to surprise him! Then I'll bring him and his friends back here for a banana split."

I jumped on my bike and sped to the soccer field - my heart pounding with anticipation. Six months had been too long of a separation. I had sent Vidhya several bank transfers to help defer costs at the orphanage, plus a Christmas package for Mahesh and his friends. There were ten small boys playing soccer with all their might. I stood at a distance, not wanting to disturb them, but felt tears of joy welling up in my eyes.

My precious rag-a-muffin boy had transformed into a strong, agile eight-year-old. He was wearing the cap and sweatshirt I sent him for Christmas and managed to kick a goal with expertise. I spontaneously broke into animated applause until I realized I had spoiled the game. All ten boys looked up and waved.

Nepalese children are, by nature, shy. They are soft-spoken and well-behaved – unlike their southern neighbors in India, where kids are boisterous and extroverted. I controlled my emotions and crouched down as they approached to be on their level. I shook hands with each boy and handed them a bag of *guchcha* (marbles)—something Mahesh had requested and could be enjoyed by all his friends.

During my week in Nepal, I would have more one-on-one time with Mahesh, so I didn't want to embarrass him with a hug in front of his pals. He knew I loved him. I invited the boys back to Ying Yang for banana splits, and there were a few squeals of excitement. The boys took turns riding my bike while I walked in back, steadying the bicycle for the younger ones.

The Ying Yang proprietor kindly pushed two tables together, and the kids sat down politely, awaiting their utopian dessert. While chattering among themselves in their local dialect, a hush suddenly fell over the table as the banana splits were served, and then there was not one peep apart from sporadic slurping. What an absolute joy it gave me to see these kids enjoying my favorite dessert. Most all the cafes and restaurants in Kathmandu had jumped on the bandwagon and added the delectable dessert onto their sprawling menus.

Vidhya explained that all ten boys lived in the orphanage but were free to go out and play after their school lessons finished at 3 pm. They had a light supper at the orphanage or could eat out with 'foreigners,' which had become the custom.

The kids were so well-behaved and appreciative - they had ongoing relationships with die-hard repetitive visitors to Nepal, like myself. Few of the children were outright adopted and would have felt lost if uprooted from the customs of their familiar homeland and friends. I knew I was probably sharing Mahesh with other wanderers and all the happier for it.

A group of sympathizers from the community were hoping to offer a technical training college for the kids as they matured. Since the infrastructure of Kathmandu was sprouting by leaps and bounds, so would its need for electricians, plumbers, and construction workers.

I needed to get my act together to join the group of sponsors that would enable this realistic dream to become a reality. Meanwhile, I would invite Mahesh and his friends to whatever meals or snacks their little hearts desired.

Momos (buffalo meat-filled dumplings) and *dal bhat*, were the staple food of Nepal. Other cheap and substantial favorites were rice served with lentil soup and vegetable or chicken curry. Of course, banana split with *anaraa* (rice cookie made with dry ground fruit and deep fried) gave a sweet ending to the meal.

Since the kids had school until 3 pm and then sports until almost 5 pm, I had the days to revisit my favorite spot - Boudhanath – the Tibetan heart of Nepal. The neighborhood is known as 'Little Tibet' and is located seven miles from the outskirts of Kathmandu.

The central Tibetan *stupa* (ancient 120 feet mound used as a depository of Buddha relics) and its massive *mandala* (Buddhist devotional image deemed a symbol of an ideal universe) was one of the largest spherical *stupas* in Nepal and the world. It is said to be 1,500 years old, and the surrounding neighborhood has become home to nearly 16,000 Tibetan refugees.

Boudhanath was a bonanza of ancient culture, artifacts, ethnic silver jewelry, and traditional rainbow-colored ensembles. Coral and turquoise were the treasured equivalent of diamonds and emeralds. I found a silversmith to mount those ancient Tibetan stones in rings and things several years ago. Lobsang, the gifted silversmith, welcomed me warmly with yak butter tea which tasted more like rancid broth since it was salty with a bitter aroma.

I had bought a bunch of semi-precious gemstones in Jaipur – some as gifts for my Nepalese and Tibetan friends and others to be worked into jewelry by Lobsang and sold in Ibiza. The joys of wheeling and dealing kept me exhilarated and stretched my imagination for new designs that my Tibetan silversmith could set into chunky jewelry. I saw he knocked out some of my designs from last year and had them on display for sale. I felt complimented beyond measure.

* * *

Back on Freak Street, I visited Ram Gopal, known as KD - the owner of the other booming restaurant/café catering to foreigners, namely Everest Snack Bar. His clientele were mainly wannabe hippies who missed the mark, plus generic backpackers and yuppies (young urban professionals) who wanted to be cool. Everyone was smoking joints, since it was cheap and legal, or munching hash brownies – except me. I enjoyed being outrageously original and was pleased not to be slotted into any category.

Freak Street had developed its own pecking order, but I felt the height of the hippie scene had morphed into a stage for the type of travelers who came to gape at the now-aging, free-spirited dropouts.

The flip side of the Kathmandu scene was made up of diplomats, who felt they were the elite echelon. However, considering the global importance of Nepal, their presidents and prime ministers had to scrape the diplomatic barrel to fill the posts for the Valley's embassies. Nevertheless, being sent to Kathmandu was like winning the lottery, but not if you were trying to climb the diplomatic ladder. This extreme duality of residents could be found sitting shoulder to shoulder, sipping borscht, at the Yak and Yeti Restaurant.

I personally felt the foreign resident heroes were the doctors volunteering their time and energy at the local clinic - mainly from *Médecins Sans Frontières* (Doctors Without Borders). I decided to whiz by the expanding clinic to see if Jean-Jacques was still there. He volunteered four months a year since the early '70s and was helping to eradicate smallpox from the nation of Nepal. Bingo, Jean-Jacques was there and invited me to dine at the up-market eatery of the Valley, the Yak and Yeti Restaurant. He kindly added that Mahesh was more than welcome to join us.

Co-owner, flamboyant hotelier, and restaurateur was the celebrated Russian ballet dancer Boris Lisanevich. He was there in person to meet, greet and seat you. Upon entering, Boris welcomed Jean-Jacques, "Bienvenue Docteur, your usual table for two?" I was a regular when in town, so Boris graciously lifted my hand to his lips and clicked his heels - more out of respect for my illustrious escort. I was wearing my Peruvian cape and fedora hat, accessorized with some Jaipur jewelry and my hand-embroidered Tibetan boots. Mahesh wore one of the new outfits I bought him and looked absolutely adorable.

As we walked across the ancient stones of the restaurant floor, weaving gracefully through the elegant tables, the men looked up and smiled while their lady friends pelted us with silence. I felt it was my duty to give the bored residents some ammunition for gossip sniping and allowed them time for some mental gymnastics to assess whether Mahesh was a love child . . . . or not. One thing was for sure – he *was* a lovable child! Jean-Jacques and Mahesh chatted in Nepali while I studied the appetizing menu.

We all settled for a piping hot bowl of Ukrainian borscht – Boris' signature recipe. The bright red beetroot soup, filled with a medley of veggies, was topped with dollops of rich sour cream and accompanied by hot, homemade bread. To seal our appetite, we finished with chocolate brownies drenched in chocolate sauce, decorated with marshmallows, and adorned with scoops of homemade ice cream.

It was great to catch up with Jean-Jacques, a truly noble human being. Even though he was handsome, he was unconcerned about his image or status as a single physician. Since his unique focus was on the relentless mission of stamping out the dreaded disease of smallpox, he would continue to return to the valley and its people.

"The devastating disease has been eradicated in even the smallest villages of Nepal," explained Jean-Jacques. "However, with a constant trickle of refugees trekking over the mountains from Mongolia, there is always a chance of reoccurrence."

When I asked, "What is the key to eradicating the disease?" Jean-Jacques replied, "Prayer and perseverance. Also, I had to win over the trust of the Nepalese people with genuine care and concern."

Jean-Jacques had become one of my heroes and I would try to emulate his heart of gold. I was still in the copper or brass range but would gradually aim for gold. While in Rio, Nico had convinced me that I needed to stay in step with the Holy Spirit – so I'd try. I still needed to decipher what mission God had for me to accomplish - then, with His guidance, I would try to walk it out.

My week in Kathmandu had bolted by too fast. It was already time to head back to Delhi, then London, and on to my sparkling island in the Med - Ibiza. I made the rounds to bid farewell to my diverse group of friends, then stopped by the orphanage to drop off a volleyball, along with a net and a wide variety of cricket equipment they needed.

I checked out of my home in the Valley - the Nepalese-owned Panoramic Hotel. Giving Mr. Tuladhar (better known as Dad) a hardy half-hug, I jumped into Jean-Jacques' sedan and balanced Mahesh on my jean-clad knees. The half-hour it took to arrive at the airport was filled with laughter and light conversation. However, I was fighting off tears but holding fast to this farewell memory with two unforgettable men who were making my world a better place to live. I'd be back!

15. IBIZA, SPAIN

My return flight to London took about forty-eight hours, including stopovers and unexpected sleepovers. All of my luggage actually made it through customs and ended up with me in Tink's living room. PHEW! I reshuffled my closet, stuffing in the winter woolies and extracting my flimsy island wear. I then loaded up my nomad silver belts, a flurry of antique gowns, and turn-of-the-century ladies' underwear. I intuitively knew that those skimpy garments would be a success on the streets and in the clubs of my fairy-tale isle.

Ibiza was my comfort zone, and for the first time, I started to think about it as *home*. WHAT? I had friends with comfy couches in London, Paris, and Rome, so I didn't need a home. I had avoided staying longer than a month anywhere for over three years and was proud of it. I had zero desire for permanent walls and furniture.

I preferred exotic travel rather than toxic monotony. All I needed was a place to lay my head to dream about my next adventure. I felt uneasy when two days were nearly the same – so what made me feel like I was going *home*? Maybe it was something I ate - or perhaps it was jet lag. But whatever it was, it was disturbing! I'd try to shake it off . . . . . quickly!

Feeling like a ruffled homing pigeon, I wondered if the Holy Spirit had programmed me to return to Ibiza. The desire seemed to be out of my control. I was even considering renting a studio for most of the summer rather than staying at *Los Caracoles* (The Snails). I would have no commitment in that humble hostel - I could fly off whenever, to wherever I pleased. As hard as it was to find logic or reason, perhaps my mission *was* to be in Ibiza for an entire season.

Deciding to go with the flow, I would follow what gave me peace rather than dissect my desires and rehash my means of income. One thing was clear: I had a passion for fashion, as frivolous as it seemed. I knew what would sell, so my two-fold mission would be to set up a cottage industry fueled by local ladies working in their homes. I would then locate a shop where l could sell my creations to fashion-hungry tourists.

Ibiza had a 'look' of its own. No matter what designer apparel the visitors arrived with, their outfits would fall short when worn on the magical "White Island." Ibiza had a fantasy fashion all of its own. I decided to search for a three-month rental and test the waters. Without getting drenched, I'd wade in with caution.

Bouncing into paradise, I arrived at the newly completed terminal of Ibiza, accompanied by the usual applause from nervous but relieved locals, then screeching breaks and muffled screams. Ah, there's nothing like Ibiza in mid-May! The familiar bougainvillea adorned the old airport to greet us, along with the rifle-toting *Guardia Civil*. Hallelujah, I'm home to my very own gemstone in the Med!

Back in Ibiza

My many suitcases zipped through customs with a mere sneer from the uniformed men, and I hopped onto a German charter bus headed to the historical Montesol Hotel. There, on the main promenade in Ibiza Town, was the landmark hotel/cafe where everyone started the day - at noon. After *muchos abrazos* (many hugs) and a piping hot coffee, I quizzed the beach and club crowd about a simple apartment for rent.

"Well, darlin'," offered NYC Arlene, "Beautiful Barry has a studio for rent in the *Calle de la Virgen* (Virgin Street) in the Peña, near the port." La Peña, a neighborhood situated on a brute rock bordering the sea and the marina, was where the *Gitanos* (gypsies) hung out. They were generational squatters who had staked their claim without any intention of budging. Without a second thought, I knew that was the spot meant for me. The news got to Barry through the grapevine and we sealed the deal over lunch.

A caravan of kind friends helped me lug my luggage onto the pedestrian-only Virgin lane and up to the studio. As we wove our way through gypsy kids, I tossed out candy (Mardi Gras style) to the teens and tots in lieu of paying protection money. It worked. I was pleased to see that New York Deena and her son Clovis lived just across the street.

I was fast-tracked into the American ex-pat clique by presumably being of Semitic origin. I was proud to be mistaken for one of the *Chosen,* having come to terms with my fairly long nose, full lips, dark curly hair, and olive complexion. I was a bit too tall and missing the curves, but hey, it felt good to be included. Most of the ex-pat community consisted of draft-dodging guys from the Big Apple and the girls who followed on their heels.

However, North Vietnamese tanks had rolled through the gates of the Presidential Palace in Saigon just two weeks ago, effectively ending the war. Nevertheless, many of the US ex-pats stayed on and continued their lazy lifestyle in Ibiza during the spring and fall, Kashmir during the sweltering heat, and of course, Goa for the winter. Others returned to their wealthy family businesses, and a few became entrepreneurs.

Ibiza, an island filled with artists, writers, and musicians, was a bona fide hippie haven. However, it was now slowly attracting celebrities and wealthy investors from all over Europe and beyond. The local Ibicencos were ultra-tolerant to the influx of quirky characters that jump-started their economy and were now beginning to cash in on the steady trickle of tourism.

It was the tipping point. I knew I'd have to jump onto the merry-go-round while it was still spinning. This summer would determine my future, but I would try to be led rather than run ahead. Weighing the pros and cons, I realized that if you work a seasonal job, you still have six months of freedom – OLÉ!

With the infrastructure slowly expanding, it would accommodate the arrival of global travelers. Without designated norms, the mix of cultures, nationalities, and perspectives eliminated the boring by-product of predetermined dress codes and behavior. That was the deciding factor – I was a merry misfit and intended to remain one.

I was still trying to balance being in this world without becoming worldly. I needed to support myself, but I wanted to generate enough money to reach out to those who didn't have a choice - especially innocent children. What about the kids who lived in the streets, surviving by their wits? What about all the youth, abandoned by death or neglect, who were forced to turn to crime or dine from a trash can?

* * *

There were already a handful of boutiques strung out in the fishermen's rustic neighborhood - parallel to the port. There was even a colorful shop on my gypsy lane. I would investigate them after I settled in and chilled out. Skipping up and down my rocky 'Street of the Virgin,' I gradually bonded with the kids, realizing how much they resembled the children of India and Nepal. After all, they were the descendants of the nomads from the Thar Desert of Rajasthan. Due to famine and persecution, they immigrated to the Balkans and Europe six hundred years ago. I guess they were mostly out of work since there were no cobras to catch and extract their valuable venom to sell as magic potions.

Yes, even the tiniest children were singing and dancing in the streets, and there was always a guitarist sitting on a step strumming and humming. Of course, the flamenco dance was a variation of the Kalbelia's colorful gyrating whirl birthed not far from Jaipur, India. The hand, wrist, and finger movements were nearly identical to their Indian nomad ancestors. It was a stunning surprise to have Kalbelia descendants on my doorstep. I brought my two-ton circular skirt with me to perform that unique desert dance in style – perhaps to the tune of the gypsy guitarist.

I was curious about the intriguing boutique at the entrance of my street. It was a small cave-like shop with a big name - Paula and Mopitz Boutique. Although it was a hole in the wall, it was fascinating. Every day, I was compelled to stop and scrutinize the three-by-three-foot window display. I was mesmerized by how much creativity oozed out of that limited space. Often, a menagerie of people gathered in front of the shop, appearing to have haphazardly fallen out of a Fellini film.

Eventually, I felt it was polite to introduce myself properly to the group. I was amazed to discover that the tall, dark, dashing guy who looked like a magician was an American stylist by instinct and super-salesman by trade. He introduced himself as Stuart. This savvy ex-pat took sales to another level.

There was a heavy chain strung across the shop entrance, and you had to deserve to enter. I realized that once past the chain, you were at Stuart's mercy. I peeked in several times and heard him tell a lady that *he* would choose what she could try on. Real *chutzpah* (audacity)! However, the Germanic-looking lady walked out of the shop with the dress, matching hat and bag, and a radiant smile.

YES, she had just purchased a piece of Ibiza - not only an ensemble, but a slice of a lifestyle she could only dream of living.

"Hey Stuart, how did you get away with that?" I asked.

He shook his head and replied, "These ladies have no idea what looks good on them, but I do." I liked his brazen confidence – I'm sure he was right.

"Are you designing these faded floral prints," I wondered out loud.

"No, my partner is an architect who is now building dreams with his hand-designed fabric and the fortunate mistakes of the local sewing ladies."

"Oh yeah, what kind of mistakes?" I softly grilled Stuart.

"The right ones," he answered - not wanting to give away too much.

A fascinating guy with long hair, a mustache, circular wire-rimmed glasses, toting a huge Ibiza basket walked into the shop as if he owned it. He carefully extracted a handful of dresses and said he'd be back later. On his way out, he paused, looked at me, and said, "Is she one of the new *chicas* you found for our next fashion show?"

"Not yet," said Stuart as he introduced me to Armin. A gorgeous Afro-American lady was perched outside the shop on a stool. Her XL floral dress appeared to have a large percentage of the island's flowers printed on it.

"Aren't you the one who attended the opening party at Pacha wearing nothing but an Ibiza basket? I noticed you cleverly cut out the bottom of the basket, stepped in, then slung the straps around your neck," said the lovely lady called Johnnis.

"Uh, yep, that was me," I admitted, "but I had a bouquet of gladioli stuffed in the basket to camouflage my skimpy bikini."

Pacha Opening Night – 1973

"And hey, weren't you the DJ - go-go girl at Lola's club in the cave?" I inquired.

Johnnis, with a twinkle in her eye and a hardy laugh, replied, "It was a good starting point until I was promoted to Paula's Boutique."

"So glad to meet y'all, my name's Marie France, but my nickname is Tyke. I've rented a studio up the road and plan on staying for the summer - let me know if you all need anything from the market."

It was comforting to meet other non-conformist seekers who were obviously looking for an alternative lifestyle . . . . . and seemed to have found one. I skipped to the market with a few gypsy kids in tow.

Sporting a flouncy straw hat covered with flowers, I accentuated a romantic appeal by wearing an early Victorian camisole. My bare midriff lent space to stack up several silver snake belts and complimented my tight blue jeans, cut off below the knee. I removed the ruffle from my vintage bloomers and sewed it onto my jeans for a romantic flare. Thus, I had the perfect outfit for a mid-morning shopping spree.

The market was buzzing with confusion from the multi-faceted residents who were propelling the expansion of Ibiza's budding commerce. The elderly local ladies were in full regalia, with traditional black shawls and full skirts reaching their hand-woven sandals. Meandering around the stalls was a full spectrum of hippies. Some were orange-clad Bhagwan followers and others serious merchants. The noble columned open-air market that displayed the local produce also served as an intimate place to secure important rendezvous.

"Well, hello, Miss New Orleans! When did you breeze in and from where? You look absolutely divine!" With my ultra-high platform sandals, I seemed to dwarf my friend, the entertaining and infamous art forger Elmyr de Hory. He and his friend Mark said they were throwing a luncheon soiree in several days and invited me to come along, "And Tyke, do bring some beautiful people, preferably handsome guys. We're always top-heavy on over-ripe ladies."

I laughed and said I'd be delighted to come for lunch and bring some good-looking guys. There were tons of gorgeous multi-national males on the island and most were hungry, so no problem. Elmyr's petulant and pejorative intonation enabled him to chop people up without even trying. On the other hand, he could be as charming as Prince Valiant and a mega-talented enigmatic artist.

"And wear exactly what you have on," shouted Elmyr over the clamor of the crowded market. Without many telephones on the island, the Montesol and the Market were the main communication venues. You had to check into one or the other daily to stay abreast and know precisely what was happening.

Fortunately, there was no supermarket, so within half a block, you also had the *panaderia* (bread shop), *carnicería* (butcher), and *lechería* (milk shop) – however, fresh yogurt was sold on the port at 'La Bomba.' By making the rounds, you had all the tidbits of gossip you could want and even more.

After scooting back to my studio to put my stuff away, I pranced down to the Montesol to check in with friends and visually announce that I had silver belts for sale. I was grilled about my journey through South America but simply replied, "You have to see it to believe it." I had learned from experience that people didn't *really* want to know how you were or the details of your travels. And if they sincerely wanted to know, they'd beg.

The yellow and white four-floor neocolonial style Montesol Hotel/café was by far the best-known landmark in Ibiza City. It was also the best place to reconnect with everyone who was anyone. It had become so popular that the servers ignored the customers. They knew full well that the clients would remain faithful because it was the island's indisputable 'in' café.

While sipping my coffee, I had greetings and hugs from a stream of friends. Not only my Ibiza pals but friends from across Europe and along the hippie trail in Nepal, India, Bali, and beyond.

"Hi Alan, are you taking a break from promoting your rock star tours to catch some fun in the sun pre-season?" I asked the bronzed Frenchman. "Hey, where's Petra? I had a blast staying in her mom's condo in Ipanema during Carnival in Rio," I bragged.

I could read Alan's body language – something had gone wrong. "Petra couldn't keep up with life in the fast lane," he replied. Alan pretended to blow it off and tried to look unfazed by the turn of events.

"Oh, she seemed happy six months ago when I stayed with you two in Paris," I exaggerated.

"Yeah, but she started with a lot of crazy talk and kept saying she felt she should go back to Brazil. Something about the Holy Spirit was nudging her to return to Rio, where she had left her heart. Anyway, her inheritance was dwindling," he laughed.

I could tell Alan was devastated, perhaps not because of lost love but because Petra's exit was a kick to his inflated ego. He was the type of guy who couldn't roll with the punch of rejection. Infidel that he was, he never imagined a lady would leave him.

"By the way, I'd like you to meet the love of my life, Juliette," cooed Alan. "You're always welcome to stay with us in Paris – you know that."

"Nice to meet you Juliette. I hope you enjoy your time here in Ibiza with Romeo," I replied with derisive laughter while extending my hand, "Good luck!" Meanwhile, my eyes filled with tears of joy and I thanked the Lord for answering my prayer. Petra was destined to be with Nico. He loved her beyond words – their love story was meant to continue on into eternity.

I needed to celebrate! "Hey Miguel," I called to the waiter, "A banana split with lots of chocolate sauce!" I was so ecstatic I could barely wait to call Petra's mother so we could revel together in the earth-shattering good news.

After exchanging updates and embraces with at least a dozen friends, I worked my way back up *La Calle de la Cruz* (The Street of the Cross). I glided past all the basket shops selling hand-woven palm fibers - crafted into sandals, hats, baskets, mats, and everything under the sun. The emerging new versatile array of residents, representing every color and persuasion, all had one thing in common – we all toted Ibiza baskets, so business was booming for the basket weavers and the merchants!

"Hi Tyke, glad you're back in town - I need you to model for my upcoming fashion show this Saturday at La Tierra. It's still too early in the season to pay you anything, but you can gladly keep whatever you wear." I gave Catherine, the petite French fashion entrepreneur, a heartfelt hug and thanked her for asking me to model her unique designs at the upcoming event.

1st Moda ADLIB - La Tierra

Her boutique, 'Tip Top,' was in a commercial position on the basket street - just one block from the port and not far from the Market. She was raised in Mexico City by French parents, so she had the advantage of speaking Spanish and the work ethic needed to organize business on this lackadaisical island. She transplanted hand-tinted cotton with lace, popular in Mexico, to the shores of Ibiza - giving an artistic, romantic flair to cotton wear.

"If you can, come by tomorrow and try on the dresses so I can make any alterations that might be needed." Catherine pleaded.

"Sure thing; how about 11 am?"

"*Parfait!* I'm up every morning by 8 am, so I'll be expecting you."

My daily diary was already rounding out, and I was feeling more and more like Ibiza was the place I was meant to be. I felt like a gradual but steady paradigm shift was taking place. I was aware that the trajectory of my life was being reshaped by a force more profound than the limitations of my mind or decision. So, I just decided to go with the flow and try and stay in step with the Holy Spirit. I was clearly being led, so I tried to follow. However, the dilemma persisted, how was I to remain in this materialistic world without becoming worldly?

What I needed was a bicycle! I always became more focused while pedaling, and it was the right speed to smell the perfume of wildflowers while absorbing the beauty of my surroundings. I planned on renting a bike but settled on a sturdy, second-hand bargain since I'd need wheels for the season. The best beach was Salinas – a mere five and a half miles each way, so I wouldn't have to hitchhike from the Montesol. OLÉ!

I bought some almond cookies for the kids on my street and knew they'd be back from school and waiting for their treat. I was trying to teach them the philosophy of 'give and take.' I expected a song or a dance in exchange for an almond delight - I could tell the children were born to perform. They'd occasionally ask me to pray for a cut or a bruise, and Voila! Their boo-boos were quickly healed. They knew that I cared, because I did.

Sebas, short for Sebastián, was a tiny kid with a huge voice. His demeanor and expression transformed when he closed his eyes and opened his mouth. He put so much passion into his renditions - it made me well up with emotion. Sebas' motivation was intrinsic – he would sing for the sake of singing. He was a sweet little angel disguised as an urchin.

As I approached my neighborhood, I noticed a lot of commotion. It looked like Hollywood was using my pot-holed dirt road as an unlikely set. Upon closer inspection, I realized they had discovered Paula and Mopitz Boutique. The petite boutique extraordinaire had an array of surrealistic models at the entrance decked out in their signature floral prints.

With Stuart directing, Johnnis was perched elegantly on her stool while the other models seemed to orbit around her. The compositions were galactic! The photographers were snap-happy and lapping it up.

The classy *DuMont Travel Guide*, with the eye-catching advert for Paula's boutique, attracted travelers and the news media. More importantly, *Die Zeit* (The Time) weekly newspaper, published in Hamburg, included a special insert aimed at intellectuals and professionals from the world of culture. Bingo! *Die Zeit* cleverly placed the eclectic Paula's Boutique entourage on the cover of its insert, enabling Ibiza and the boutique to become household names in *Deutschland*.

Armin became the prototype of a professional (architect) who ran away from society to seek love, peace, and freedom. Dividing his time between self-discovery in the simplicity and beauty of the countryside and earning a living, he became a tangible dream for others to follow. *Stern* and *Bunte* magazines jumped on the bandwagon and rushed out to cover the attraction. Meanwhile, the bi-product produced was a ton of free publicity lavished upon Ibiza.

I wonder if the big-wig locals and multi-national developers would ever realize what initiated Ibiza's booming tourism. Clearly, the creative and colorful hippies of the 70s attracted the news media, thus propelling the economy.

What I gleaned from this astute observation was that it was time to jump in. Ibiza was a frontier town, and the gold rush was undoubtedly beginning. Spain had loads of inexpensive destinations with fun in the sun, but the main attraction to Ibiza was the eccentric hippies and their sought-after lifestyle.

I would look for a boutique to rent and start next season. I'd spent enough years in discos and clubs to be sure of the quirky fashion that would rock with the clubbers. I'd have my niche and excel in it.

My island was only twenty-one miles long and twelve miles wide, but it was the center of my world. Perhaps Ibiza would become the world's music capital, and I would be there to dress the trance dancers. Now the challenge was to balance peace with prosperity, like the wings of a dove – I'd have the Holy Spirit for equilibrium.

* * *

Skipping up to my studio, leaping over kids, and avoiding stray chickens, I could hear a familiar tune I had known since childhood. Yes, it *was* "Amazing Grace." However, it was sung with semi-Spanish lyrics and intense gypsy fervor. The *Gitanos*, the musical nomadic ethnic group, originated from Rajasthan's deserts. Their secret language, Caló, was the only Indo-Aryan language spoken exclusively outside the Indian subcontinent.

In 1973 the Spanish dictator, Francisco Franco, resigned as prime minister due to advanced age and illness – thus ending the reign of one of Europe's longest dictatorships. Juan Carlos became king, and the slow transition to democracy began. The *Herald Tribune* article that my mother mailed me was informative, but I wasn't sure how the present political situation could affect my life. I wondered what mom was insinuating; the only uproar going on in Ibiza was the 'love revolution.'

Meanwhile, the gypsy population throughout Spain faced persecution under Franco. However, on the heels of democracy, they would encounter unprecedented opportunities and equal status as Spanish citizens. They would also have the freedom to establish their own Evangelical church. Any non-Catholic denomination was labeled a cult or sect during the Franco reign. That said, a large portion of the Catholic Church at that time was intertwined with superstition and sometimes meshed with ancient deities.

The gypsy evangelical denomination was called Philadelphia, taking its name from the community referenced in the last book of the Bible - Revelation. The revival started to sweep through the nation within the Gypsy communities. The teachings were Biblical, stressing justification by faith in Jesus Christ. These evangelicals based their faith on Scripture rather than what was handed down through the grapevine. How amazing that God Almighty would choose the gypsy (*Gitano*) community in Spain to reveal His grace-saturated truths.

I was surprised to see and hear that there was a Philadelphia fellowship on my dead-end road. The gypsy-*Gitanos* had a reputation for nefarious dealings such as drug trafficking, petty theft and thimblerig (the fraudulent gambling game with three shells and a pea). I wondered what came first – the egg or the chicken. Did the gypsies resort to bad behavior due to persecution, or were they being persecuted for their bad behavior? God only knows.

Meanwhile, I hoped they'd allow me to join their hallelujah street service – I knew I was destined for flamenco-style worship. I noticed that at 8 pm each evening, a group would gather, and the leader would read from the Bible. And then, the flamboyant assembly would sing and dance, praising the goodness of *Jesucristo* (Jesus Christ). I knew many of the melodies and could lip-read their local lyrics. I was accepted, therefore breaking the barriers for a *payo* (non-gypsy) to participate. Of course, I looked like an alien, so they probably weren't sure if I was ethereal or human.

* * *

I would soon embark on my nightly circuit. First, I'd cruise by *Mono Desnudo* (Naked Ape) and check out who had checked into the island since yesterday. I'd ordered a Tequila Sunrise as usual, and even though I didn't drink, it looked stunning. Since my friends admitted I always looked 'out of it' naturally - I accepted that as a compliment.

Mono Desnudo was popping with interesting people. I wore one of my 20s beaded silk chiffon gowns, purchased at the Antique Clothes Market on King's Road. I discovered the fastest way to sell a vintage dress was to wear it. By the time I'd gotten to Pacha disco, I had sold my slightly worn dress at least five times. I invited my customers to meet me at the Montesol at noon the following day, where I'd finalize the sales. I had brought only about twelve of those dresses with me and wished I had scooped up more.

"Hey Tyke, you're back! How was Carnival in Rio?" Tomas was a good friend from Berlin, and his handsome friend Udo was with him.

"Groovy! I wish you could have been there," I replied. "Hey, would you two guys like to join me for lunch tomorrow?" I knew Elymr de Hory would adore having those two blue-eyed, blond guys with unique muscular physiques as guests and decoration at his luncheon soiree. They'd enjoy the banquet and perhaps find some cool chicks there.

"Sure thing Tyke, we'll pick you up in my Wolksvagen wan." Most all my German friends spoke excellent English but often confused W's and V's. Never mind, the verbal reversal was charming.

"Great, I'll meet you two at the Montesol at noon, and we can have a coffee first, then listen to the juicy news. Elmyr expects us at 1 pm, and it will only take fifteen minutes to get to his house at *Los Molinos* (The Windmills)."

"We're heading to La Tierra if you want to join us," Tomas asked.

"Thanks; I'll catch up with you two in a jiffy." I saw several professional transients from the hippie trail that I wanted to see before they breezed out of town again. We had a good chat in between hysterical laughter. They must have been high as a kite, and I always managed to have contact highs - it was a lot cheaper and better for my health, I decided. My waist-long wavy hair was decorated with a drooping flower, so I pinched a fresh one from a nearby vase and was ready to move on.

"Ana, YEA, you're back from Argentina. I've been asking about you! You made my time in Buenos Aires a real dream! How is Bautista and his tango school, and what about Nacho? When are his polo matches in Europe, and when will he arrive in Ibiza?" Ana's British boyfriend and sponsor had bought the lease for La Tierra bar from NYC Arlene, so Ana had become the reigning queen of the 'in' bar and the proprietor.

"Tyke, you look divine – I must have the dress you're wearing!"

"Sure Ana, it's yours – tomorrow – I'll try not to work up a sweat at Pacha!" We hugged and laughed as she gave me the lowdown on Bautista, Nacho, and the rest of the gang from Buenos Aires. Ibiza people were professional travelers. You crossed them wherever you went – both in the Northern and Southern Hemispheres and everywhere in between.

It was nearly midnight and time to boogie at Pacha club, so I grabbed a taxi with a few friends and headed to the other side of the harbor. What had once been considered the countryside was now within the city limits. Pacha had been transformed from a centuries-old farmhouse into a celebrated club. Its founder, Ricardo Urgell, greeted us with a giant smile. He was bronzed to a toast and remained that way year-round. We strolled in without paying since we were considered influencers and did our best to dance up a storm.

The club only opened two years ago, but its fame and popularity have grown globally. The regulars were there and moving with the music. Renee, a curvy redhead Jewess from the US, was wearing a friendly boa constrictor draped around her neck. "Feather boas are sissy stuff," she hissed. Cute Dutch Annemie with her handsome Spanish boyfriend took center stage, and all eyes were on her.

Alba, the lovely Italian princess, was swaying with her swanky, charming suitor. Dora, the German designer, and her local love were seated on the red-carpeted steps observing the glamour. I was a solo dancer – preferring to rock out at my own rhythm. I had special praise steps to lift up the name of YESHUA. The next thing I knew, it was 3 am, the disco lights flashed on and off, and then the familiar announcement, "*Estamos cerrando – vete a casa!*" (We are closing – go home!).

* * *

Tomas and Udo were at the Montesol punctually at noon, and I'd finished selling my slightly worn 20s beaded gowns for an elegant price. After a leisurely coffee and catching up with friends, we headed out to Elymr's place for a mouth-watering meal, and hopefully, I'd clench a deal for my unique silver cobra belts.

Wearing the lively market outfit that Elymr had requested, I ensured my Victorian camisole left enough bare midriff to accentuate the stack of silver belts I wound around my tanned tummy. My flouncy straw hat was filled with flowers, and my hair was left wild since it was saturated with the salty brine of the sea. I substituted my ruffled denims for my embroidered Kalbelia skirt. After all, the skirt was part of my belt story and would provide oomph if I was allowed to give a dance demo.

Elmyr and his friend Mark greeted us enthusiastically, but their eyes were glued to Tomas and Udo. Their lovely sea-view home was filled with elite visitors - mainly with borrowed or invented titles they carried without effort. The Yugoslavian *'Princess'* Smilja Mihailovitch, who created the *Moda Adlib* Fashion Show, needed a showcase to entertain her aristocratic friends from Madrid or perhaps Transylvania.

I had modeled in those initial shows since they were held in the cozy patio of the 'in' bar - La Tierra. I wore Catherine's Tip-Top designs because they were so romantic and appealing. Smilja shrieked when she focused on my cobra belts and proposed I give her one – thus promoting my nomad treasures amongst her lavish friends.

"No dice, your highness, my belts don't need promotion – they promote themselves without even trying," I replied with a toothy smile.

Meanwhile, Elymr, the dapper and famous art forger, had sold over a thousand art forgeries to reputable art galleries worldwide. He had garnered celebrity status on the island and was now holding court and basking in his tarnished glory. His fame escalated when Clifford Irving's book, *Fake,* exposed his brilliant forgeries and became an international bestseller. A year ago, Orson Welles followed up with a documentary essay film, *F for Fake.*

On that note, Elymr asked me if I'd be so kind as to auction off one of his signed paintings. The auction venue would be Pacha, and the money would go to charity. By now, his fame as an artist had escalated, and his signed work (with his own name) had found a lucrative market. His charitable donation would help cleanse his reputation.

"Absolutely, Elymr, what a splendid, benevolent idea," I replied. I was confident I could convince my artist friend to have follow-up auctions for the street children of Bolivia, Brazil, and Nepal. Why not? The more he gave to charity, the more charitable he would appear. He would be remembered for his good works rather than his dubious deeds.

Auctioning Elmyr's Painting – Pacha

When one by one, the ladies at the soiree wanted to know more about my belts - I offered to demonstrate the Kalbelia dance that the nomads of Rajasthan made famous. I brought a tape with the background dance music, just in case. "YES, we want to see the dance," they begged in unison.

I'd do my best to give them an entertaining display. As I shimmied into my backbend position, applause broke out and only paused when I bent my head backward and grasped the ring between my teeth. I gyrated around the room until I was breathless, ending with a triple pirouette. As you can imagine, I returned home beltless, with a naked midriff and cash to last me the summer.

Tomas and Udo were speechless, with their eyes like saucers and mouths wide open. "Tyke, what a sales pitch - they didn't know what hit them," laughed Udo. "You must have gypsy blood pulsating through your veins." We laughed until we cried as Tomas drove back to town shaking his head.

They dropped me off at the market, and I made my way up Virgin lane to chill out in my apartment before the Philadelphia worship service, and then my nightlife circuit would begin.

* * *

As I chilled out in my apartment, the reoccurring theme was nagging me - how do I remain in this world without becoming worldly? I was often frustrated with my seeming lack of ability to progress more rapidly in my walk with Yeshua. I often walked sideways and backward while trying to advance forward.

Needing some fresh air, I walked up to the 13th-century cathedral atop the walled *Dalt Vila* (upper town). The fortified walled city, with its imposing *Portal de ses Taules* gateway, was only a few blocks away - just at the foot of the market.

Walking up the ramp, I always felt a romantic nostalgia attached to the dramatic history of the beautiful old walled city. The cobblestones were worn with centuries of use, and the stately whitewashed mansions required repair. However, the bright magenta bougainvillea and the shrill songs of the birds seemed to speak of vanity – "Look at me, listen to me, I'm perfect and dazzling!"

The views from the castle and its ramparts were nothing short of spectacular. Sitting on the wall overlooking the sea, I tried to follow my mom's instructions and opened the weekly *Herald Tribune.*

There was an exciting interview with Buzz Aldrin, the astronaut, about his eight-day mission to the moon and back. When his capsule was shot up to the moon, I always thought it arrived in one clean, direct hit. However, he explained that there was a course correction every ten minutes from start to finish.

That spoke volumes to me. I realized that I would probably need a course correction every ten minutes of my life. However, I held on to a highlighted verse in my Bible;

"For it is by grace you have been saved, through faith – and this is not from yourselves, it is the gift of God – not by work, so that no one can boast." (Eph. 2:8-9) I counted on the Holy Spirit to help me recalibrate every six hundred seconds. I knew there was no way I could ever earn salvation through self-effort. That's why God Almighty devised His rescue plan. However, I wanted to be a good PR agent for JESUS. I could feel my heart being tenderized, and I was becoming acutely aware of others' needs – especially children.

As I meandered back down the mountain, I thought about life as a painting with ambiguous images. Those dual illusions are pictures that elicit a perceptual "switch" between alternating graphic interpretations. I needed to focus on the space beyond the obvious . . . . to capture the Truth. Yes, faith begins where reason and logic end.

It's all about God's love operating, whether I have done anything to deserve it. Grace dismantles my worldview – as if living a good life and being nice to people will be enough to tip the balance at the end of time. It's not so much about what I do, but it's all about what Jesus did – and *my* faith in His finished work.

I admit God's rescue plan is too good to be true. And so is His unconditional love. Why should I receive God's riches at Christ's expense? How can I refuse God's amazing GRACE? I don't know. I give up – but I give in.

So what about my MISFIT status? The way I look at it, some of us are just too unique and too creative to fit into a conventional mold. It would stifle our creativity to conform to society's structured norms. Therefore, God created special places for us unique people to set us apart for His purposes. I was relieved to discover that God loves misfits and has a place for each of us in His perfect plan. Our cracks allow His light to shine in. Do I have to leave behind my quirky, eccentric behavior? Do I have to outgrow my idiosyncrasies? Will I have to act my age? I concluded – NEVER!

My challenge will be to allow the Holy Spirit to become my algorithm. If I am really destined to make my life in Ibiza, so be it. If I am destined to remain single – so be it. However, when I looked into the enormous grey eyes of that gorgeous guy at the club, I saw my future . . . . and that had never happened before. I believe that eyes *are* the window to the soul, and his eyes were soft but strong and had a depth that drew me in . . . . . .

Stay tuned; the best is yet to come!

ABOUT THE AUTHOR

Born in New Orleans, I left for a two-month vacation to Europe in the early 70s. Spurred on by wanderlust, I traveled a large portion of the globe, seeking a two-fold quest; discovering the world and myself. Modeling to fund my extensive travels, I lived a nomadic lifestyle for seven years until my passion for fashion ignited a desire to settle on the semi-unknown Spanish island of Ibiza, afloat in the Mediterranean. It was a boom town, and everything was possible.

I manufactured my own designs with the talents of the local ladies and opened a trio of boutiques to reach the upcoming onslaught of tourists. After years of riding the undulating fashion wave, I've now embarked on my writing journey. "Rio or Bust" is a humorous travelogue sequel to "Banana Split Misfit," thus covering a large chunk of both the Northern and Southern hemispheres.

My late husband and I lived in our 1727 historic farmhouse in the center of the island for thirty years - now, I reside in a charming village looking out to sea.

> *"Disturb us, Lord, to dare more boldly,*
> *To venture on wider seas*
> *Where storms will show your mastery;*
> *Where losing sight of land,*
> *We shall find the stars.*
> *We ask You to push back*
> *The horizons of our hopes;*
> *And to push into the future*
> *In strength, courage, hope, and love."*

Poem attributed to Sir Francis Drake

All proceeds from my books are donated to vulnerable children worldwide through World Vision International, Christian relief and development organization.

You can contact me on the Destinee Media website:
http://www.destineemedia.com/tyke-fortier.html

BANANA SPLIT MISFIT

Banana Split Misfit is available on Amazon.
https://www.amazon.com/dp/193836760X

315

Printed in France by Amazon
Brétigny-sur-Orge, FR

11788968R00176